The Bench
and the
Ballot

The Bench and the Ballot

Southern Federal Judges
and Black Voters

Charles V. Hamilton

New York   Oxford University Press   1973

To Carol and Valli
and they know why

Preface

In 1972 black voters in several Southern states went to the polls and elected many of their own race to public offices at all levels of government—congressional, state, county, and municipal. In eleven Southern states, there were 3,448,565 registered black voters. This represented an increase from 1,530,634 in 1965. There is no question that the most significant contributing factor to this increase was the Voting Rights Act of 1965.

That new law, of course, was not enacted in a political vacuum. It was preceded by years and decades of persistent struggle on the part of many people working in different ways and at different political levels trying to gain the right to vote for Southern black citizens. A major part of that struggle was acted out in Southern federal courts with judges as the critical decision-makers. This activity pre-dates the twentieth century, but the concentrated drama took place in the eight-year period immediately preceding 1965, beginning with the passage of the Civil Rights Act of 1957.

This book is a study of that struggle in those courts during that time. It examines the advantages and disadvantages of a policy that relied on the courts to register black citizens. A great deal has been written about the benefits and burdens of using the federal courts to implement school desegregation—South and North—but there has been relatively little written about the courts' role in voter registration. This study analyzes the different judicial styles and temperaments of various Southern judges in their conduct of the mandate given them by Congress. And above all it attempts to put this eight-year struggle in a meaningful context for those interested in the courts, social change, and contemporary political events. This book, then, is a study of recent judicio-political history and the impact of that history on current developments.

This study focuses on some fifteen cases brought in federal courts in four states—Alabama, Mississippi, Louisiana, and Tennessee—before five Southern federal district court judges and the United States Court of Appeals for the fifth circuit. Interviews with attorneys of the United States Department of Justice in Washington, D.C., the official files of the Department of Justice, and interviews with Southern black voter registration workers provide the principal sources for this research.

Before beginning a detailed examination of the case materials, the book presents three chapters which give the historical background and the post-1957 political setting for the cases. Specifically, Chapters Three and Four on the congressional and executive roles in the enactment and implementation of the Civil Rights Act of 1957 and 1960 are intended to illustrate some of the expectations and efforts of those two branches of government in the matter of black voting rights. The relevance of this material to a study of this nature stems largely from the belief that the work of the judiciary is affected in great part by the other two branches of government. Some alternative proposals rejected by the Congress and the reasons therefor provide an indication of the expectations of some congressmen in the execution of the enacted legislation. Likewise, because suits under the two laws had to be initiated by the Department of Justice, the attitude of the executive branch was vitally important to indicate not only how much work the courts would receive in this field, but to show the orientation of the men who had the job of prosecuting the laws before the Southern courts. Several observers have suggested that the office of the Presidency, as a position of considerable influence, can do much by pronouncement and performance in setting a tone for the general acceptance or rejection of a law. A President who made repeated and sincere statements supporting the civil rights laws and then followed those pronouncements with active efforts at prosecution of alleged violations could lend great support to a Southern federal judge who might conceivably find himself in a community that disagreed with the goals of the laws.

The organization of the core data is based first on the work of four specific judges and second on the efforts of the Southern federal courts in handling the problem of economic intimidation. This latter problem was selected for separate treatment because many persons believed that the major impediment to Southern black voting—and thus a major obstacle to judicial enforcement of the civil rights laws—stemmed from the fact that black people were intimidated by economic and physical means in their attempts to register and vote. Unless these acts of intimidation could be curbed successfully by the federal courts, some people believed, the judicial approach as an effective solution would fail. This view was buttressed by doubts of the efficacy of the judicial solution in this area, based largely on the sometime subtle methods of intimidation employed. The presentation of the detailed data, then, in Chapter Eight is necessary to test this view in light of the alleged acts of intimidation and the performance of the courts in dealing with these acts.

Finally, the study describes the politics involved, the progress that has been made, and it examines the nature of the problems that still remain to be solved.

As always, there are more than a few individuals to thank for their assistance. Professor C. Herman Pritchett, John Lewis of the Voter Education Project, Robert Browne of the Black Economic Research Center and the many lawyers in the Department of Justice who patiently pulled out files and answered questions are but a few. Fellow workers and friends in voter-registration efforts in the South will recognize their contributions to this volume. I am also grateful to Miss Vivian Kaufman for her work in tediously typing the manuscript and to my editor, Mr. James Amon, for important helpful suggestions. All of these persons contributed to whatever merits the book might have, but they are hardly responsible for its weaknesses.

C.V.H.

New York   May 1973

Contents

The Bench
and the
Ballot

I Introduction: Colloquy on the Judicial Approach

In 1957 and 1960, the Congress of the United States passed, and the President signed, bills giving the federal courts the task of ensuring that black people in the Southern states would be able to register and vote uninhibited by restrictions based on race. This book examines the performance of some federal courts in the execution of that assignment over the eight-year period following 1957. Several observers questioned the efficacy of requiring the federal court system to serve as overseer of voter registration in the Southern states, and it is with some of these questions that this study is primarily concerned. Were the apprehensions wholly or partially justified?

The federal court system is composed of three levels: the Supreme Court of the United States; courts of appeals; and district courts. The first was specifically established by Article III of the United States Constitution. That Article (Section I) reads, in part: "The judicial power of the United States shall be vested in one supreme court, and in such inferior courts as the Congress may from time to time ordain and establish." Judges of all federal courts are appointed by the President of the United States "with the advice and consent of the Senate."

The Judiciary Act of 1789, one of the first laws passed by the first Congress under the new Constitution, established the district courts. This, the initial, trial level, has been referred to as the work horse of the federal judicial system. In 1970 there were 90 district courts throughout the country, presided over by federal district court judges. Approximately 100,000 cases are filed each year in these courts. A constant argument of lawyers and judges alike is for the creation of more judgeships, precisely because the present ones are always overworked. District court judges hear about 14,000 cases a year.

The Southern federal district courts are in the Fifth Circuit Court of Appeals. Cases from the district courts are appealed to the circuit level. There are a total of eleven U.S. courts of appeals.

This society does not like to think of its judges, and certainly not its federal judges, as political figures. Judges are expected to be "above partisan politics," inasmuch as this is the only way they can administer their judicial duties objectively and without taint of political favoritism. The merits of a case as supported by duly admissible legal evidence are the only criteria to guide judges in the performance of their duties. But the fact is, of course, that the judge is appointed by the President, and the appointment more frequently than not has to be cleared with the United States Senator or senators from the state in which the federal judge will preside. This is referred to as "senatorial courtesy." Thus, while the judge is not expected to *perform* politically, it is quite clear that the jurist is a part of the political process. Some appointments certainly are rewards for past political support. Professor Jack W. Peltason has written: "To be seriously considered for a judicial appointment, a lawyer should be a member of the right political party—the one controlling the White House—a resident of the judicial district in question, of unimpeachable reputation, of good health, and preferably not too old. If he is related to the state's political leaders so much the better." [1]

Objections to Utilizing the Federal Courts

The major arguments against using the federal courts as overseers of voter registration fell into five categories, with many expressing all these objections; but at least five distinct kinds of objections were raised. The first focused on the nature of the judicial process. The courts were slow, reactive, passive, negative, and cumbersome. In suits alleging racial discrimination in the right to vote, long delays would be the rule, and consequently, the registration of significant numbers of black citizens in the near future would be unlikely. In speaking of the federal judiciary generally, and of the United States Supreme Court specifically, one observer wrote:

> The Supreme Court . . . is limited because its process is essentially reactive. The Federal judiciary cannot initiate cases or seek out violations of liberty but must choose from those cases appealed by others. It cannot take immediate action upon observing a violation of constitutional rights. Moreover, once it does act, in the carefully prescribed realm of "case or controversy," it cannot, except by implication, suggest alternatives. Its role is largely negative—reconciling, cautioning, and retarding the policies of the other branches and other levels of government. The Federal courts, in a word, possess "no self-starter," and by definition, leadership cannot exist under circumstances of counteraction alone.[2]

On February 14, 1960, a conference was held at the University of Notre Dame Law School to discuss various proposals for ensuring the right to vote. The meeting was attended by fifty-three participants—senators, congressmen, governors, lawyers, law professors, civil rights leaders, government lawyers.

1. Jack W. Peltason, *58 Lonely Men* (New York: Harcourt, Brace and World, 1961), p. 6.
2. Richard P. Longaker, *The Presidency and Individual Liberties* (Ithaca, N.Y.: Cornell University Press, 1961), p. 13.

At that conference the then governor of Michigan, G. Mennen Williams, expressed the belief that the federal courts would not provide the required "spirit of 'Let's get this job done.' " He questioned whether the judicial approach was forceful enough. He recognized that a judicial finding of discrimination was necessary, but after that he said, "I think this should be a somewhat more persuasive method than just sitting back and waiting for somebody to come in and knock down the door to register." He viewed the judiciary as reactive, waiting for something to happen. For Governor Williams this was insufficient. He wanted a process that would go out "in the backwoods" and get people "who perhaps don't even know what it means to register." This, he felt, was needed in his own state of Michigan as well.

Those of you who are acquainted with the political process know that registration in the North just doesn't happen by opening your doors and inviting the public to come in. Now how much more difficult is it going to be to make any appreciable dent in the non-registered in the South. And if what we want to get is a number of Negroes registered so that it will make an appreciable step toward freedom and democracy, then I think we have to have a system that is going to afford some encouragement as well as legal possibility. And therefore, I think that we've got to envisage a system which is going to have a responsibility and obligation to get a job done to be fighting for democracy rather than permitting it to happen.[3]

Governor Williams did not view the problem as a legal one. This was not a matter of what the Supreme Court was going to do in the final analysis; it was to him a matter of devising a system that would be as simple as possible and "almost self-executing."

Others at the conference followed a similar line by emphasizing the complex and cumbersome potentialities of a judicial approach. Congressman John Brademas of Indiana asked how often a judicial

3. From the Proceedings of the Notre Dame Conference, reprinted in *Congressional Record*, February 29, 1960, Vol. 106, Part 3, pp. 3875–3903, 86th Congress, 2d. session.

finding of a pattern of discrimination would be required. Senator Paul Douglas of Illinois envisioned an endlesss process of judicial appeals resulting in the "danger of undue delay." He made the following comment in reference to legislation proposed by the Attorney General in 1960 to provide for court-appointed referees:

Suppose you get a verdict from a referee asking for the court that John Jones should be permitted to register. Then a series of questions come from this. Can the appeal be taken from the referee to the district court which has appointed the referees so that there may be a review of the referee's findings? If so, is the decision of the referee suspended during that time, or is it in operation? Then suppose the district court affirms the decision of its referee and the appeal is taken to the circuit court, what is the status of the finding during that time? Is it suspended or is it in operation? Now if all these matters are suspended prior to appeal, not only will the first election have passed, but the next election will have passed, and indeed perhaps there may be two or three more elections which will have occurred before the final opinion is handed down. So that this has been in my mind ever since the Attorney General made his proposal, and it's upon this point that I would really like some enlightenment from experts in judicial procedure.[4]

Some participants pointed to the fact that a judicial approach would necessitate a lawsuit "in every recalcitrant voting district in the South." What would prevent Southern legislatures from creating "tens of thousands" of these districts simply to frustrate enforcement? * In addition, there was considerable question whether the federal government had sufficient legal manpower to meet this eventuality.

In 1960 Professor Paul A. Freund of Harvard, in a memo to then Senator John F. Kennedy of Massachusetts analyzing the

4. *Ibid.*
* None of the conference participants voiced an objection to methods of some kind to strengthen the voting laws. The major disagreement centered on how best to go about it. The ultimate goal of substantially increasing Southern black voter registration and political participation was accepted by all.

various proposals, assumed that under a judicial approach appeals would be taken from referee and lower court decisions. This, he felt, would result not only in delays but "uncertainties inherent in the bringing of law suits by the Attorney General." [5]

The second type of objection dealt generally with the influence on the courts of community pressures and local attitudes. In addition, some persons pointed out that a few Southern judges might not view these as pressures at all, but rather simply as external forces serving to buttress their own predilections against black voting. Southern federal district judges were not good agents for enforcing the right of black people to vote, this argument went, because these judges could not escape the strong white community sentiment against enforcement.

In his book on Southern federal judges and school desegregation, *58 Lonely Men,* Professor Jack W. Peltason made the following comment:

All policy-makers in a free society are the focus of contending pressures. Judges are no exception. The judiciary is subject to competing claims in a somewhat different fashion from, say, the legislature, nevertheless the difference is one of degree and not of kind. And just as the laws enacted by the legislature reflect the dominance of certain values in the community, so do the decisions of judges. It is so today; it has always been so.[6]

This situation, coupled in some instances with a judge's personal segregationist or anti-black-voting bias, would contribute even more to delay and other evasive efforts. One participant at the Notre Dame conference stated, "I don't mean to disparage the judiciary, but I think it is fair to say . . . that some of these judges are suffering from invincible bias in this area, and for those judges no form of legal draftsmanship will do very much good." And to this person, the problem was less one of the inherent complex nature

5. *Congressional Record,* Vol. 106, Part 3, p. 3897.
6. Jack W. Peltason, *op. cit.,* p. 247.

of the judicial process or the evasive tactics of Southern registrars, because "a vigorous judge of integrity will see that he [the registrar] pays a price for it." But simply stated, "I think the difficulty is the willingness of the judge to carry out the law, rather than the detail of this procedure." And while he did not wish to be specifically condemnatory, neither was he generally optimistic.

That this willingness was lacking in some federal judges and would serve to frustrate the primary aim of the Civil Rights Act of 1960 was pointed out by Professor Peltason. His studies of Southern federal district court judges and school desegregation had left him more than a little skeptical about the basic position of this branch of government. In 1961 he wrote:

Southern federal judges have shown no greater desire to protect the Negroes' right to vote than they have to desegregate the schools. In Georgia, Judge T. Hoyt Davis even went so far as to declare the 1957 Act unconstitutional. Other judges discovered technical reasons for refusing to enjoin voting officials from discriminating against Negroes. Only Judge J. Skelly Wright has so far used the Act of 1957 to protect Negro voters. But in 1960, the Supreme Court reversed the Judges who were dismissing complaints filed by the Department of Justice. Henceforth, though litigation is inherently slow, southern judges will have to find other reasons to refuse to act.[7]

He also pointed to federal district Judge Benjamin C. Dawkins, Jr., of Louisiana, whom he described as "among the more ardent segregationists serving on the federal bench." [8] Dawkins held court in Shreveport in northern Louisiana, in the midst of the strongest segregationist area of the state. He was the judge who not only refused to interfere when white citizens' councils manipulated the law with the help of Monroe City officials to "purge" 2500 black voters from the registration rolls, but accused the black plaintiff of "bad faith . . . sheer stubborn vindictiveness." It was Judge Dawkins who made the statement, "It is all part of the game," when

7. *Ibid.*, p. 251.
8. *Ibid.*, p. 133.

he enjoined the United States Commission on Civil Rights from holding hearings in Shreveport, and subsequently admitted his order might be reversed.[9]

While the second objection cautioned against using the federal courts because for various reasons they might not produce the results sought by the civil rights laws, the third objection focused on what would happen to the courts if they did produce. It was not good for the prestige and effectiveness of the federal courts to require them constantly to supervise politically controversial matters such as school desegregation and the right to vote.

If they are given the task of forcing many unpopular reforms on their local communities, they may cease to be effective instruments for the administration of justice. Judges function best when they are handling issues of little political explosiveness. If large numbers of southerners, for reasons just or unjust, come to consider federal judges to be nothing but 'yankee agents,' even civil rights advocates may lose more than they may gain from immediate legal victories. These men will not only be lonely but ostracized.[10]

Peltason quickly followed this statement with his judgment that "it was not likely that federal judges would use the 1960 Civil Rights Act in such a fashion as to arouse the ire of Southerners. As the story of school integration illustrated, they are apt to be something less than aggressive. Judicial decisions here, as elsewhere, are not likely to make any major departure from the norms of the community." [11]

It was not what would happen to the Judge Dawkinses or Judge Davises that bothered those who raised this third type of objection; indeed, these judges would probably be heralded by anti-black-voting advocates as wise jurists and champions of the Constitution. But what would be the effects on those judges who ordered blacks placed on the registration books? And if this were not a problem,

9. United States Commission on Civil Rights, *Report,* 1959, p. 101.
10. Peltason, *op. cit.,* pp. 252–53.
11. *Ibid.*

given the premise of community retaliation, then it meant the Civil Rights laws were defective in using the judicial approach.

Frequently one heard or read a fourth type of objection which focused on the function to be performed rather than on the judicial process or the relation of the judges to the local communities. The registration of black people in the South in conformance with the Fifteenth Amendment, it was contended, was more properly an administrative function. This was not basically a job that the judiciary should be required to do. Professors Charles L. Black, Thomas I. Emerson, and Louis H. Pollak of the Yale Law School concluded that the judicial approach was impractical; it would unduly burden the federal judiciary. They also emphasized the third objection of not drawing the courts "so extensively and so minutely into explosive political controversies of this nature." And their article read:

> Responsibility for the strictly executive function of voter registration must be assumed by the executive, with the courts performing their usual function of judicial review in those occasional cases where a doubtful issue of law emerges.[12]

Some saw this judicial assignment as "a passing of the buck of the responsibility which belongs on Congress and the Executive." And again, combining the third type of objection, Professor Roger Cramton of the University of Chicago Law School observed at the Notre Dame conference, "The courts will lose the respect of private citizens if functions which are essentially non-judicial are heaped on them repeatedly over a period of years. The court should be restricted to the traditional functions." [13] What functions worried Professor Cramton? He stated, "I do not think that our federal courts are in a position to run the affairs of a great nation, nor should they be put in that position." He referred specifically to the

---

12. *Congressional Record,* Vol. 106, Part 3, p. 3901.
13. *Ibid.,* p. 3883.

"somewhat kindred functions in relatively narrow circumstances such as the bankruptcy jurisdiction." He spoke of the courts' work "in the organization and the administration of the school systems, at least in the South." And now the proposals were made to have the courts oversee the registration and voting process.

Another student of these matters felt that the time had come for emphasis on enforcement of certain principles rather than on the legality of those principles. Professor Richard P. Longaker classified the right to vote free from racial restrictions as such an example, and suggested enforcement was not a primary function of the judiciary. He wrote, "By 1960, the problem no longer was to find in law the validity of the principle of equal rights but rather to establish its vitality." [14]

This problem of the denial of the right to vote under the Fifteenth Amendment, another observer felt, was "a problem political in its nature, calling for a political solution." [15] Professor Harris Wofford, legal adviser to Father Theodore Hesburgh of the Civil Rights Commission, likewise stressed the burden on the federal judiciary in school segregation suits as well as the "slow progress through long drawn-out cases. . . ." By a political problem requiring a political solution, he was referring to action by the political branches of the national government—the Congress and the Presidency. His statement presented to the Notre Dame conference read, in part:

A congressionally enacted administrative procedure by which qualified citizens are registered in districts practicing discrimination thus seems to be the most appropriate remedy.

The U.S. Government has three engines to propel it. So far in this matter, it has been flying on one engine—the Federal judiciary. This problem cannot be adequately solved by the action of one branch of Government—and the platitudes of the President. It is time that the

14. Richard P. Longaker, "The President and the Civil Rights of Negroes," *American Government Annual, 1962–1963* (New York: Holt, Rinehart and Winston), p. 53.
15. *Congressional Record,* Vol. 106, Part 3, p. 3895.

other two branches of the Government exercise their full responsibilities so that resort to the courts can be, as it should be, a last resort.
The Attorney General's plan, if taken alone or in its present form, is another example of this administration's practice of trying to turn over
its political problems to the courts.[16]

An additional argument lending weight to this fourth objection
called attention to the fact that there was another function aside
from the enforcement aspect to consider—an educational function.
Professor Nathaniel L. Nathanson of the Northwestern University
Law School stressed the importance of continuing education in this
field, and he was of the opinion that an administrative apparatus
was better suited for the performance of this dual role (education
and enforcement) than a judicial approach. Ultimately, he concluded, the courts would be necessary to sanction the work of the
administrative agency. "But, insofar as we have primarily a long-
range job to do here of education and enforcement in a hostile
area, it seems to me that the now old-fashioned, but once new, administrative process is the more suitable." [17] He recognized limitations on the administrative process but he also equated the right-to-
vote cases with those cases arising under the National Labor Relations Board. What constituted an unfair labor practice was fairly
clear, and likewise to him, the voting cases would not present an
administrative agency with the kinds of problems that confronted
agencies like the Federal Communications Commission. "Here [in
voting cases] the objective is quite clear. We don't have the problems of formulating a standard out of vague considerations from
God knows what kind of policy." [18]

    The fifth type of objection was based on apprehensions about
the inability of the judicial system to deal effectively with what some
people felt to be the major deterrent to black voting in the South—
economic reprisals. Interestingly enough, one found this criticism

16. *Ibid.*
17. *Ibid.*, p. 3888.
18. *Ibid.*

most prevalent among Southern black voter registration workers who emphasized their special knowledge of these problems as a result of their "working everyday in this business of trying to get our people registered." Several such activists in Alabama, Georgia, and Mississippi constantly repeated in 1959, 1960, and 1963 that "unless they [the federal government] provide some means to protect Negroes from losing their jobs and things like that, then we can forget it. People just ain't going to risk it." A judicial approach with the requirements of legal evidence would simply not be able to deal with the problem of economic reprisals, they believed. "How're you going to legally prove that the boss man told you that if you registered or even tried to register, let alone vote," one representative of the NAACP in Mississippi said, "that you needn't come back to his job?" Those who saw this as the major problem usually concluded by suggesting some form of summary registration for all citizens, but they ultimately admitted that even this was not an absolute guarantee against intimidations:

"Now I don't believe in a law making people vote," one black person in Alabama stated in 1960, "but neither do I see any protection for a man who'll lose his job or lose his home or what if he votes. I just don't know. Ain't no unions down here to speak of—so I just don't know. But I do know that until they lick that, they ain't done nothing. That I know because, remember now, I'm knocking on people's doors every evening the Lord puts here. I can talk voting and rights and all like that, but that man's looking at his six kids running 'round him and wondering what's going to happen to them."

The president of the NAACP branch in Cleveland, Mississippi, made the following observation in January 1963:

When we register or even attempt to register a hundred Negroes, that means automatically we will have to find jobs and homes for a hundred people, because they are bound to lose both in Bolivar County and for that matter all over the Delta. People come to my house everyday—you stay here, you'll see it—with such problems. Now you can't always prove that, but I'm telling you what is fact.[19]

Arguments Favoring a Judicial Approach

In this colloquy on the use of the federal judiciary, there were those who pointed up certain positive factors as well as inevitabilities associated with such an approach. The major objections outlined above, so stated the pro-judiciary people, overlooked the enormous equity powers of the federal courts. The courts were flexible and adaptable to an extent not usually recognized by many persons. One Washington, D.C., attorney, Adam Yarmolinsky, emphasized this point at the Notre Dame conference:

equity can accomplish anything, I would suppose, and has accomplished almost anything that the administrative process can accomplish. And I think that this is particularly true when we're talking about the operation of a system that is going to be working largely in rural areas . . . in situations where we're not looking for the kind of expertise that theoretically you get out of the ICC or the FCC or the CAB or whatever. I'm inclined to think that it's more natural, more straightforward to stick to the judicial process.[20]

In the same vein, another person felt that the "enormous reservoir of ill-defined equitable remedies" has never been seriously thought about in terms of the advantages and limitations "in managing litigation that is aimed at producing results with which dominant segments of the community vigorously disagree."

The federal district courts had their limitations, the pro-judiciary advocates conceded, and many of the objections set forth above might have been quite valid, but more practical considerations overruled these objections. It was inevitable that the judiciary

19. Interview with Mr. Amzie Moore, president of the Cleveland, Mississippi, branch of the NAACP.
20. *Congressional Record,* Vol. 106, Part 3, p. 3888.

would be involved directly and minutely in any system designed to assure black people the constitutional right to be free from restrictions in voting based on race. The Southern states would demand judicial review of administrative action. They would demand their day in court. "So it seems to me," one professor of law stated, "that everyone is going to be better off if we simply start off in court in the first place."

Others felt that unless the judiciary performed the job of ensuring the right to vote, there was the great likelihood that the job would not get done. The Congress, because of its strong loyalties to local, rural constituents, could not be expected, according to one student of the federal courts and civil rights, "to give us a clear statutory enforcement of the Fourteenth Amendment." [21] While many persons concluded that the executive branch should, in the future, assume greater responsibilities in the enforcement of voting rights, the experience of seven years of the Eisenhower administration was not encouraging. A typical observation along this line was as follows:

If the executive branch of the Federal Government wanted to play, was willing to play—as I hope it will be in the future, but I don't think it has been in the past—a leading role in the securing to the colored citizens their right to vote, the executive department of the government has all kinds of ways to do so, not only through the high office of the President, which would put these judicial officers, if they were appointed not in the position of the lonely enforcers of what is right and just, but as people surrounded by friends and supporters.[22]

Dr. John A. Morsell, assistant to the executive secretary of the National Association for the Advancement of Colored People felt that too much emphasis had been put on the point that Southern federal courts were already overloaded with school desegregation cases. "The actual amount of school litigation now pending," he

21. Robert J. Steamer, "The Role of the Federal District Courts in the Segregation Controversy," *Journal of Politics,* Vol. 22 (1960), p. 421.
22. *Congressional Record,* Vol. 106, Part 3, p. 3888.

stated at the Notre Dame conference, "or in my view likely in the immediate future, is not voluminous. And I do not believe that it really imposes as tremendous a burden on the courts as might appear to be the case." [23]

These arguments, pro and con, continued up to the time of passage of the Civil Rights Act of 1960. Many opponents of the judicial approach were disappointed with the law that was passed, but virtually everyone adopted a wait-and-see attitude. In addition, as a subsequent chapter illustrates, most observers were resigned to the fact that the political environment was not right at that time for legislation designed to go beyond a judicial approach to voting rights.

23. It should be noted that Dr. Morsell felt that fear of reprisals was a major factor in the minds of many Southern black people. To help alleviate these fears, Morsell favored some type of *ex parte* judicial proceeding that would not require black citizens to endure cross-examination by "hostile" states' attorneys.

2 The Federal Courts and the Black Vote Before 1957

One might view the legal developments of the struggle by black Americans against suffrage discriminations since the turn of the century in three stages.[1] The first, the state action stage, is associated with the court battles to overcome the "grandfather clause" and the white primary. This stage culminated in *Smith* v. *Allwright* in 1944 and ended with *Terry* v. *Adams* in 1953. Essentially, it left the way open for blacks to participate in the most important election in the Southern states—the primary election. Involved in the unfolding of this story were several Southern federal judges who contributed significant decisions along the way.

Shortly after the 1944 decision, Southern officials and opponents of black voting turned their attention more to methods designed to keep black citizens from the polls altogether by denying them the privilege to register. This second stage, the registrar-oriented phase, was characterized by stringent literacy tests, "understanding" and "good character" clauses, purges, and the discriminatory

1. Lawsuits were initiated before 1900, of course, but the period here is chosen in order to limit the presentation without substantially affecting the content. Reference will be made to earlier cases where necessary.

was the general procedure throughout the 1880s, 1890s, and the first decade of the twentieth century.

The State Action Stage

One of the surest devices for disenfranchising black citizens was the "grandfather clause." This method had many variations from state to state,[6] but the fundamental purpose was to deny the vote to those persons in the state who could not pass a stiff registration test. Those failing this examination would be permitted to vote, nonetheless, if they or their ancestors voted in the state or some other jurisdiction before a certain specified date—1860, 1866, or 1870. Since blacks usually were slaves in the Southern states or could not show that they personally had voted before the particular year, they were effectually prohibited from voting. The signal case overruling this device was decided by the United States Supreme Court in 1915.[7] The state of Oklahoma had amended its constitution in 1910 to provide that all persons could vote in the state who were able to read and write any section of the state constitution. This requirement was to apply to "no person who was, on January 1, 1866, or at any time prior thereto, entitled to vote under any form of government, or who at that time resided in some foreign nation, and no lineal descendant of such person shall be denied the right to register and vote because of his inability to so read and write sections of such constitution." The focus of the case was on the 1866 standard. The Fifteenth Amendment,[8] of course, was adopted in 1870. The federal district court

6. See Monnet, "The Latest Phase of Negro Disfranchisement," 26 *Harvard Law Review* 42 (1912); Mangum, *op. cit.;* C. Vann Woodward, *Origins of the New South, 1877–1913* (1951).
7. *Guinn* v. *U.S.,* 238 U.S. 347 (1915).
8. The Fifteenth Amendment reads as follows: "Section 1. The right of citizens of the United States to vote shall not be denied or abridged by the United States or by any State on account of race, color, or previous condition of servitude. Section 2. The Congress shall have power to enforce this article by appropriate legislation."

and the Circuit Court of Appeals for the Eighth Circuit held the state provision invalid. The Supreme Court upheld this contention. Because the federal courts could find no "discernible reason" in setting up the 1866 standard other than to abrogate the Fifteenth Amendment, the state provision was disallowed. The Supreme Court opinion read in part:

It is true it [the state provision] contains no express words of an exclusion from the standard which it establishes of any person on account of race, color or previous condition of servitude prohibited by the Fifteenth Amendment, but the standard itself inherently brings that result into existence since it is based purely upon a period of time before the enactment of the Fifteenth Amendment and makes that period the controlling and dominant test of the right of suffrage. In other words, we seek in vain for any ground which would sustain any other interpretation but that the provision, recurring to the conditions existing before the Fifteenth Amendment was adopted and the continuance of which the Fifteenth Amendment prohibited, proposed by in substance and effect lifting those conditions over to a period of time after the Amendment to make them the basis of the right to suffrage conferred in direct and positive disregard of the Fifteenth Amendment.[9]

Mr. Chief Justice White wrote for the Court that he could find nothing about the 1866 date that would give it special characteristics respecting voter qualifications unless the Fifteenth Amendment was the motivating factor.

The Supreme Court was not of the opinion that the Fifteenth Amendment conferred a positive grant of the right to vote; merely that the Constitution prohibited the use of standards of race, color, or previous condition of servitude in denying the franchise. But where the state had used such standards exclusively as in Oklahoma, then the Fifteenth Amendment operated automatically to strike down the state law and thereby left the persons with the right to vote under remaining constitutional provisions of state law. Such was the situation in Oklahoma. The literacy clause of the

9. 238 U.S., p. 364.

Oklahoma constitution was likewise invalid because it was so inextricably connected with the so-called grandfather clause. One could qualify to vote under either provision of the Oklahoma amendment.[10]

Had the grandfather clause been upheld, it would have been a foolproof method for total disenfranchisement of blacks. Short of that, the next most effective way to exclude black voters was to exclude them from those elections which had the chief significance in the Southern electoral process—the primary elections. In one-party areas like the South, where general elections served only to confirm political choices made in the earlier party primaries, they might vote en masse in the general elections where there usually was no opposition of importance to the Democratic nominee. Interestingly enough, the two cases that formed the framework for the legal development of this situation had nothing to do with black voting.

The first case, *Newberry* v. *U.S.,* involved a successful candidate, Truman H. Newberry, for the United States Senate from Michigan.[11] He ran for office in 1918 and was accused of violating the Corrupt Practices Act of 1910 which restricted campaign expenditures in securing nomination as well as election. He was convicted in the lower court, but in 1921, the Supreme Court ruled in his favor on the grounds that the Constitution used the term "election" to mean the "final choice of an officer by the duly qualified electors." The majority of five justices held the Corrupt Practices Act of 1910 not applicable to primaries:

Moreover, they [the primaries] are in no sense elections for an office, but merely methods by which party adherents agree upon candidates

10. A subsequent attempt by Oklahoma to circumvent the Guinn decision was overruled in *Lane* v. *Wilson,* 307 U.S. 268 (1939). Oklahoma passed a new election registration law which permitted only a twelve-day registration period, but exempted from the registration requirement those who had voted in the 1914 election under the unconstitutional grandfather clause.
11. *Newberry* v. *U.S.,* 256 U.S. 232 (1921).

whom they intend to offer and support for ultimate choice by all qualified electors. General provisions touching elections in constitutions or statutes are not necessarily applicable to primaries—the two things are radically different.[12]

Although this ruling was considered by some persons to be definitive on the question of primaries, one member of the Court, Justice McKenna, limited the scope of the decision. He was willing to vote for Mr. Newberry because the Corrupt Practices Act was passed in 1910, before the Seventeenth Amendment was enacted in 1913. That Amendment provided for the direct election of senators, and Justice McKenna felt that a case coming after then could conceivably have a different result. This case stood for twenty years until 1941, when in another non-black voting case, *U.S.* v. *Classic*,[13] the Supreme Court specifically stated that primaries were "integral" parts of the election process within the meaning of the Constitution.

In the intervening period, however, from 1921 to 1941, the state of Texas, taking its cue from the generally accepted interpretation in the Newberry case, proceeded to initiate a white primary. At first, the Texas legislature explicitly prohibited black participation in Democratic party primaries. The Supreme Court overruled this in *Nixon* v. *Herndon*[14] in 1927, but it left the Newberry doctrine intact. The basis for the Herndon decision was the "state action" of Texas in direct violation of the equal protection clause in the Fourteenth Amendment.

As early as 1930, however, a federal district court in Virginia did not feel compelled to follow the Newberry ruling in overruling a white primary as it existed in that state. A black citizen of Virginia, James O. West, was denied the privilege of voting in a Democratic primary in Richmond, Virginia. He filed for damages

12. 256 U.S., p. 250.
13. 313 U.S. 299 (1941).
14. 273 U.S. 536 (1927).

alleging an infringement of the rights guaranteed to him by the Fourteenth and Fifteenth Amendments. The election judges admitted that West was excluded from voting in the direct primary because of a resolution adopted by the state Democratic Convention in 1924, pursuant to the authority of the Virginia legislature. The resolution declared that only white persons could participate in a Democratic primary. The Virginia statute gave the political party the power to establish qualifications for those who could participate in the party primary. The state law made no mention of race. The election judges insisted that their action was based on the commands of a private group—the political party—and not on action by the state. Their point was that the state statute did not give the political party power to exclude racial groups, but merely recognized the existence of that power where it had always resided. But the federal district court found that Virginia laws provided an optional form of nominating candidates by primaries, and that this form involved less expense on the political party exercising that option inasmuch as the cost of the primary was borne by the public treasury of Richmond, Virginia. The court reviewed the history of the primary and quoted language from an earlier Virginia case (*Commonwealth* v. *Willcox* (69 S.E. 1031)) that read in part: "the primary when adopted by a political party becomes an inseparable part of the election machinery." The opinion in *West* v. *Bliley* cited *Nixon* v. *Herndon* and stated that while the Virginia statute was different from the Texas statute, the result was the same. "The State of Virginia was attempting to delegate to the political party what the state itself could not do constitutionally." The last paragraph of the opinion took cognizance of the fact that the court's decision would meet with disfavor from some sections of the community, but the court has no constitutional alternatives:

That its [the decision's] effect may be to change a custom that has long obtained in the political system in effect in this state, and therefore meet with the disapproval of many, is a consequence which un-pleasant though it may be, may nevertheless not be avoided in the performance of the duty devolving on the court.[15]

A three-judge circuit Court of Appeals upheld the district court the following year.[16]

Texas, however, with its sights focused on *Nixon* v. *Herndon,* proceeded to pass a law authorizing the state executive committee of the political party to bar blacks from the party primary. This the Democratic party executive committee of Texas proceeded to do, but in 1932, in *Nixon* v. *Condon,*[17] the Supreme Court once again found "state action" in the legislative authorization. And once again, the decision was reached without overruling Newberry. The only alternative remaining was the complete withdrawal of state participation whatsoever, leaving the political party itself to draw up whatever rules it desired regarding participation in its primaries. This was done in the Democratic party convention early in the 1930s, thereby excluding blacks. In *Grovey* v. *Town-send* [18] the Supreme Court found no state action, but rather held that the political party was a private organization engaged in a private function (i.e., the primary election), and it upheld the doctrine in Newberry.

Here the matter rested until the Classic case, involving United States prosecution of Louisiana election officials for vote frauds in a primary election in which candidates for Congress were chosen. The important point to be noted here is the five-judge majority opinion that concluded:

Where the state law has made the primary an integral part of the procedure of choice, or where in fact, the primary effectively controls the choice, the right of the elector to have his ballot counted at the primary is likewise included in the right protected by Article 1, Sec-

15. *West* v. *Bliley,* 33 Fed. Rep. 2d. 177 (1929), p. 180.
16. *Bliley* v. *West,* 42 Fed. Rep. 2d. 101 (1930).
17. 286 U.S. 73 (1932).
18. 295 U.S. 45 (1935).

tion 2. And this right of participation is protected just as is the right to vote at the election, where the primary is by law made an integral part of the election machinery, whether the voter exercises his right in a party primary which invariably, sometimes or never determines the ultimate choice of the representative.[19]

This was the trigger that set off a new round of attacks on the white primaries. From Texas, again, came *Smith* v. *Allwright,* alleging essentially the same facts as in *Grovey* v. *Townsend,* only now there was the *Classic* opinion for the black plaintiff to cite. This Mr. Smith did, and the Supreme Court in 1944 reversed the district and appellate courts and overruled *Grovey* v. *Townsend.* While the political party conducted primaries in Texas, it did so under state authority. Only those nominees certified by the party could appear on the ballot for the general election as a candidate of a political party. "The party takes its character as a state agency from the duties imposed upon it by state statutes; the duties do not become matters of private law because they are performed by a political party.[20] The court reached its decision without referring to the earlier Virginia case of *West* v. *Bliley.*

This effectually spelled the death of the white primary, although there was left some "mopping up" to be done by lower federal courts. In Georgia a federal district court found in 1946 that although a state statute had made primaries optional by the political party, if and when a party exercised this option, the state adopted the party action as official for purposes of including the results on the official election ballot.[21] The fifth circuit court upheld this view,[22] and the Supreme Court denied certiorari.[23]

South Carolina's subsequent attempts at a foolproof white primary were also defeated by a federal district court. The state

19. 313 U.S., p. 318.
20. 321 U.S., p. 663.
21. *Chapman* v. *King,* 62 F. Supp. 639 (1946).
22. 154 Fed. 2d. 460 (1946).
23. 66 S. Ct. 905 (1946).

withdrew completely from the electoral process leaving the political party to set up any rules it saw fit to make. But in *Elmore* v. *Rice*[24] the lower court stated, "We need hardly look back of 1941 when the famous case of *U.S.* v. *Classic* was decided and a few years later in 1944 *Smith* v. *Allwright*. These two cases now completely control and govern the matters under discussion. . . . It is time for South Carolina to rejoin the Union. It is time to fall in step with the other states and adopt the American way of conducting elections."

The Court of Appeals for the fourth circuit upheld the lower federal court in the Rice case and in a later case also coming out of South Carolina, *Baskin* v. *Brown*.[25] A most interesting sidelight to these appellate court decisions, for purposes of this book, was the identity of the chief judge who wrote the three-judge opinions. That judge was John J. Parker, who nineteen years before had been nominated by President Hoover for a vacancy on the Supreme Court. His nomination was fought strenuously by the NAACP because that organization felt that Judge Parker was highly unfriendly to the idea of blacks' voting. Walter White, in his book, *How Far the Promised Land,* described the NAACP's activities in the anti-Parker campaign as one of the major factors in the birth of black voters as a political force to be considered in decision-making.[26] The NAACP recalled a speech made by the judge in 1920 that was reported in the Greensboro (N.C.) *News.* W.E.B. DuBois, then Editor of *The Crisis,* wrote

Its clear meaning was
A. He believed in the disfranchisement of Negroes,
B. That no Negro had ever sat in a state Republican convention that he had attended,
C. That Negroes did not wish to enter politics,

24. 72 Fed. Supp. 516 (1947).
25. 174 Fed. 2d. 391 (1949).
26. Walter White, *How Far the Promised Land* (New York: Viking Press, 1954), pp. 78–79.

D. That the Republican Party did not wish the Negro to vote,
E. That the participation of the Negro in politics is a source of evil and danger.[27]

And yet, in *Baskin* v. *Brown* in 1949 Judge Parker issued a strong opinion for the NAACP against the South Carolina white primary. Following the unsuccessful withdrawal attempt which *Elmore* v. *Rice* defeated, the Democratic party of South Carolina had adopted rules under which control of the primaries in that state was vested in clubs to which blacks were not admitted to membership, and voting in the primaries was conditional on the voter's taking an oath that he believed in social and educational separation of the races and was "opposed to the proposed Federal so-called FEPC law."

Judge Parker quoted his Rice opinion wherein he said that an "essential feature of our form of government is the right of the citizens to participate in the governmental process." He reiterated that the state or the political party could not do indirectly what the Constitution and the courts had prohibited them from doing directly, that even though the election laws did not mention race specifically, they could be so administered to discriminate against blacks. In this instance, the Democratic party of South Carolina was in fact taking over and performing

a vital part of its [state's] electoral machinery. . . . Courts of equity are neither blind nor impotent. They exercise their injunctive power to strike directly at the source of evil which they are seeking to prevent. The evil here is racial discrimination which bars Negro voters from any effective participation in the government of their state; and when it appears that this discrimination is practiced through rules of a party which controls the primary elections, these must be enjoined just as any other practice which threatens to corrupt elections or direct them from their constitutional purpose.[28]

27. W. E. B. DuBois, "The Defeat of Judge Parker," *The Crisis* (July 1930), Vol. 37, No. 7, p. 226.
28. 174 Fed. 2d., p. 394.

And then, as if speaking with his Supreme Court nomination experiences of twenty years earlier in mind, Judge Parker concluded his opinion on the subject of judges and biases. The South Carolina officials had asked that the lower court judge disqualify himself, charging the judge with bias and prejudice against South Carolina.[29] Judge Parker upheld the lower court, stating, "It is the duty of a real judge to acquire views from evidence. The statute never contemplated crippling our courts by disqualifying a judge, solely on the basis of a bias (or state of mind) against wrongdoers, civil or criminal, acquired from evidence presented in the course of judicial proceedings before him." [30]

Judge Parker might well have been suggesting that notwithstanding his personal social and political views as expressed out of court on the broad subject of the wisdom of blacks' voting, he would, in his role as a judge, treat specific cases in this field on their merits. This must have been pleasing language to the NAACP counsel in the Baskin case, but language hardly calculated to make that organization entirely satisfied with the results of its earlier efforts to keep Judge Parker off the Supreme Court bench.

With these cases and a later decision in 1953 by the Supreme Court,[31] the white primary virtually was rendered useless as a legal device for curtailing the effectiveness of black voters. There was one other legal attempt in the late 1950s to conduct a primary election confined to white voters. This was in Haywood County,

29. The federal district court judge was South Carolina-born and bred J. Waites Waring, who, in *Elmore* v. *Rice,* had admonished the state to "rejoin the Union."
30. 174 Fed. 2d., p. 394.
31. *Terry* v. *Adams,* 345 U.S. 461 (1953). In this case, the Jaybird organization in a county in Texas had been holding pre-primary primaries since the 1880s. Consistently over the years, the nominee chosen in the Jaybird pre-primary went on to win the primary and the general election. In a sadly divided decision (there were three separate concurring opinions and one dissenting opinion), the Supreme Court ruled for the black plaintiff, giving the plaintiffs the right to participate in the Jaybird pre-primary.

Tennessee, in the summer of 1958 and was promptly invalidated by the district court.[32] In 1958, the *Race Relations Law Reporter* concluded that "the most significant body of law to grow up concerning voting rights has been that pertaining to primary elections." [33]

The Registrar-Oriented Stage

With this occurrence, the emphasis shifted from the state legislatures and state statutes as front lines of defense against black enfranchisement to boards of registrars and discriminatory administration of voter registration tests. If the grandfather clause and white primary could not perform the job of total exclusion, then this other method, if successful, surely could cut into the number of blacks who would vote. Increased attention turned to literacy tests, voucher-systems, purges, and various methods of slowing the registration process. Professor V. O. Key wrote in 1949:

No matter from what direction one looks at it, the southern literacy test is a fraud and nothing more. The simple fact seems to be that the constitutionally prescribed test of ability to read and write a section of the constitution is rarely administered to whites. It is applied chiefly to Negroes and not always to them. When Negroes are tested on their ability to read and write, only in exceptional instances is the test administered fairly. Insofar as is known, no southern registration official has utilized an objective test of literacy.[34]

Various practices of Southern registrars have been documented in this regard.[35] The particular methods varied from county to

32. *U.S.* v. *Fayette County Democratic Executive Committee*, Civ., No. 3835, Nov. 16, 1959.
33. Note: "Voting Rights," Vol. 3, *Race Relations Law Reporter*, 371 (1958).
34. Key, *op. cit.,* p. 576.
35. See Margaret Price, *The Negro Vote in the South* (Atlanta: Southern Regional Council) (1957) and *The Negro and the Ballot in the South*

county: requiring black applicants to read, write, and interpret, to the satisfaction of the registrar, sections (usually very long and complicated) of the state or federal constitution; requiring two registered voters (in some counties these had to be two white voters) to vouch for the "good character" of the black applicant, and limiting each voucher to only two applicants per year;[36] permitting only one or two blacks at a time to complete the registration application, thus allowing only four or five blacks to make application in one day—in some places it took as long as two hours or more to complete the application process; having registrars resign and thus cause the county to be without means for registering prospective voters for months at a time.[37] These practices were most commonly associated with those counties of heavy black populations.

The legal battle against this second set of obstacles to black suffrage was spotted with victories and defeats for individual black plaintiffs. But perhaps the most significant fact is that the attack had to be launched by private parties. This was expensive, tedious, and not particularly rewarding in terms of registering sizable numbers of black citizens. Walter White wrote in 1954, "An estimated five hundred thousand dollars has been spent by Negro citizens on legal cases challenging disfranchisement, many of them ending in defeat." [38] The spottiness and relative ineffectiveness of the legal victories contributed to the argument in favor of new congressional legislation in 1957.

Macon County, Alabama, has provided the setting for significant case law and research concerning the denial of black voting

---

(Atlanta: Southern Regional Council) (1959); *Hearings before the U.S. Commission on Civil Rights,* Montgomery, Alabama, December 1958; Note, "Use of Literacy Tests to Restrict the Right to Vote," 31 *Notre Dame Lawyer,* 251 (1956).

36. As in Macon County and Cullock County, Alabama, before 1960.

37. Charles V. Hamilton, *Minority Politics in Black Belt Alabama* (Eagleton Institute, New York: McGraw-Hill) (1962).

38. Walter White, *op. cit.,* pp. 65–66.

rights. We shall have occasion in a later chapter to examine developments there in the late 1950s and early 1960s. But as early as 1945, following a suit by a black, William P. Mitchell, a federal district court rejected the efforts of the plaintiff to become registered. Mitchell alleged that he correctly made application for registration in Macon County on July 5, 1945, and had produced the required two vouchers, but was subsequently denied registration. He sought an injunction against the registrars and damages in the amount of $5000. The suit was filed in the federal district court on behalf of other persons similarly situated—a class action.[39] The district court judge dismissed the complaint on two grounds: first, the black plaintiff could not maintain a class action; and second, the plaintiff had not exhausted the remedies provided by state law. The court held that other black citizens in Macon County "who [as alleged in the complaint] possess all the qualifications to be registered as voters and possess none of the disqualifications of voters is indefinite, unclassified, and is not recognized by the public or anyone as a group or class." The judge said:

Registration is an individual matter, each case is considered on its own merits and demerits. . . . The question of unconstitutional discrimination in registration cannot be determined by groups or classes but must be determined as to each individual.[40]

The court then proceeded to examine the procedure in the state registration process. The steps were, first, action by the county board of registrars, and then, if the applicant was refused registration, appeal to the circuit court of Macon County, and from that court to the Supreme Court of Alabama. That was Alabama law. Mitchell had not contested that law; indeed, by pursuing the first step of applying to the county board, he had availed himself of a part of that law. It was then incumbent upon him to exhaust his

39. 62 Fed. Supp. 580 (1945).
40. *Ibid.*, p. 582.

administrative remedies under state law. Since registration of the plaintiff could be ordered at any step along the way, the entire process remained an administrative procedure.

Mitchell appealed, and the fifth circuit Court of Appeals reversed and remanded on April 24, 1946. The appellate court believed that the Alabama procedures providing for review of the board's action were judicial in nature not administrative, and there was precedent[41] holding that an appellant did not have to pursue whatever remedy may have been open to him in the state courts. Under the Alabama law providing for state court review, the Alabama courts were required to perform judicial functions not administrative tasks.

So Mitchell went back to the federal district court for a hearing on the merits. On January 8, 1947, the district court ruled for the defendants.[42] The court once again dismissed the class action section of Mitchell's complaint[43] and proceeded to find that the black plaintiff had satisfied all the statutory requirements for registration except one: whereas he had listed two vouchers, neither of these persons had, in fact, appeared before the board, as required by law, to vouch personally for Mitchell.[44] One listed voucher, a black citizen, stated that he was Mitchell's neighbor, but he (the voucher) did not know that Mitchell had given him as a reference, and he had never given consent to Mitchell's doing so. The other voucher, a white citizen, testified that he went to the board to vouch for Mitchell but left before doing so because of the large crowd in the registrars' office. The court found no act of racial discrimination.

Mitchell appealed to the circuit Court of Appeals, but before a decision at that level was rendered, an incredible thing hap-

41. *Lane* v. *Wilson,* 307 U.S. 268 (1939).
42. 69 Fed. Supp. 698.
43. In *Thornton* v. *Martin* (1 *Race Relation Law Reporter,* 213 (1955)), the court declared that a class action was permissible in registration cases.
44. Alabama law required the applicant to list two persons who could vouch for his bona fide residence.

pened. The registrars produced a photostatic copy of Mitchell's registration certificate, showing that Mitchell had been certified as a registered voter. The certificate, represented as having been "found," was dated January 20, 1943, two and one-half years before the initial filing of the suit and was presented after the case had been in the courts for more than two years. Mitchell had never been notified that his earlier application had been accepted (thus he had not voted in intervening elections), and no mention was made of it to him in his subsequent attempts to register. "It is doubtful whether we won anything from all that drawn out court battle," Mitchell stated years later, adding: "One Negro was registered." He did not bring up, although he could have, the cost in attorney's fees. Other blacks, however, were registered in Macon County without having to resort to protracted court action. Indeed, on the day Mitchell appeared before the board of registrars, July 5, 1945, ninety blacks applied to be registered; ten were successful. Seven white persons applied; all seven were registered.[45]

In 1949, a three-judge federal district court in Alabama unequivocally invalidated an attempt in that state to curtail black voting by granting substantial arbitrary powers to boards of registrars.[46] A proposed amendment to the state constitution was adopted at the November 7, 1946, state elections, requiring that only those persons could register who were able to "understand and explain any article of the constitution of the United States in the English language." The white primary had been nullified; this was the fall-back to the next line of defense. The three-judge court overruled the Boswell amendment (so-called after the sponsor of the amendment) on three grounds: its lack of a standard, its unconstitutional purpose, and its actual effect in administration. What constituted "understanding" of a particular section of the Constitution? Supreme Court justices frequently disagreed. It boiled

45. 69 Fed. Supp., p. 701.
46. *Davis* v. *Schnell*, 81 F. Supp. 872 (1949).

down to giving the board members arbitrary power to grant or withhold the right to vote. This arbitrariness was not sanctioned. The court took judicial notice that the amendment was racially motivated; the legislative history of the amendment left no doubts on this point. The object, according to its sponsor, state legislators, and other public and private spokesmen in the state, was to circumvent *Smith* v. *Allwright* and to maintain "white supremacy" in Alabama. The court felt it was only stating the obvious intent of the amendment. The trial evidence supported the contention that registrars had, in fact, used the "understand and explain" provision to reject black voter applicants and not white applicants.

All black plaintiffs were not as successful as the ten plaintiffs in the Davis case against alleged discrimination on the part of registrars. The following testimony was given by a black citizen, the Reverend John H. Scott, at hearings held by the Commission on Civil Rights in New Orleans on September 27, 1960:

Vice Chairman Storey: Have you ever had any suit in connection with voter registration?
Rev. Mr. Scott: Yes, sir.
Vice Chairman Storey: When and where?
Rev. Mr. Scott: In 1951 we filed a suit against the registrar of voters in East Carroll Parish. Our attorney from this city filed the suit for us, Louis Barry, who is out of town. It is quite discouraging.
Vice Chairman Storey: Just tell us this. What happened to the suit?
Rev. Mr. Scott: Well, the suit dragged along until—from one court—not one court to another, but from one attorney in court to another, on technical grounds. I believe it was in 1957, from 1951 until 1957, and at that particular time, Jurist Ben Dawkins put us out of his court, said he had no jurisdiction, it belonged to the three-judge court, and after that our attorney went off to California. So I don't know. He just dropped the suit or whatever.
Vice Chairman Storey: You didn't get any relief from the suit?
Rev. Mr. Scott: No, sir.[47]

47. *U.S. Commission on Civil Rights Hearings,* New Orleans, Louisiana, September 27, 1960, pp. 21–22.

The practices of registrars continued to be a major factor in curtailing black voting beyond 1957 and into the 1960s. There remained various ways by which registrars could perform the duty of taking registration applications that would result in serious deterrence to black registration.[48]

The Extra-Legal Stage

The first and second stages are similar to the extent that they have their foundation in constitutional or statutory enactments. While most of the devices used have been voided as attempts to perform essentially unconstitutional acts, foundation in the law is a major factor that distinguishes these obstacles from the third stage—intimidations and reprisals. The third category is mainly noted for its illegality, or rather its attempt to stand outside the law at the outset, and perhaps for this reason alone it may ultimately be the most difficult to handle. Even within this category, there are differences in the degree of difficulty in curtailing these practices. One might say that physical intimidation is more easily curbed than economic reprisal; economic reprisal against large numbers of blacks similarly situated is more easily solved than reprisals against one or two isolated individuals; and economic reprisal against one black by several persons is easier to remedy than acts by one individual against another. The information in a later chapter deals with these gradations.

The legal activity in this specific area before 1957 was neither voluminous nor effective. Since many sources attested to the flagrant and prolific existence of reprisals and intimidations as weapons to deter blacks, one might ask why there were relatively few

48. In *Sellers* v. *Wilson*, 123 F. Supp. 917 (1954), the registration statute was held valid, but it was claimed the board of registrars, in order to prevent black applicants from registering, refused to meet as required by the statute. The court found that the allegations of discriminatory treatment were true, but since the defendant members of the board had resigned, no injunctive relief could be granted.

lawsuits on this subject. There are several answers. Federal statutes, enacted during Reconstruction, were either repealed or severely limited in application by the courts.[49] The federal government was empowered to bring only criminal suits, and the criminal statutes were unwieldly and difficult to apply.[50] Section 241 of the federal Criminal Code penalized conspiracies to "injure, oppress, threaten, or intimidate any citizen in the free exercise or enjoyment of any right . . . secured . . . by the Constitution or laws of the United States." [51] The other criminal provision, section 242 of the Code, forbade action "under color of law"—state officials or persons acting in concert with them who interfered with "rights . . . secured or protected by the Constitution or laws of the United States." Section 241 applied to actions by either state officials or private persons which interfered with voting in federal elections, and apparently to discrimination by state officials in state and local elections as well.

Private parties were enabled to bring civil actions for damages under three federal statutory provisions. One statute condemned racial discrimination in both state and federal elections. While this did not in itself provide for civil actions, two other sections did—sections 1983 and 1985 of Title 42 of the United States Code. Section 1983 allowed suits against persons acting "under color of any statute, ordinance, regulation, custom or usage" to deprive citizens of rights secured by the Constitution and laws of the United States. The injured party could sue for injunctive relief or damages.[52] Section 1985 authorized actions for damages (but not injunctions) against private persons (as well as those acting under

49. See *Report,* U.S. Commission on Civil Rights, 1961, Book I, Part 2, Ch. 4; Book 5, Part VII, Ch. 4, 5; also Carr, *Federal Protection of Civil Rights* (1947), pp. 57–77, 85–115. For a definitive treatment of Section 242 USC, see Shapiro, 46 *Cornell Law Quarterly* 532 (1961).
50. *Report,* U.S. Commission on Civil Rights, 1961, *op. cit.*
51. 18 USC 241.
52. This section served as the basis for *Nixon* v. *Herndon, Smith* v. *Allwright,* and *Rice* v. *Elmore.*

color of law) who conspired to prevent another from voting in a federal election. Section 1985 did not apply to state elections. One source stated, "Civil cases, with their flexible remedies and relative ease of proof, could be brought only by private persons, who are not always able to bear the expense and difficulty involved in long and complicated litigation." [53]

In *Ex parte Yarbrough* (1884),[54] the Supreme Court upheld the constitutionality of Section 241 by saying that Congress had a direct interest in seeing that elections at which members of Congress were chosen were free of violence and fraud. In *Yarbrough,* eight private persons were charged with conspiring to intimidate a black citizen in the exercise of his right to vote. The defendants had beaten, bruised, and wounded a black man "on account of his race, color and previous condition of servitude." They were convicted, and the Supreme Court upheld the conviction.

The power of Congress to protect the right of the franchise under the Fifteenth Amendment arose again in *James* v. *Bowman.*[55] That case involved an indictment under Revised Statute Section 5507, which prohibited interference with the right to vote of persons whose right is guaranteed by the Fifteenth Amendment. The Supreme Court held the statute invalid on the ground that it purported to prohibit individual action whereas the Fifteenth Amendment prohibited action only "by the United States or by any State."

The issues raised in *Terry* v. *Adams* and *James* v. *Bowman* deal with "state action." In both cases, the Supreme Court was examining the act of the organization or the congressional law in light of the language in the Fifteenth Amendment. That language clearly prohibits states from discriminating. At a later point in this book, when we discuss "extra-legal" activity, we will see how the acts of private persons are not properly covered by these

53. *Report, 1961*, U.S. Commission, *op. cit.*, p. 75.
54. 110 U.S. 651 (1884).
55. 190 U.S. 127 (1903).

cases. Whether the Jaybird pre-primary is constitutional or not
depends on its connection with the state—the *nature* of the act
is important. Likewise, whether Congress can, under the Fifteenth
Amendment, prohibit acts of bribery in elections depends on the
courts' construction of "state action." When we discuss private,
extra-legal acts of intimidation we will see that the basis for congressional prohibition is not the Fifteenth Amendment but Article
1, Section 4 of the Constitution, which gives Congress power to
regulate the "times, places, and manner" of federal elections. Thus,
under the Fifteenth Amendment, the major concern is the nature
of the "private" act, while under Section (b) of statute 1971 of
the Civil Rights Act of 1957, the central concern is the motivation
of the private party performing the act. One conclusion of this
book is that the issue of motivation is more difficult to resolve
than the issue of the nature of an act. There are more overt
circumstances by which one can make a judgment in the latter instance. And because the other possible motives—contract and
property rights—are valid rights for protection, the courts must
take a long, hard look before they dismiss them.

The matter of intimidation, especially economic reprisal, remains a most serious deterrent to black voting in several Southern
areas.

3 The Congress Enacts

Accent on Voting

Circulating among civil rights organizations and leaders in the South in the mid-1950s, often one would hear comments about the need for a new approach to the problems of Southern blacks. Most frequently this assertion contained the notion that what was needed was an involvement of masses of black people. Many black leaders were impressed with the enthusiasm, unity, and results of the protest from 1955 to 1957 of thousands of black citizens in Montgomery, Alabama, against segregation on the city buses. In the South there had never been such a sustained and organized protest of masses of blacks. This movement caused several black leaders to start thinking in terms of mass organization in other areas. Other foci were immediately chosen—public parks, municipal golf courses—but the major target became voter registration. The object was to organize countless numbers of blacks throughout the South who would qualify as registered voters and, as voters, use their power to change the political status quo of their particular communities and states. On the scale contemplated, this was new, and many black leaders felt, if properly organized, it was possible. For years, relatively small local organizations—voters' leagues and civic associations—had worked toward increasing the black electorate in particular communities. But this involved holding "voting clinics" attended by perhaps no more than five persons at a time and going through the tedious process of trying to get a handful of applicants successfully past the board of registrars. Many black leaders believed the benefits to be derived from voting strength would constitute not just one of the strongest tools black people could have, but indeed the strongest. The problem was reaching the point of significant strength. Registration officials were in control, and lawsuits in courts were protracted, expensive, and too often fruitless. After 1956, more and more black leaders, national and local, began thinking in terms of mass participation. One associate of Dr. Martin Luther King in the Montgomery bus boycott said, "We'd come to those mass rallies on Monday nights—and sometimes more nights than that—and we'd just see the hopes and—you know—the spirit of the people. Man, I'm telling you, it was something. Thousands, I mean. And we just figured, man, if we could get these many to voting wouldn't that be the day. And that's really what inspired us to move on. We believed, 'cause we saw, our people could stick together."

Long years in the courts over educational desegregation had proved successful in terms of legal victories, and there promised to be many more years of this type of activity. But a school desegregation suit did not involve thousands, and the victorious outcome still left political control of the local communities in the hands of persons who, for the most part, were unsympathetic to the demands of voteless black people.

On May 17, 1957, Dr. King articulated the long-term goals of those who envisioned an increased Southern black electorate:

Give us the ballot and we will no longer have to worry the federal government about our basic rights. Give us the ballot and we will no longer plead to the federal government for passage of an anti-lynching law. We will by the power of our vote write the law on the books of the South and bring an end to the dastardly acts of the hooded perpetrators of the salient misdeeds of bloodthirsty mobs into the calculated good deeds of orderly citizens. Give us the ballot and we will fill our legislative halls with men of good will and send to the sacred halls of congress men who will not sign a Southern Manifesto because of their devotion to the manifesto of justice. Give us the ballot and we will do justly and love mercy. And we will place at the head of the southern states governors who have felt not only the tang of the human but the glory of the divine. Give us the ballot and we will quietly and non-violently, without rancor or bitterness, implement the school decision of May 17, 1954. Give us the ballot and we will help bring this nation to a new society based on justice and dedicated to peace.[1]

In the spring of 1957, King called a meeting of approximately fifty Southern black ministers in Atlanta, Georgia, and formed the Southern Leadership Conference. The name was subsequently changed to the Southern Christian Leadership Conference (SCLC).[2] One of the major programs of SCLC was to conduct a South-wide voter-registration campaign among blacks.

On June 14, 1957, the *Montgomery Advertiser* published a news story under the headline,

KING REVEALS PLAN TO REGISTER
3 MILLION NEGROES FOR '58 POLL

A campaign to prepare three million Southern Negroes for voting in the 1958 elections was announced today by Dr. Martin Luther King. King, one of the leaders in the long Negro boycott of buses in Montgomery, Ala., laid his plans before Vice President Nixon and said he will present them soon to the Southern Leaders Conference, an organization of southern ministers.

"Across the South we now intend to extend the voting clinics to help Negroes overcome the contrived and artificial obstacles to their registering and voting," King said in a statement issued after he met Nixon.

1. Part of a speech delivered in Washington, D.C., May 17, 1957.
2. One observer at that meeting stated the reasons for the change: "They wanted the advantages that would come from having a religious label. Nobody could tab us communist if we were christians. I always felt like this was a compromise, but I went along."

"We hope the campaign will culminate in simultaneous mass attendance at the registration offices in 10 cities across the South."
At a news conference held later, King said the 10 cities hadn't been
selected yet.[3]

Several black leaders felt this emphasis on voting was long over-
due; indeed, many believed it should have been given priority over
the school desegregation campaign. Their thinking was fourfold.
First, there were stronger constitutional guarantees against vote
discriminations: the Fifteenth Amendment was unequivocal in its
prohibitions. Second, voting was ostensibly freer of the social
implications connected with the integration of public schools.[4]
Third, perhaps because of the first two, there was much more support, North and South, in Congress and out, for the protection of
voting rights than for desegregation of public schools. Fourth, if
successful, a voter-registration campaign could result in many
more direct gains for the masses of Southern blacks by the wise
utilization of the franchise.

3. *Montgomery Advertiser,* June 14, 1957.
4. Martin Luther King's speech quoted above would appear to argue against
this. Also, see Myrdal's treatment of the ranked order of the various
measures of segregation and discrimination against Negroes. The theory of
"no social equality" is buttressed by some nine measures of segregation and
discrimination. The crux of the theory is sex. In this popular theory sex
becomes the principle around which the whole structure of segregation of
the Negroes down to disenfranchisement and denial of equal opportunities
on the labor market is organized. "Intermarriage," says Myrdal, is to be
avoided at all cost. "The southern man on the street responds to any plea for
social equality: would you like to have your daughter marry a Negro?" The
ranked order of discrimination then proceeds: (1) ban on intermarriage
and other sex relations involving white women and colored men takes
precedence before everything else. It is the end for which the other restrictions are arranged as means; thereafter follow (2) all sorts of taboos
and etiquettes in personal contacts; (3) segregation in schools and churches;
(4) segregation in hotels, restaurants, theaters, and other public places
where people meet socially; (5) segregation in public conveyances; (6) discrimination in public services; and finally, inequality in (7) politics, (8)
justice, and (9) bread-winning and relief. Myrdal, *An American Dilemma,*
pp. 586–88. So, while voter registration is far down the list of prohibited
activity, it is still related to the primary taboo of sex relations.

Several explanations have been given for the existence at this time within the South and the country generally of an atmosphere more receptive to black enfranchisement than at an earlier time. Essentially, many observers agreed, World War II was a major catalyst. The United States had entered the war to fight a brand of racism it could not tolerate indefinitely in its own society. The racial practices and pronouncements of Nazism were repugnant to millions and, as if to guard against these even further, many were inclined not to permit flagrant racial discriminations, especially in regard to voting, in this country.

Walter White attributed much of the spirit of change to what he called the liberalizing philosophy of the New Deal.[5] Legal victories over the white primary system accumulated and were gradually preparing the South for the time when black voters at the polls would not be a rarity. Having cited the social distinctions between voting and school desegregation, Professor Richard Longaker added his explanation for 1957 having been the year that a Congress was able to pass a civil rights law:

For the first time in eighty-two years a civil rights proposal coincided with favorable national newspaper and organization sentiment and with the political ambitions of Senate leaders such as William Knowland, Richard Nixon, and Lyndon Johnson.[6]

For whatever reasons—and there obviously were many factors operating with varying degrees of significance—1957 could be classified "a civil rights year" in the Congress. How much civil rights? What kind of law? These were questions that had to be worked out over the summer of 1957.

President Eisenhower's administration submitted a proposal to Congress that contained four major features:

5. Walter White, *How Far the Promised Land,* pp. 71–74. White also felt that President Roosevelt's wife, Eleanor Roosevelt, was a major factor in providing "moral leadership . . . on human rights" throughout the country.
6. Longaker, *Presidency and Individual Liberties,* pp. 43–44.

1. Establishment of a special Civil Rights Division within the Department of Justice.

2. Creation of a Federal Civil Rights Commission armed with subpoena powers to compel witnesses to testify and produce records.

3. Authority for the Department of Justice to intervene in the name
   of the United States on behalf of individuals in instances of actual
   or threatened violations of civil rights—such as the right to vote
   or attend an integrated school.

4. Federal district judges would be empowered to issue injunctions
   against such real or threatened violations on the motion of federal prosecutors. Persons disobeying those injunctions could be
   fined or imprisoned for contempt by federal judges without a jury
   trial.

The House of Representatives acted first on the President's proposals.[7] A Southern motion in the House to include a jury trial
provision in contempt prosecutions was defeated by a vote of 251
to 158. On June 18, 1957, the bill was passed by the House by a
vote of 286 to 126 and sent to the Senate (H.R. 6127).

The Jury Trial Battle

Throughout July and August 1957 the Senate focused its attention
on two major features of the civil rights bill passed by the House.[8]
The first modification involved what was referred to as Part III,
that section of the bill permitting the Attorney General to seek
injunctions to enforce public school desegregation and other forms
of racial integration. While this measure was proposed by the
Department of Justice, it was not supported by President Eisenhower. In fact, in a press conference held early in July, the Presi-

7. This, of course, was not exceptional. The House was not the major
obstacle. Four times, beginning in 1942, the House of Representatives
passed anti-poll tax laws by better than two to one votes, but each time
Senate filibusters killed the bills.
8. For a detailed account of the maneuvers in the Senate in 1957 and the
effect of rules on the fate of a bill see, Howard E. Schuman, "Senate Rules
and the Civil Rights Bill: A Case Study," *American Political Science Review*, December 1957, pp. 955–75.

dent expressly indicated his intention to confine the coverage of
the bill mainly to voting rights. Eisenhower's position made the
deletion of Part III a relatively easy matter.

The major battle in the Senate, therefore, ensued over efforts to
add a provision guaranteeing the right of a jury trial to those persons charged with contempt of federal court injunctions. These
efforts received support from varied sources. Most observers agreed
that Southern senators insisted on the jury trial provision because
Southern white (or predominantly white) juries would not be
likely to convict local registration officials or others of discrimination against blacks. Senator Paul H. Douglas (D., Ill.) diagnosed
the case with the observation that federal judges—in the South
as elsewhere—had life tenure "so that they are in a sense insulated
against the passions and prejudices of the community." But, he
added, "white jurors, on the other hand, who might wish to see
justice, have to go back into and be subject to the pressures of
their communities." [9]

One student of constitutional law pointed out that the public
posture of many of the Southern senators in defending the jury
trial as an essential part of protection of individual rights was at
variance with the practices prevailing then and over a period of
years in their own states.[10] Indeed, one of the intellectual leaders
of the Southern forces in the Senate, a former North Carolina
state supreme court associate justice, Sam J. Ervin, Jr., had joined
in opinions while on the state supreme court affirming the position
that a jury trial was not a right in contempt cases arising out of
disobedience to injunctions.[11]

But the Southerners were joined in their jury trial fight by other
influential leaders, one of whom was the powerful labor union
leader, John L. Lewis, who feared the power of court injunctions.

9. *Chicago Sun-Times,* editorial, July 10, 1957.
10. Walter F. Murphy, "Some Strange New Converts to the Cause of Civil
Rights," *The Reporter,* June 27, 1957, pp. 13–14.
11. *Ibid.*

His experiences as a labor leader undoubtedly influenced his judgment. Lewis explained his position by stating, "The strong and harsh power of injunction has been in the past so often abused and indiscriminately used that enlargement thereof, even for worthy purposes, must carry with it reasonable protection to all citizens who may be charged with violation and therefore cited and tried for contempt." [12]

More than one source commented on the coalition of Senate forces favoring the jury trial provision. It was not a new coalition, but the summer of 1957 saw civil rights as an additional issue over which this group could come together. James Reston of the *New York Times* called it "one of the oddest coalitions of strange political bedfellows ever gathered together in Washington." [13] Professor Howard Schuman identified them as the Southern and Western Democrats together with the "remaining hard core of the Republican right wing." Both Reston and Schuman commented on the quid pro quo that operated. Reston wrote:

Most observers here agree that it is always difficult and even dangerous to analyze the reasons for votes in the Senate, and that too much can be made of personal and political influence. Therefore, nobody was making any open charges of "trading" between the Western and Southern Senators.

Moreover, it has been clear from the start that this jury-trial question clearly disturbed many men in the Senate—Senator O'Mahoney is a vivid case in point—who are suspicious by experience of adding any new injunctive powers to the arsenal of the Federal Government. This, plus the conviction that powerful minorities cannot be easily coerced to abide by procedures that are hateful to whole regions of the country, were undoubtedly the main reasons for the Senate's decision to try one step at a time. In any decision that finds the Senate so evenly divided, however, it is also true that personal and regional political considerations combine to influence votes. And

12. *New York Times*, August 3, 1957.
13. *New York Times*, August 3, 1957. Included in this coalition were Senators Lyndon B. Johnson of Texas, Margaret Chase Smith of Maine, Richard B. Russell of Georgia, Mike Mansfield of Montana, John F. Kennedy of Massachusetts, and John O. Pastore of Rhode Island.

while everybody in the Senate will, of course, explain his vote on the grounds of personal conviction, these other political factors undoubtedly had some effect. On many practical matters, the South and West tend to collaborate, even though this coalition brings together men of vastly different political philosophies.

The South needs Western votes in maintaining supports for cotton, tobacco and peanuts. The West looks to the South for protection of its wool, silver, lead, zinc and beet sugar industries. The West helps the South on irrigation projects, especially since the South dominates the chairmanships of most of the key Senate committees involved in these matters.[14]

In past years the Senate filibuster had been the weapon used to defeat civil rights measures, but except for an unsupported twenty-four-hour speech by Strom Thurmond of South Carolina on August 29, when the bill in its final form was presented for a vote, there was nothing to resemble a filibuster in the summer of 1957. Senator Russell of Georgia disclosed that every Southern senator was willing to conduct a filibuster, but it was felt that such a maneuver would not only have failed, but "was certain to make a bad bill infinitely worse." [15] Instead, the Southerners decided to use the threat of a filibuster in a tactic designed to weaken the bill as much as possible. This, of course, meant that the Senate would pass some kind of civil rights bill in 1957.

On August 7 by a vote of 72 to 18, the Senate did pass a revised version of the bill sent to it by the House.[16] The Senate version of the bill permitted federal prosecutors, with or without the consent of the victims, to obtain injunctions against actual or threatened denial of the right to vote. Persons refusing to obey these injunctions could be fined or imprisoned for civil contempt by a federal judge sitting without a jury. In criminal cases the judge would be required to hold a jury trial.

14. *New York Times,* August 3, 1957.
15. *Congressional Record,* August 30, 1957, pp. 15171–72.
16. Opposed were 17 Southern Democrats and Senator Wayne Morse (D., Oregon), an all-out civil rights proponent who denounced the Senate version as one that would raise "hopes and expectations which will not be satisfied."

The First Law in Eighty-two Years

With this action by the Senate, the focus shifted to the reaction of the House of Representatives to the much altered version of its bill. What format would be used to work out a reconciliation? Would the House be asked simply to adopt the work of the Senate or would a formal conference committee be required?

The majority leader of the Senate, Lyndon B. Johnson, reportedly did not want a formal Senate–House conference to iron out the differences.[17] Such a procedure offered the strong possibility that House conferees would reject what the Senate had done, force Southerners to conduct a filibuster and defeat any hope of a civil rights bill emerging from Congress that year. Some observers noted that Democratic congressional leaders wanted and expected the President to have the burden of vetoing the legislation. On the other hand, to get the House to concur in the work of the Senate meant extreme skill had to be exerted on the House Rules Committee, which could recommend either a conference or concurrence.

As forces lined up for the impending battle, accounts circulated about the possibility of a compromise. Unnamed administration sources stated the President would be amenable to a plan that limited jury trials only to voting cases.[18] Some supporters of the Senate version were speaking of a willingness to limit the jury trial provision to voting and labor cases alone. Republican leader of the House, Joseph W. Martin, Jr., of Massachusetts, said the President had made no threat of a veto if the Senate version passed intact.

The Republican floor manager for the House bill, Representative Kenneth B. Keating of New York, declared that he would insist the bill be sent to a full-scale Senate–House conference for changing "anemic" Senate provisions. He also suggested that the

17. *New York Times,* August 3, 1957.
18. *New York Times,* August 4, 1957.

Republicans would recommend a Presidential veto and a special session of Congress unless major changes were made.

House Speaker Sam Rayburn of Texas asked the House to accept the Senate version of the civil rights bill, and he offered as a compromise the prospect of limiting the jury provision to criminal contempt charges in voting cases only. His task was to get seven members of the House Rules Committee (composed of four Republicans, four Northern Democrats, and four Southern Democrats) to report a "rule" to that effect to the floor of the House. Rayburn had the four Northern Democratic votes plus the vote of Representative Thornberry of Texas, so he needed only two additional members of the committee to agree with him.

In insisting on a joint conference between the House and Senate, House Republican leaders had the active support of Vice President Richard Nixon as well as William P. Rogers, Acting Attorney General, "and other administration officials." [19] Representative Keating reported that he had received a telephone call from Mr. Nixon urging him to "stand fast for a 'strong' bill," that Nixon agreed with him (Keating) "that it would be 'abject surrender' to accept the Democratic plan [of avoiding a formal conference]." [20] Spokesmen for each party filled the air and the press with charges of "partisan politics."

Several civil rights organizations, including the NAACP, had urged passage of the Senate version as the best possible plan. During the week of August 12 the AFL–CIO issued a statement calling on Congress to approve the bill as passed by the Senate. It read, in part:

The trade union movement has never taken an "all or nothing" position in the legislative field. We are always prepared to accept progress even when we expected the progress would be greater. In this instance, the Senate-approved measure provided for a Civil Rights Commission, operating with subpoena powers, which can do much to focus public

19. *New York Times,* August 11, 1957.
20. *Ibid.*

and congressional attention on the problems which cry out for justice.[21]

What was the thinking of the chairman of the House Rules Committee, Democratic Representative Howard W. Smith of Virginia, and a very outspoken opponent of any civil rights legislation? He told reporters, "I am inclined to follow the course most likely to result in no bill. Am I making myself clear?" [22] And of course, before the committee members could vote a "rule," they had to be called into meeting; the power to call a meeting rested with the committee chairman.

After several days of impasse, a thaw appeared. Representative Martin called a meeting of the four Republican members of the Rules Committee and Keating proposed that spokesmen for the Senate and House meet informally to determine whether a majority of both houses was insistent on preserving the jury trial amendment. If this were so, he explained, it would then be clear to all that the forces opposing jury trials "had their backs to the wall" and that the time had come to be "realistic" and accept an attainable bill instead of no bill.[23] Keating indicated he had discussed his plan with Martin and Nixon. The Republican forces consented to the maneuver originally suggested by Rayburn, but they gave warning of their intention to propose stronger amendments to the bill once it was on the House floor.

Forcing Rules Chairman Smith to call a committee meeting would require a majority of the committee and at least a ten-day delay. There was evidence that Rayburn would have a committee majority and that in view of this Smith would not refuse to convene the committee. But the four pro-civil rights Democratic committee members submitted a written request to Smith for a committee meeting. Rayburn had two additional votes in Thornberry of Texas

21. *New York Times,* August 14, 1957.
22. *New York Times,* August 15, 1957.
23. *New York Times,* August 16, 1957.

and Trimble of Arkansas. The other two Democrats on the committee were Smith, the chairman, and Colmer of Mississippi. Rayburn needed Republican help, but the Republicans were insisting that he come directly to them and ask for it. "If the Northern Civil Righters want a bill the President will sign," Martin stated, "they had better come to us." [24]

On August 21 Eisenhower held a press conference at which he expressed a strong desire for a civil rights bill during that congressional session, called for an end to any "all or nothing" attitude, and seemed to indicate that he would accept the Senate version as the best that could be had. Within five hours the House Republican leadership conditionally offered to go along with the Senate version. The Republicans suggested that jury trial apply only where the penalties involved were above $300 in fines or above ninety days' imprisonment. If these terms were accepted, they would provide the necessary votes to break the Rules Committee stalemate. Rayburn's immediate reaction was that "This is very deep stuff. I must have time to digest it." [25]

Then the House Democrats proceeded to study the latest Republican proposal. Finally, a bi-partisan, two-chamber agreement was reached between Senators Johnson and Knowland and Representatives Rayburn and Martin. The "leadership compromise" provided that a federal judge should determine whether a jury trial was to be granted in criminal contempt prosecutions arising from violation of federal voting-right injunctions; that if he elected to proceed without a jury, convicted the defendant, and fined him more than $300 or sent him to jail for more than forty-five days, the defendant could demand to have the case tried over before a jury.

The House Republicans then proceeded to join the Democrats in a move on the Rules Committee. The Committee, by a vote of 10 to 2, recommended that the House concur in the Senate's text

24. *New York Times,* August 21, 1957.
25. *New York Times,* August 22, 1957.

of the bill, with the above-described alterations. The House passed the revised bill by a 279 to 97 vote.

The Senate approved the bill, 60 to 15, on August 29. Only the President's signature was needed, and that was added on September 7.

The law was heralded as much for its being the first piece of civil rights legislation passed by the Congress in eighty-two years as it was for any optimism about its ability to ensure voting rights for blacks. Its effectiveness would depend on its implementation by the federal government. The act created the United States Commission on Civil Rights for a two-year term as a bi-partisan agency to study civil rights problems and report to the President and Congress. The Civil Rights Section of the Department of Justice was raised to the status of a full division and a position of Assistant Attorney General was established to head it.

While obviously all parts of the law were important, the heart of the act was the section outlining the constitutional right to be protected and the procedures to be followed. It authorized the federal government to bring civil actions for injunctive relief where discrimination denied or threatened the right to vote. Previous statute law (42 USC, section 1971) provided that the right to vote in any election should not be denied a qualified voter because of race, color, or previous condition or servitude. Under the 1957 act, this earlier provision was now called subsection (a) and four additional subsections were added. Subsection (b) expanded this protection by prohibiting actual or attempted intimidation or coercion which might deprive a person of his right to vote in a federal election. This laid the foundation for equitable relief. The Attorney General was authorized to institute civil actions for relief in the name of the United States under subsection (c). In addition, the previously existing criminal codes were available to the federal government.[26] Civil action could be commenced "when-

26. 18 USC, Sections 241, 242, 594 (1952).

ever a person has engaged or there are reasonable grounds to
believe that . . . [he] is about to engage" in a deprivation of
voting rights protected by subsections (a) or (b). Subsection (d)
gave the federal district courts jurisdiction in these civil proceedings without requiring that state remedies first be exhausted. Subsection (e) provided protection for the defendant cited for contempt of the federal court order; the defendant should have notice,
the right to a hearing, the benefit of counsel, the right to compel
witnesses to appear in his behalf, and a jury trial under the circumstances described earlier.

In essence, the 1957 act made a major change over previous
laws by giving the federal government an equitable remedy in civil
proceedings. A decree in equity could prevent an attempted deprivation of the right to vote before it occurred and provide continuing protection. One student made the following observation
of the new law:

Equity has the additional advantage of providing quick relief in the
form of a temporary injunction pending the outcome of the suit. However, the major reason why Congress felt an equity action was desira-
ble is that means of enforcing the decrees of a court of equity are as
compelling as is a criminal sanction, and certainly more compelling
than money damages at law. The decree in equity, moreover, has the
advantage over a criminal prosecution in that violation of such a
decree can be proven more easily. Equity, by its power to punish for
contempt, acts upon the person of the defendant.[27]

The equity procedure was also seen by another as a major advance
over previous laws:

Effectively administered Part IV should go a long way toward making
the right to vote meaningful. Certainly most forms of private action
interfering with the right to vote sink to the low station of some
species of intimidation; the more subtle forms of deprivation have in
the past seemed to stem from some kind of official activity. In addi-

27. Comment: "The Civil Rights Act of 1957 and Contempt of Court," 43
Cornell Law Quarterly, 661 (No. 4), Summer 1958, p. 666.

tion, the flexible process of equity lends itself to the actual ferreting out of these subtleties much more propitiously than the doctrinaire approach of the "common law side," not to mention the technicalities of the criminal law.[28]

The Half-Loaf / Whole-Loaf Controversy

It is quite understandable that an issue as important and as controversial as civil rights should, in 1957, have evoked a great deal of interest, comment, and disagreement. Before the ink was dry on the act—indeed, even before it was finally passed—advocates of varying points of view were engaged in debate on the merits of the bill. Positions began to solidify, especially after the Senate passed its modified version in early August. Walter Lippmann felt that the bill as revised by the Senate was a wise bill, one that did not commit the administration to performing beyond its capabilities. He stated:

Supposing that a wide bill, such as the one which came from the House, could be passed, it would be almost impossible to enforce it. For it would unite the resistance of the southern states, and it would place upon the Department of Justice a more impossible task than did the old and thoroughly discredited Prohibition Amendment.[29]

We should be concerned about the problems of enforcement, Lippmann admonished, and less about broad, sweeping promises. "Does not the history of the problem of civil inequality in this country," he asked rhetorically, "prove conclusively that declara-

28. Dorsey E. Lane, "The Civil Rights Act of 1957," 4 *Howard Law Journal,* No. 1, January 1958, p. 46.
29. *Chicago Sun-Times,* August 18, 1957. One answer to this view has emphasized the distinction between use of available methods and authorization of them. See Dixon, *George Washington Law Review,* April 1959. He recognized that particular circumstances might operate to cause moderation and caution in enforcing the law, "but to reject the mere authorization of methods of enforcement in the face of a sectional policy which approaches nullification of the Constitution is to countenance a cancer of anarchy in the body politic."

tions of rights can be nothing but empty sounds if the resistance is strong enough?"

Black leaders got into the controversy on both sides. Roy Wilkins, executive secretary of the NAACP, and Martin Luther King accepted the Senate version of the bill after stating that they obviously had wanted a stronger bill. A major Chicago black weekly newspaper attacked them bitterly in an editorial entitled: "King, Wilkins Fumble on Civil Rights":

In accepting the Senate version of the tattered civil rights bill, Roy Wilkins, executive secretary of the NAACP, and Rev. Martin Luther King of Montgomery, Alabama, have committed the gravest tactical blunder that has ever been made by Negro leadership throughout the whole course of our turbulent history in America.

It is a blunder so colossal as to carry with it an unmitigated implication of an unconditional surrender. Under the assumption that half a loaf is better than none—a hobo psychology—these gentlemen spelled out in concrete terms a formula for appeasement in what is fundamentally a battle for Constitutional rights and simple social justice. It is a reprehensible concession which has set in motion the sequence of events that may lead to disastrous consequences.

The tragic irony of the situation is that Wilkins and King capitulated at the critical hour when the backers of the bill were still fighting to strengthen it and when the prospects were bright for a satisfactory revision. Word had gone out from the White House that the President was not satisfied with the Senate version of the bill and that there was strong possibility he might veto it. Therefore, there was no cause to toss in the towels when the battle was still raging. If they could not campaign for a stronger proposal, the least Wilkins and King could have done was to zipper up their lips.

Instead they appeared to have allowed themselves to be bamboozled by Walter Reuther and James Carey of the AFL–CIO, who wanted the jury trial amendment for labor disputes. King and Wilkins have echoed the views of labor-politicians who are stirred by anxiety for labor interest.

It takes more to establish democratic rights than obsequious deference to labor Czars who have no real identification with the longings of our people.

We will grant that there is room for honest differences of opinion in almost any controversy, but there is no room nor occasion for weakness and vacillation in demanding our full civil rights. By their unwarranted surrender Mr. Wilkins and Reverend Mr. King have done a great disservice to the cause of first class citizenship. They have come close to forfeiting their claim to national leadership.[30]

Wilkins's response was that he admitted he chose a position which "may not be popular at the present time," but "we believe that we have chosen a course which is practical rather than emotional."

Dr. Ralph J. Bunche of the United Nations sent a telegram to President Eisenhower after the Senate modification and while the House was deliberating in late August:

The bill in its present form is disappointingly weak. I heartily support every effort now being made to strengthen it.[31]

Jackie Robinson, the well-known baseball player, also wired the White House after the Senate added the jury provision:

Am opposed to civil right bill in its present form. Have been in touch with a number of my friends. We disagree that half a loaf is better than none. Have waited this long for bill with meaning—can wait a little longer.[32]

There were those who advocated the "half-loaf" rather than no bill but proceeded to chastise Senator Johnson for his position. Eleanor Roosevelt and Adlai Stevenson preferred to have "the little that will come with this bill than to have nothing." She added:

I think the southern Senators, led by Sen. Lyndon Johnson, have won a costly victory—because this fight for civil rights is not going to stop. If the people of Africa are on the move, the people of the United States are also on the move. Our people are not going to be satisfied with crumbs such as this civil rights bill gives them. It will bring us

30. *Chicago Defender*, August 31, 1957.
31. *New York Times*, August 20, 1957.
32. *Ibid.*

no peace, but it is better to pass it and see what we can achieve with even this slight change.[33]

Many wanted more than the 1957 act provided; many wanted none of the features it offered; and many saw great value in the mere existence of the act itself. Some pointed out, in connection with the latter view, that the chief significance of the act lay in the fact that it was passed at all, "that it restored civil rights as a legitimate subject for congressional action after a lapse of over eighty years." [34] Such a position probably offered little consolation to the "whole-loaf" advocates who generally saw little meaning in "small steps forward," and who talked for the most part in terms of the already ninety-odd years since the abolition of slavery and of 1957 as being too late for "tidbits." Politics might be the "art of compromise," but an American citizen's civil rights, they argued, should not be the object of political bargaining.

The political institutions of the society were called upon to make certain decisions, and one could reasonably expect—or should have at any rate—that political methods would be utilized in the process.

Revisions: Registrars or Referees

The pass-it-and-see attitude endorsed by many in 1957 [35] began to crystallize into renewed efforts at the first session of the next Congress for another civil rights law.

In the sixteen months after the passage of the 1957 act the Department of Justice instituted one suit against election registrars

33. *Chicago Sun-Times,* August 13, 1957.
34. Milton R. Konvitz, *A Century of Civil Rights* (1961).
35. On August 9, 1957, the *New York Times* editorialized: "If a law does in fact emerge, let us regard it as an experiment in which honest men of both races and on both sides of the Mason and Dixon line may take part. . . . Let us see what can be done. If the prospective law does not improve an unhappy situation, let us study how that law can be strengthened and improved."

in the South—Terrell County, Georgia. The Civil Rights Commission did not hold its first public hearing until December 8, 1958 (in Montgomery, Alabama), largely because a staff director was not finally confirmed by the Senate until May 1958. Many were beginning to suggest in the early months of 1959 that a new law was needed.

In the first two months of the new congressional session, thirty-eight bills were introduced into the Senate and 205 into the House.[36] These included proposals to extend the life of the Commission on Civil Rights, punish acts of bombing churches and synagogues, and guard against destruction of voting records by local registrars.

During the first session of the Eighty-sixth Congress in 1959, hearings on civil rights bills were held by a House subcommittee and a subcommittee of the Senate Judiciary Committee.[37] But as before, the major obstacles to the passage of a bill lay in the House Rules Committee and the chairman of the Senate Judiciary Committee, James O. Eastland of Mississippi. Various legislative maneuvers by civil rights opponents resulted in the abandonment in late August and early September of 1959 of any effort to secure a comprehensive bill at that session. Senate majority leader Lyndon Johnson, however, dramatically stated, "I serve notice on all members that on or about 12 o'clock on February 15 [1960], I anticipate that some senator will rise in his place and make a motion with regard to the general civil rights question." Senate minority leader Everett Dirksen of Illinois concurred in this promise: "If the Lord is willing and I am alive."

One item could not be postponed, and that dealt with the Civil

36. Dixon, *loc. cit.* This House figure may be misleading inasmuch as many of the bills were identical in content. The House, unlike the Senate, required a member to introduce a bill in his own name. The Senate permitted several members to co-sponsor a single bill.
37. For a very detailed study of the legislative maneuverings centered on the passage of the 1960 bill see Daniel M. Berman's *A Bill Becomes a Law: The Civil Rights Act of 1960* (1962).

Rights Commission which, under the 1957 act, was scheduled to die two months before the next session. Bi-partisan congressional leadership developed, and a rider extending the life of the commission for two years was attached to a foreign aid measure and passed. This was given greater significance because on September 9, 1959, the commission issued its first full-scale report, minutely documenting, among other things, denials of voting rights in the South and recommending the establishment of federal registrars to register persons where such discriminatory practices were proven. So attention focused on February 1960 and a promised civil rights battle in the Congress. The fact that 1960 was also a Presidential election year did not escape the attention of many persons.

In the second session of the Eighty-sixth Congress which opened in January 1960 a major rivalry developed between two types of procedures or plans for strengthening the 1957 law. The first was the "registrar plan" initially proposed by the Civil Rights Commission. Any individual could submit an affidavit to the President alleging that he had been unable to register with state voting officials for reasons of race, color, or national origin. He would also have to swear that he believed himself qualified under state law. If the President received nine or more such complaints from a single county, he would refer them to the Civil Rights Commission for verification. After an investigation had weeded out any petitions that lacked merit, the President would designate a federal officer or employee in the area to act as a temporary voting registrar. The registrar would respect any qualifications state law imposed on registration. He would issue registration certificates conferring the right to vote on disenfranchised persons, and he would continue to serve until the President determined that his services were no longer needed. This registrar plan was based on the "time, places, and manner" clause of Article I, Section 4 of the Constitution and consequently applied only to federal elections.

The Department of Justice countered this plan with a "referee proposal." Attorney General William P. Rogers suggested procedures that involved the federal judiciary and applied to state and local as well as federal elections. The referee procedure would begin with a suit under the Civil Rights Act of 1957. In such a suit, the Attorney General would ask that specific individuals be enjoined from discriminating against voters because of their race. If he obtained the injunction, he would then go beyond what the 1957 law had authorized the court to hold that a "pattern or practice" of voting discrimination existed in the area. After making such a finding, the judge could appoint a voting referee to receive applications from prospective voters claiming that racial discrimination had kept them from the polls. The referee would take evidence in each case and then report his conclusions to the judge, who would have to accept them unless convinced that they were "clearly erroneous." The judge would then issue a decree listing individuals whose qualifications for voting had been substantiated. State election officials would be notified that these persons were entitled to vote, and the referee could be at the polls to observe any infringement of this right. In the hearing before the referee, the applicant would be heard *ex parte* (with no one appearing on the other side). This provision was introduced to guard against the situation whereby a black witness would have to face possible stiff cross-examination by Southern officials.

Senator Thomas Hennings, chairman of the Senate Committee on Rules and Administration which conducted hearings on the bills, offered a plan combining what he considered to be the strong features of both the registrar and referee plans. He offered a plan for "federal enrollment officers." There would have to be a suit under the 1957 law, followed by a judicial finding of habitual discrimination against black voters. After this prerequisite had been met, purely administrative steps would follow. The President would appoint enrollment officers to register blacks living in the affected area, and the Department of Justice could obtain court

injunctions to prevent interference at the polling places. State
officials could challenge the registered black person only at one
place and at one time—at the polls on election day. In the event
of such a challenge the black voter would still be permitted to cast
his vote, although on a provisional basis. The ballot would not be
counted at once. State officials would have an opportunity to
challenge the black's qualifications in federal court. If their charges
were substantiated, the ballot of the black voter would be dis-
carded. Some criticized Hennings' enrollment officer plan because
it required the proof of habitual discrimination.[38] This would require several suits over several years, the critics felt. It can also
be pointed out that the plan would have destroyed the secrecy of
the black voter's choice.

The fourth and final major proposal was suggested by Senators
Paul Douglas and Jacob Javits. The President would be authorized
to appoint federal registration officials for any locality where he
had reason to believe that discrimination was taking place. His
action would apply only to federal elections, and Douglas and
Javits were willing to rely on the referee plan to deal with state
elections.

As promised, on February 15, 1960, by an ingenious maneuver
that was at once praised and condemned by their colleagues,
Senators Johnson and Dirksen combined to obtain consideration
of civil rights on the Senate floor. The vehicle was an insignificant
bill already passed by the House authorizing the use of an unused
army officers' club in Missouri as a temporary replacement for a
county school that had been destroyed by fire. Johnson asked
unanimous consent that the Senate proceed to consideration of
the bill. There was no objection. Then Johnson pulled his surprise;
he announced that the bill was then available for amendments—
civil rights amendments. The Senate has no rule requiring that
amendments be germane to the subject matter of the bill. Dirksen

38. Thomas I. Emerson, "Negro Registration Laws," *Nation,* CXC, March
19, 1960, p. 241.

then introduced as an amendment the seven-point civil rights program requested by President Eisenhower in 1959 and the Attorney General's referee proposal. The Judiciary Committee had been circumvented, and a civil rights measure was on the Senate floor. Southern senators began a filibuster; Johnson called for around-the-clock sessions. Civil rights proponents, against Johnson's will, sought a cloture petition to end the filibuster. The petition suffered a major defeat—53 to 42 against the petition. Not only were the civil righters unable to obtain the necessary two-thirds vote of senators present, but they fell short of a simple majority.

Sentiment built for a compromise civil rights bill with emphasis on voting. Johnson and Dirksen favored this. More than one observer commented on the almost unbeatable alliance of the two Senate leaders. "The unusually close cooperation between Johnson and Dirksen was patent at virtually every stage of the civil rights struggle. . . . Johnson and Dirksen were a study in togetherness. The alliance between the two leaders made Johnson's power almost absolute. It meant that on occasion when the liberals deserted his leadership, he could compensate for their defection with votes that Dirksen controlled." [39] Johnson, sensing that a bill devoted almost exclusively to voting would be passed by the House, counseled the Senate to await action by the lower chamber.

On the other side of Capitol Hill consideration of a civil rights bill (H.R. 8601) was delayed by the inaction of the House Rules Committee. A discharge petition was started and when the required number of 219 signatures was in sight, Chairman Howard Smith announced that the Rules Committee would hold hearings. With the aid of the four Republican members, the Committee reported the bill by a vote of 7 to 4. The House bill contained the following six points:

39. Berman, *A Bill Becomes a Law,* pp. 70–71. See also Anthony Lewis, "The Professionals Win Out Over Civil Rights," *The Reporter,* May 26, 1960, pp, 27, 30.

Title I A fine of as much as $1000 and imprisonment up to sixty days for interference with the school desegregation order of a federal court.

Title II A fine of $5000 and a jail term of five years for fleeing across state lines after bombing any building.

Title III Preservation for two years of records pertaining to the election of federal officials and their availability to the Department of Justice.

Title IV A two-year extension of the Civil Rights Commission, with a new authorization to take sworn testimony.

Title V Educational opportunities furnished by the federal government for children of military personnel in areas where regular schools had been closed to prevent desegregation.

Title VI Separability of the various titles. (This meant that if the Supreme Court invalidated any portion of the act, the other provisions would remain in force.)[40]

The House adjourned and reconvened as a Committee of the Whole. Several amendments proposed by Emmanuel Cellar (D., N.Y.) were ruled out of order by the Chairman of the Committee of the Whole, Francis E. Walter (D., Pa.). After extensive legislative in-fighting, the House passed a bill containing the provisions of the original measure reported out of committee and including voter referees.

H.R. 8601 was sent to the Senate and within one hour Senator Johnson had it referred to the Senate Judiciary Committee with instructions that the measure be reported back within five days. Johnson favored what the House had done, and he was in no mood to see those results bottled up by the customary tactics of Senator Eastland and his colleagues. The more ardent civil rights supporters would not like the bill, but Johnson felt the liberals were more manageable than the opponents of the bill. The House-passed bill stipulated that hearings before the voter referee should be *ex parte*. The Senate Judiciary Committee, at the instance of

40. Berman, *op. cit.,* p. 17.

Senator Estes Kefauver (D., Tenn.), amended the bill to provide that the hearing was to be held in a public place, with two days' notice given to the state or county registrar so that he could attend with counsel and make a transcript of the proceedings. Two other amendments pertaining to voting stated that local officials should be required to preserve election records for only twenty-two months instead of two years, and election records coud be examined by federal investigators only at the place where the records were regularly stored.

Senator Kefauver's amendment was clarified on the floor of the Senate by providing that the referee hearing was to be *ex parte,* but in proceedings that would be open to the public. The Senate concurred in this change, 69–22. Heated exchanges took place between Senators Johnson and Javits over the latter's attempt to establish a permanent Commission on Equal Job Opportunity. Johnson called for an immediate vote on Javits's proposal; Javits protested that he was not prepared for such a vote. Senator Joseph Clark (D., Pa.), feeling that the Senate leadership was less considerate of civil rights proponents than of Southern senators, engaged Senator Dirksen in a heated debate.

On April 8, the Senate passed the bill as amended amidst congratulatory statements by Johnson and Dirksen commending the role played by the other, pronouncement by Senator Byrd (D., Va.) that "In the main the result has been a victory for the South," and a strong denunciation of the bill by Senator Clark as nothing "more than a sham which will fool some people into believing that we have done something for the disfranchised citizens who have been discriminated against for years, but which in fact, is not going to do them any good at all."

The amended bill went back to the House, but the congressional battle was over. Professor Berman reports that no serious opposition was raised in the House Rules Committee because the Southern members felt it would be futile or because they were pleased the bill was no stronger than it was.[41] Several congressmen made anti- or pro-civil rights speeches for the record, and then the House concurred in the Senate action by a 288 to 95 vote.

The Second Law in Three Years

On May 6 President Eisenhower signed the Civil Rights Act of 1960. Part IV of the act had four steps. First, the Government had to file a suit under Section 1971(a) and (c) and obtain a court finding that a person had been deprived of the right to vote on account of race or color. Second, the court must find that "such deprivation was or is pursuant to a pattern or practice." Third, for at least a year after such finding any person of the race found to be discriminated against in the area could apply for an order declaring him qualified to vote. To be entitled to such an order, a person would have to prove that he was qualified under state law to vote, and had, since the finding by the court, been denied the opportunity to register or qualify to vote. Fourth, the court could hear the applicants itself, or it could, at its discretion, appoint referees from among qualified voters in the district to rule on the applications.

Another significant provision of the act, Part III, declared voting records to be public and required their preservation for a period of twenty-two months following any general or special election. The importance of this provision, as pointed out in the 1961 report of the Civil Rights Commission was that it made records available to the Attorney General before a suit had been filed. This was unlike ordinary judicial discovery procedure.

Prior to the enactment of the 1960 law, several persons agreed that whatever method was devised to ensure the equitable treatment of Southern blacks in their efforts to vote, that method

41. *Ibid.*, p. 109.

should be "no more complicated or cumbersome than the method available to other citizens in the State or district who are registered." [42] Senator Paul Douglas' comments following the passage of the 1960 law questioned the achievement of that goal:

> Mr. President, the bill which the Senate is about to pass sets up an elaborate obstacle course which the disenfranchised Negro in the South must successfully run before he will be permitted to vote at all. At every strategic point there are high technical walls which Negroes must scale, and along the course there are numerous cunningly devised legal pitfalls into which he may fall. The delays and the discouragements have been multiplied so . . . that the bill would permit only a very few additional Negroes to vote. The precise nature of these unnecessary hurdles, pitfalls, and water jumps which have been constructed by the framers of the bill . . . will be revealed to the country in the months and years ahead. . . . [The bill] is grossly inadequate to right the great wrongs which are now practiced. . . . Ninety years after the 15th Amendment and ninety-three years after the 14th, this is not good for the American tradition of equal opportunity.[43]

One Washington observer, however, did not absolve the liberal, pro-civil rights forces in the Senate from considerable blame for the type of bill that was ultimately enacted. "The liberal group had neither a plan nor a leader," he wrote.[44] Anthony Lewis felt that one of the major strategic blunders of the liberals was to attempt cloture in March 1960. Not only did this maneuver take "Senator Johnson off the hook" (he no longer had the burden of finding some way out of the impasse caused by the Southern filibuster), but it failed, and it failed in the most disastrous way. "If a master strategist had been planning a debacle for the liberals, he could hardly have done better. The failure to win even a simple majority undercut the frequently repeated liberal argument that on civil rights legislation a majority of the Senate is undemocrat-

---

42. Notre Dame Conference, *op. cit.*
43. 106 *Congressional Record*, April 8, 1960, pp. 7261–62.
44. Lewis, "The Professionals Win Out . . . ," *loc. cit.*, pp. 27–30.

ically thwarted by Rule 22. The vote demonstrated more dramatically than anything Senator Johnson could have devised that there was no majority in the Senate for all-out civil rights legislation. From that moment on, it was evident that only a much narrower bill could be passed—one limited primarily to voting rights." [45] The liberals should not have tried to destroy the referee plan, but should have accepted it and then tried to improve it.

Its [liberal bloc] members seemed unable to recognize that they simply do not constitute a majority of the United States Senate. Instead of aiming at limited objectives as the Southerners did, or of thinking as Senator Johnson does, of what concessions have to be made to obtain a majority, the liberals refused to abandon any one of their proposals no matter how much it alienated the controlling central group in the Senate.[46]

45. *Ibid.*
46. *Ibid.*

4 The President Reacts

There are many, frequently conflicting points of view concerning the role of the President in regard to civil rights. But all generally say that whatever the role, he must do something. At times action may take a negative form, as when President Eisenhower repeatedly refused to endorse the Supreme Court's decision on school segregation in 1954 on the grounds that such action by the President was improper and would set an undesirable precedent. Those who cite reasons for Presidential action, however, usually have positive manifestations in mind. The language frequently used reads "with crusading zeal";[1] "imaginative action";[2] or "robust conviction." [3]

Positive Presidential support for civil rights activity has several rather immediate practical consequences. Professor Peltason's study of Southern federal judges and their implementation of the 1954 decision led him to state that the Presidential

nonintervention policy [into the matter of school boards ordering desegregation] has had its impact on the judges as well. Nor were those

1. Martin Luther King, "Equality Now: The President Has the Power," *The Nation,* February 4, 1961.
2. *The Federal Executive and Civil Rights,* Southern Regional Council, 1961.
3. *Ibid.*

judges who did act encouraged by the fact that if they ran into opposition, the President's backing was by no means assured. In this
situation, the most recalcitrant judge and the most defiant school
board were allowed to set the pace.[4]

Presidents must be mindful of the black vote, another pointed out,
"which is now of crucial political significance." [5] In addition, the
President is the main guardian of American prestige abroad, and
"Presidents must respond to Negro aspirations or face the prospect
of damaging" this prestige.[6] President Eisenhower referred to this
last factor in his address to the nation during the Little Rock crisis
in 1957:

At a time when we face grave situations abroad because of the hatred
that communism bears toward our system of government based on
human rights, it would be difficult to exaggerate the harm that is
being done to the prestige and influence, and indeed to the safety,
of our nation and the world. . . . Our enemies are gloating over the
incident and using it everywhere to misrepresent our whole nation.[7]

So a President must be responsive to many constituencies—black,
white, North, South, domestic, foreign. The posture he assumes becomes centrally important in the resolution of many issues. His
position alone may not be decisive, but his power, unlike that of
any other individual's in the society, is able to set a tone, to articu-
late a direction—in essence, to lead. For these reasons, we turn
now to the leadership exercised by the two Presidents in the right
to vote issue between 1957 and 1963.

1957—An Administration Against Itself

Whatever is said about President Eisenhower's lack of firm, consistent leadership on civil rights in the summer of 1957 (and there

4. Peltason, *58 Lonely Men,* p. 55.
5. Longaker, *Presidency and Individual Liberties,* p. 8.
6. *Ibid.* p. 11.
7. *New York Times,* September 25, 1957.

has been a great deal said about this), the fact remains that it was
an Eisenhower bill that was introduced into Congress. This meant,
of course, that Congress could not easily overlook it.[8] But while the
bill bore the prestige of the President's name, it cannot be said that
it consistently had his all-out support. President Eisenhower soon
backed away from the important provisions of Part III allowing
the Attorney General to seek injunctive relief to support school desegregation and other civil rights. The President gave the impression that he was not fully informed on the contents of the bill that
bore his backing. Early in July 1957 at a press conference he was
asked if he would be willing to accept a bill limited to voting rights.
He replied, "Well, I would not want to answer this in detail because I was reading part of that bill this morning, and I—there
were certain phrases I didn't completely understand." [9] One answer
earlier, in dealing with a question pertaining to Senator Russell's
charge that the administration bill passed by the House was a
"cunning device" to enforce integration of the races in the South,
the President said:

Well, I would say this: Naturally, I am not a lawyer and I don't participate in drawing up the exact language of proposals. I know what
the objective was that I was seeking, which was to prevent anybody
illegally from interfering with any individual's right to vote, if that
individual were qualified under the proper laws of his state, and so
on.
I wanted also to set up this special secretary in the Department of
Justice to give—to give special attention to these matters, and I
wanted to set up a commission, as you will recall. Now, to my mind,
these were simple matters that were more or less brought about by
the Supreme Court decision, and were a very modest move.[10]

It was not clear exactly how the President related the Supreme
Court to these requests. It was not necessary for Mr. Eisenhower
to be a lawyer to distinguish between a bill covering only voting

8. Longaker, *op. cit.*, p. 45.
9. *New York Times*, July 4, 1957.
10. *Ibid.*

rights and a Civil Rights Commission and one pertaining to injunctive relief of the nature provided by Part III. The President apparently had not carefully studied the bill prepared by his own administration. Such lack of knowledge and vacillation could hardly help but lend support to those in the Congress seeking a much watered-down bill or no bill at all. Eisenhower should have known the basic policy content of the bill, whether he could understand "certain phrases" or not.

His personal philosophy became clearer at a press conference two weeks later. Again the question was based on Part III. He said:

I personally believe if you try to go too far too fast in laws in this delicate field, that has involved the emotions of so many millions of Americans, you are making a mistake. I believe we have got to have laws that go along with education and understanding, and I believe if you go beyond that at any one time, you cause trouble rather than benefit.[11]

However sincere, it was not the type of statement calculated to support the type of bill drawn up by his administration. This type of statement should have been made at an earlier stage in the circle of those drafting the bill, and if the President was firm in his belief, then he should have insisted that his subordinates abide by his wishes and not propose the kind of bill that ultimately left the executive branch.

Later in the summer, when the Senate voted to add the jury trial provision in criminal contempt proceedings, President Eisenhower termed this "bitterly disappointing." It is difficult not to conclude that his earlier actions had lent weight to the Southern cause. He had repudiated a major part of his own administration's bill; he had shown an unconscionable lack of knowledge about broad policy issues in that bill; and he had made the "time-and-education" statement so frequently used by those who, at varying points along the civil rights route, wanted to move slowly or not at all. It is not ap

11. *New York Times,* July 8, 1957.

propriate here to assess the validity of that position, but it provides
the opportunity to point out that if Professor Neustadt's theory
about a President and his "professional reputation" [12] is valid, then
Mr. Eisenhower violated many if not all of the essential rules of the
politics of leadership.

1960—Administration Moderation

Early in 1959, the country received a definite indication of the
thinking of the Department of Justice (later concurred in by President Eisenhower) concerning the administration's approach to civil
rights. Moderation was the keynote. Attorney General William P.
Rogers specifically opposed the grant of further injunctive powers at
that time. In putting his case against federal suits in school segregation cases, he stated:

If we start a lot of litigation it might harden resistance so much it
would set back the cause. We prefer compliance to come from the
people even if it takes a while. In Virginia there has been a tremendous development in the thinking of the people. I think there has been
general recognition these last few months (when some schools were
closed) that the Supreme Court decision is the law of the land. There
has been general recognition that the alternatives are compliance or
no public schools. There has been general recognition that abandonment of public schools would be tragic. As a result there has been a
search for ways to comply. I think it would not have worked out as well
if the Federal Government had moved in there and started lawsuits.[13]

Similarly, he told a House Judiciary subcommittee that "sometimes progress can be made faster without litigation. If you have
everyone in a state against you, you can't do much law enforcement
that isn't pretty disastrous." [14]

12. Richard E. Neustadt, *Presidential Power* (1960).
13. Testimony in civil rights hearings before the Subcommittee on Constitutional Rights of the Senate Committee on the Judiciary, 86th Congress,
1st Session, March 20, 1959.
14. Civil Rights Hearings before the Subcommittee No. 5 of the House
Committee on the Judiciary, 86th Congress, 1st Session, March 11, 1959.

On Sunday, January 3, 1960, the *New York Times* ran a front-page news story entitled, EISENHOWER WARY ON PLAN TO WIDEN CIVIL RIGHTS LAW; UNLIKELY TO PRESS CONGRESS FOR U.S. VOTE REGISTRARS TO PROTECT NEGROES. The story indicated that "the Administration has not fixed its position on civil rights. But official thinking indicates strongly that it will stand pretty much on the relatively modest proposals made by President Eisenhower."

The same week, amidst an "atmosphere of heightened interest in civil rights," [15] President Eisenhower delivered his State of the Union message, but he gave very little direction to Congress on civil rights. In an over-all forty-six-minute speech, he merely stated:

Still another issue relates to civil rights. In all our hopes and plans for a better world we all recognize that provincial and racial prejudice must be combatted. In the long perspective of history, the right to vote has been one of the strongest pillars of a free society. Our first duty is to protect this right against all encroachments. In spite of constitutional guarantees, and notwithstanding much progress of recent years, bias still deprives some persons in this country of equal protection of the laws.

Early in your last session, I recommended legislation which would help eliminate several practices discriminating against the basic rights of Americans. The Commission on Civil Rights has developed additional constructive recommendations. I hope that these will be among the matters to be seriously considered in the current session. I trust that Congress will thus signal to the world that our Government is striving for equality under law for all our people.[16]

He did not endorse a single recommendation of the Commission; he did not spell out the particular recommendations he wanted "seriously considered."

The *New York Times* pinpointed this woeful lack of Presidential leadership at a time and on a subject when greater executive attention was sorely needed. "Inasmuch as the civil rights issue will be one of the first, one of the most important and one of the most

15. Berman, *A Bill Becomes a Law,* p. 40.
16. *New York Times,* January 8, 1960.

controversial of all domestic issues to come before this session of the Congress," the editorial commented, "the President's comments on it are disappointingly vague." [17] President Eisenhower's remarks were described by the *Times* as definitely not lending support to those who wanted a strong civil rights bill: "The almost casual treatment he gave the question [civil rights] will not make the fight for an effective civil rights bill this session any easier." [18]

At his first press conference after the address, the President was asked, "Do you agree with the majority of the Commissioners that a law is needed to provide federal registrars when Negroes are denied the right to register or vote?" He answered:

I don't know——as a matter of fact, I don't even know whether it is constitutional. What I am saying is, or what the Commissioners said, this was one plan that they thought might have some measure of validity, and, therefore, they wanted to study it. Now, the way I feel about this civil rights, we have one bill that was put in last year in which extensive hearings have been heard——had; and I should like to see the Congress act decisively on this particular proposal, and such other proposals made as——that now become almost controversial from the moment that they are presented——would not enter into the proposal or to the process of examining and passing the bill that was already put before the Congress. . . . You see, I don't have any—— what I am trying to get at is, I have no objection to the study of the others. As a matter of fact, I want to study them because I would like to see what everybody thinks about it. My big problem is, though, let's get this bill already proposed on which they have had hearings, let's get that acted on.[19]

Many careful observers in Washington felt that the President's doubts about the legality of the registrar proposal weighed heavily against supporters of a strong bill. "This encouraged southern congressmen to believe that if another civil rights bill is passed at this session," one Washington correspondent for the *Atlanta Constitu-*

17. *Ibid.*
18. *Ibid.*
19. *New York Times,* January 14, 1960.

tion wrote, "as it most probably will be—it will not be extreme legislation." [20]

Words like "moderate," "extreme," "weak," and "strong," have been used in describing positions taken regarding civil rights issues generally. It is best to remember, however, that these are relative terms—relative to the person using them, to the issue being described, and to another position on the same subject. And of course, one's assessment of a "moderate" approach as opposed to a "strong," "radical," "extreme" approach depends in large measure on the evaluation of the ability of the particular solution to perform a desired purpose. Many called President Eisenhower's stand in 1960 "moderate," but compared with the Southern senators and representatives who wanted no bill at all, he might seem "radical" or "extreme." On balance, however, those who favored a bill in 1960 compared the administration's referee proposal to the Civil Rights Commission's registrar plan, and in the final assessment the former was the more moderate. One writer, commenting on the commission's plan, took note of the "bi-partisan, moderate, indeed, conservative commission" as of the "greatest significance" in the registrar plan.[21] The commission had become convinced, through its extensive investigations in the South, "that lawsuits were an ineffective answer to the voting problem." Two of the three Southern commissioners, Robert G. Storey of Texas and Doyle E. Carlton, former governor of Florida, endorsed the proposal for federal registrars.[22] The administration's plan required complex legal ac-

20. *Atlanta Constitution,* January 14, 1960.
21. *New York Times,* September 13, 1959.
22. Interestingly enough, this same point of the basic conservative and deliberative caliber of the commission was made in April 1963 when the commission sent a message to President Kennedy suggesting the possibility of the President investigating the powers he might have to withhold certain federal funds from Mississippi as long as that state continued to permit, or itself practiced, racial discrimination. Again, some observers were impressed that if close scrutiny of the Southern situation had led such a relatively conservative body of men to make such a relatively radical proposal, then, indeed, the racial situation, in Mississippi at least, must be bad.

tion, and there was already testimony by the Attorney General that the Department of Justice did not look upon the filing of many lawsuits as tactically wise.

So if the referee plan was "moderate" vis-à-vis the registrar proposal, this was based on one's assumption that the judicial approach was generally less effective than an administrative procedure— effective, that is, in ensuring the right of black people to register and vote free of racial discrimination. But the administration's plan prevailed. While 1957 and 1960 may have been civil rights years, this was no guarantee of a particular kind of bill. And given the controversial nature of the subject, a plan burdened with Presidential doubts of its constitutionality (although he had professed many times he was not a lawyer), not to mention his lack of endorsement, had little chance of passage.

One student of these problems has stated that the experiences of 1957 and 1960 indicated that civil rights legislation would not come in an omnibus package, but rather in piecemeal fashion.[23] Speaking of 1960, he wrote:

It is difficult to evaluate the role of the White House except to say that the President once again concentrated his support on the voting aspects of the bill. His leadership brought many hesitant Republicans into line. But the directives emerging from the White House were frequently unclear and lacked the vigor to pull together a divided Republican Party and to resolve divisions within the administration itself. The executive capitulated too easily to pleas for compromise, while an aura of presidential "neutrality" on the question of civil rights and a reluctance to strain the conservative alliance between Northern Republicans and Southern Democrats were always in the background.[24]

23. Longaker, *Presidency and Individual Liberties,* p. 54.
24. *Ibid.*

1961–1963 Emphasis on Executive Fiat

The Presidential campaign of 1960 was highlighted by the famous television debates between the major candidates, but for many black leaders the most spectacular single event was a telephone call made by the Democratic nominee, Senator John F. Kennedy, to the wife of Dr. Martin Luther King, Jr. King had been arrested in Atlanta, Georgia, about ten days before the election for participating in sit-in and picketing demonstrations against segregated department store facilities. Senator Kennedy called Mrs. King to express his concern for her husband's safety. "He wanted me to know," Mrs. King related, "he was thinking about us and he would do all he could to help. . . . I have heard nothing from the Vice President or anyone on his staff. Mr. Nixon has been very quiet." Several Republican spokesmen complained that this was nothing more than a political maneuver calculated to gain black votes. Robert F. Kennedy, the Democratic nominee's brother and campaign manager, telephoned the Georgia judge who had set the sentence. The following day, October 27, 1960, King was released from the Reidsville State Prison on bail, pending appeal.

Black communities in Northern and Southern cities were deluged with Democratic campaign literature featuring the event. Black leaders issued strong statements. Dr. Gardner Taylor, president of the Protestant Council of New York and pastor of one of the largest black congregations in the country, said, "This is the kind of moral leadership and direct personal concern which this problem has lacked in these critical years." The Reverend Ralph Abernathy, King's co-worker and president at that time of the Montgomery Improvement Association (the organization formed to conduct the bus boycott) stated:

I earnestly and sincerely feel that it is time for all of us to take off our Nixon buttons. I wish to make it crystal clear that I am not hog-tied to any party. My first concern is for the 350-year long struggle for our people. Now I have made up my mind to vote for Senator Kennedy

because I am convinced he is concerned about our struggle. Senator
Kennedy did something great and wonderful when he personally
called Mrs. Coretta King and helped free Dr. Martin Luther King. This
was the kind of act I was waiting for.

Two days before the election, King issued a statement that received wide distribution in many Northern black communities. He
stated that he thought Kennedy would take a "forthright position"
on segregation whereas he (King) felt there had been "too much
disagreement and double talk" from the Republicans.[25] In a piece
of Democratic campaign literature distributed just prior to the
election entitled "The Case of Martin Luther King," King was
quoted as saying, "I hold Senator Kennedy in very high esteem. I
am convinced he will seek to exercise the power of his office to
fully implement the civil rights plank of his party's platform." [26]

The impression of this incident on many Southern black leaders
was not so much that of a candidate in search of votes but rather
of a man who might carry this kind of personal intervention into
the White House and thus set a "tone," provide the "moral leadership," and simply "speak out." It might be added here that many
blacks had relatively simplistic views about the power of a President and his ability to accomplish major goals.[27] These attitudes

25. *Chicago Sun-Times,* November 7, 1960.
26. Theodore H. White, in *The Making of the President* (1960), following
a pattern of understandable caution but tempted by the attractive opportunity of making such an observation, stated: "One cannot identify in the
narrowness of American voting of 1960 any one particular episode or decision as being more important than any other in the final tallies: yet when
one reflects that Illinois was carried by only 9,000 votes and that 250,000
Negroes are estimated to have voted for Kennedy; that Michigan was carried
by 67,000 votes and that an estimated 250,000 Negroes voted for Kennedy;
that South Carolina was carried by 10,000 votes and that an estimated 40,000
Negroes there voted for Kennedy, the candidates instinctive decision must
be ranked among the most crucial of the last few weeks."
27. Martin Luther King suggested that a "vigorous President could sig-
nificantly influence Congress" in voter registration. "A truly decisive President" would campaign in Congress and "across the nation until Congress
acted." He would act to deprive a state of a portion of its congressional

were nurtured through eight years of relative silence on the part of Eisenhower. Frequently some black leaders would have settled for a strong affirmative statement supporting civil rights. "He may not be able to do anything," one black leader in Alabama stated of Eisenhower in 1959, "but at least he could say he believed in what the Supreme Court did in '54. Harry Truman spoke out all the time." So to some black political activists in the South in 1960, Senator Kennedy had laid the foundation and given definite indication that he would provide vigorous, moral leadership on civil rights issues. One further point of the telephone call was that even if Kennedy was motivated by political considerations (as some blacks were convinced he was), at least it was an admission that there were black votes well worth an effort. Because of this act, many black leaders felt catered to and cared about, and these were feelings infrequently experienced by them in the national political arena.

Shortly after President Kennedy took office, a clear pattern of action developed in the executive branch on civil rights. Kennedy was not going to ask Congress to pass additional legislation on the subject for the time being; he was giving indications of intent to move through his executive powers to deal with problems of economic concern to the nation, but especially to the low man on the economic totem pole—the black citizen. In March 1961 President Kennedy issued an executive order on job opportunities forbidding racial discrimination in employment by firms doing business under federal government contracts and subcontracts. Vice President Johnson was appointed to head a committee with power to cancel contracts of non-complying companies.

This emphasis on executive action was manifested in other areas as well. The President spoke out on behalf of those seeking to implement school desegregation. Working closely with the Presi-

------

representation if some of the state's citizens were unconstitutionally denied the right to vote. King wrote, "It is leadership and determination that counts and these have been lacking of recent years."

dent in these endeavors was the newly appointed Attorney General, Robert F. Kennedy. The *New York Times* reported:

His brother Robert, the Attorney General, has been doing a great deal on civil rights—most of it unpublicized. It became known that he had telephoned lawyers and political leaders in Louisiana to try to get them to call off their war against desegregation in New Orleans. It is not generally known that he has called Governors and other leaders in almost every state of the South, for such purposes as obtaining voting records and getting the bail on a Negro demonstrator lowered.[28]

An informed observer in Washington wrote that "as soon as the department's [Department of Justice] new hierarchy can gets gears meshed, investigations and suits under the 1957 Civil Rights Act will begin." [29]

Why the administration's reluctance to ask Congress for additional civil rights legislation? The President himself stated that he would recommend new laws "when I feel that there's necessity for congressional action with a chance of getting that congressional action." There was widespread belief, however, that the reason was politics. In the opinion of the *New York Times,* "The President needs every southern vote he can get in Congress for his economic and social program, and he believes it would be foolish to alienate any of those votes at this time." [30] The President needed every congressional vote he could get for his minimum wage law, another observer pointed out.[31] "This increasing Southern support for the President's program has been carefully cultivated by the White House. The President knows full well that if the White House puts its prestige and power behind the Clark–Celler civil rights bills [introduced in Congress early in 1961], this Southern support would

28. *New York Times,* March 12, 1961.
29. *Ibid.*
30. *Ibid.*
31. See Roscoe Drummond, "The President and Civil Rights," *Chicago Sun-Times,* May 13, 1961.

drop radically—almost certainly below the point absolutely needed for administration success." [32]

But if the new President was not going to ask Congress for more legislation, it was generally recognized that he had to have an alternative approach in addition to personal negotiation by the Attorney General, strong statements, and executive orders in the economic field, if only to fulfill some of the campaign promises and implications. This alternative soon emerged in the form of a concerted effort on the part of the Department of Justice to implement the voting provisions of the 1957 and 1960 civil rights laws:

It would seem to me that the only freedom of maneuver open to Mr. Kennedy is timing. He would like to delay civil rights legislation until next year, while Attorney General Robert F. Kennedy sees what headway he can make by rigorous endorsement of present laws.[33]

So the major civil rights emphasis of the Kennedy administration rested primarily on action by the executive branch, specifically in the field of black voting rights.[34] Much of the thinking underlying this emphasis centered on the premise that political rights paved the way to all other civil rights. As Southern blacks gained the ballot and began to exercise it, public officials and aspirants for public office would contend for that vote. Another factor influencing the thoughts of administration leaders dealt with the fact that voting would probably meet less resistance in the South because of the lack of social problems associated with it.[35] The Attorney General and

32. *Ibid.*
33. *Ibid.*
34. Interestingly enough, in May 1961 an item appeared in the press entitled: "Ike Speaks Out on Race Issues." The former President felt he had more license to declare his views as a private citizen. He believed that the 1954 desegregation decision was "constitutionally correct," but he did "not agree with all the reasoning which went along with it." "The former President sees the right to vote without discrimination as the transcendent, priority right of all civil rights. . . . He feels that when the right to vote is protected and used, it will do more than anything else to guarantee all other civil rights." *Chicago Sun-Times,* May 20, 1961.
35. *New York Times,* January 1, 1962.

his assistants recognized three major obstacles to an increased black electorate: state statutes, arbitrary administration of voting laws, and black apathy. The first two, with diligent action by the Department of Justice could in all likelihood be overcome. The third involved, in the words of Burke Marshall, head of the Civil Rights Division, "hard work" on the part of black leaders to get blacks out to register and vote.

Legal action and voter-registration drives become the main forces for voting rights. The second approach received financial aid from the Taconic Foundation in the amount of $262,000.[36] Five organizations[37] received funds which were distributed and coordinated by a new foundation, the Voter Education Program, under the general direction of the Southern Regional Council.

Administration emphasis on voting and its lack of emphasis on new legislation received criticism from some sources that suspected its motives and questioned its results.[38] Some saw in this a definite attempt to divert the energies of black social action groups from direct action efforts such as sit-ins, freedom rides, and mass protest demonstrations. The Attorney General called upon the black leaders to accept a "cooling-off" period in the midst of the freedom rides in the spring of 1961. Direct actions involved masses of blacks in civil disobedience protests. This direct mass action created a

36. Louis Lomax, *The Negro Revolt* (1962); see also *New York Times,* August 25, 1962.
37. The NAACP, Southern Christian Leadership Conference, Student Non-Violent Coordinating Committee, the Congress on Racial Equality, and the Urban League.
38. See Howard Zinn's *Albany: A Study in National Responsibility* (1962), for a very strong criticism of the Kennedy administration's handling of civil rights problems arising from mass, peaceful protests of Southern Negroes. The administration, Professor Zinn wrote, was largely concerned with "law and order," with alleviating violent situations, but did not emphasize the immorality of segregation. As a result, it has moved firmly to enforce a Negro's right to attend the University of Mississippi under federal court order, but it has complimented the orderly handling and avoidance of wide-scale violence by some Southern police officials with mass public, peaceful, anti-segregation demonstrations by Southern Negroes. Over 1000 Negroes were arrested.

vital and much needed contact between black leadership and the
rank-and-file that less dramatic activity did not provide. In commenting on "a turn from civil disobedience to conventional politics," one writer observed:

The civil rights movement could be patronized and tamed by Kennedy
just as the labor movement was by Roosevelt. A tendency toward
bureaucracy and toward a loss of vital contact with the rank-and-file
is already apparent in the Southern civil rights organizations, including the student groups. Commitment to the indirections and artificiali-
ties of the political game would rapidly accelerate this trend.[39]

A national officer of the NAACP, Herbert Hill, labor secretary,
made the following statement to this writer:

The NAACP officially rejects Kennedy's idea that there is no need for
new legislation now, that he is going to do everything through executive orders, etc. This is sheer hypocrisy, and we are appalled. This is
a highly political administration. We know about the good Negro appointments, but the Alabama appointment hasn't escaped our attention. We are going to give the Justice Department more time.[40]

Meanwhile, the Department of Justice, pursuing the attack from
the legal side, proceeded to file suits under the 1957 and 1960 acts.
By February 12, 1963, some 33 cases had been brought by that
Department: eleven in Mississippi, nine in Louisiana, six in Alabama, four in Tennessee, and three in Georgia.[41]

Two years' experience in the federal courts and recommendations based on investigations by the Department of Justice and the
Civil Rights Commission undoubtedly contributed to the issuance
of a special message on civil rights to Congress by the President on
February 28, 1963. The message specifically covered five areas and
recommended congressional legislation in three. It noted the prog-

39. Staughton Lynd, "Freedom Rides to the Polls," *The Nation*, July 28,
1962, p. 31.
40. Interview with Herbert Hill, labor secretary of NAACP, May 10, 1961.
41. *Freedom to the Free*, A Report to the President by the U.S. Commission on Civil Rights (1963), p. 198.

ress in race relations made in the preceding two years through "executive action, litigation, persuasion and private initiative," but added that congressional action was needed in voting, education, extension, and expansion of the Commission on Civil Rights. No new legislation was recommended in employment or public accommodations. The President felt that judicial delay and discriminatory administration of registration laws were the two major defects in the 1957 and 1960 acts. To alleviate these, he recommended temporary federal voting referees to register persons pending the outcome of a lawsuit in a particular county; voting suits brought under the civil rights acts should be accorded quick treatment in the federal courts; the law should specifically prohibit the application of different tests, standards, practices, or procedures for different applicants seeking to register and vote in federal elections; completion of the sixth grade should, with respect to federal elections, constitute a presumption that the applicant was literate.

On April 9, 1963, twenty-three Democratic senators introduced a bill (S. 1237) covering the President's requests for changes in the voting provisions of the 1957 and 1960 acts. The bill was referred to Senator Eastland's Judiciary Committee.

The discussion in the present and previous chapters describes the thinking of many persons involved in the enactment of the laws and the expectations of some officials and black leaders. Generally, few expected the federal judiciary to take the tools handed it and use them in a manner that would result in appreciable gains in Southern black voter registration. The major debates in Congress had centered on the use or non-use of a jury and the appointment or nonappointment of voter referees. The presence of a jury and the absence of voter referees meant to some that the purposes of the laws would be frustrated. The material in the following chapters examines the work of the Southern federal courts and shows the extent to which the debates were relevant and accurate.

The Kennedy administration approached the matter of filing lawsuits from a different point of view than the Eisenhower Administration. The latter was reluctant; the former, much more persistent. This difference in orientation is not without significance in studying the work of the judiciary. The courts could expect considerable assistance from the Department of Justice in disposing of the cases, in devising methods for implementing court decrees, and in keeping the courts informed on voter registration activity in the various areas. The vigorous prosecution of alleged voting denials could provide comfort in many ways for those Southern judges who exhibited a willingness to carry out the law. This becomes very clear when we look at the situation in Alabama in the next chapter.

5 Judicial Aggressiveness

Registrar Practices in Three Black-Belt Counties

Alabama is a hard-core Southern state. It was the last state to admit black students to previously all-white state universities on a continuing basis; until the mid-1960s, the only black student to attend the University of Alabama under a federal court order did so for only three days in 1956 and was subsequently expelled for reasons upheld by the federal courts. The largest city in the state, Birmingham, had been labeled by black leaders as "the Johannesburg of the United States" because of the rigid, apartheid-like laws and practices; the black-belt Alabama counties had been the focus of many investigations of denials of civil rights by the Department of Justice and the Civil Rights Commission. And yet it was in Alabama, in the United States District Court for the Middle District, that one found the best illustration of aggressive judicial action in voting cases by a federal judge, Frank M. Johnson. The three cases examined here arose out of three black-belt counties—Macon, Bullock, and Montgomery.

Macon County had been the scene of several legal battles over the years involving the right of black people to vote. I have noted

Mitchell v. *Wright*. Mitchell and the local civil rights organization, the Tuskegee Civic Association (TCA), to which he belonged, had been at the forefront of the later voting cases, also. In 1957, when the Alabama legislature gerrymandered the boundaries of Tuskegee, the county seat, to exclude 420 black voters from the city, the president of the TCA, Professor Charles G. Gomillion, and fifteen other local black citizens filed suit alleging denial of voting rights. In 1960 the Supreme Court agreed with the black plaintiffs (Justice Felix Frankfurter writing for a unanimous court) that such a legislative act was racially motivated and consequently violated the Fifteenth Amendment to the Constitution.[1]

Macon County had black-belt county characteristics to the extent that the population was predominantly black (eight blacks to one white), but it was highly uncharacteristic of black-belt counties generally in other significant ways: the majority of the blacks earned their living from the local, private black college, Tuskegee Institute, the school that Booker T. Washington built, and the federal Veterans Administration hospital; this meant that the educational as well as economic level of a sizable number of blacks was higher than that of most other Alabamians—white or black. The TCA had systematically documented an eight-year history of denials of the right to vote in the county.[2] The TCA was able to show that from 1951 through 1958, some 1585 applications for voter certificates were made by black citizens. Only 510 certificates were issued—32 per cent. The TCA kept records from 1951 of every black person who appeared at the registrars' office, the number admitted, and the length of time needed for each to complete the application. Officers of the TCA either appeared personally or

1. 364 U.S. 339 (1961). See also Lewis Jones and Stanley Smith, *Voting Rights and Economic Pressure* (B'nai B'rith), 1959, and Bernard Taber, *Gomillion* v. *Lightfoot*.
2. *Eight-Year Summary of Registration Efforts of Negroes in Macon County: Reactions of the Macon County Board of Registrars* (prepared by William P. Mitchell and Charles V. Hamilton and entered in the records at the hearings of the Commission on Civil Rights held in Montgomery, Alabama, December 8, 1958.)

had someone stationed in the courthouse to record this information at every meeting of the board of registrars, as well as the time the board started work, the length of time it remained in session, and the days it was supposed to meet but did not. When the Civil Rights Commission finally held its first public hearing on December 8, 1958, it chose as its main target Macon County. The first witness called was William P. Mitchell. There followed a long list of blacks (twenty-seven in all)—college professors, public school teachers, medical technicians, ministers, businessmen—who testified as to how and when they had been denied the right to vote simply because they were black. The Department of Justice, could not have found a better case from the standpoint of documented evidence and presumed qualifications of applicants.

The United States filed its first case under the Civil Rights Act of 1957 in February 1959 against the board of registrars of Macon County, the state of Alabama, and two named individuals as members of the board. The federal district court, Judge Johnson sitting, dismissed the action on the grounds that the two individual registrars had resigned in good faith in December 1958; that the board was not a suable legal entity; and that the Civil Rights Act of 1957 did not authorize such action against the state.[3] In his opinion, however, Judge Johnson stated that his interpretation of the Alabama law that registrars could resign in good faith did "not permit any widespread conspiracy to defeat the law, it does not necessarily permit the paralyzation of governmental functions that are necessary to organized society, and it does not permit any 'hiatus or interregnum,' since the remedy of mandamus, if the circumstances warrant and justify its use, is always available to require the appointing board to fill, if they refuse to act within a reasonable time, any vacancies that may be created, such as these." [4] Judge John-

3. 171 Fed. Supp. 720 (1959).
4. 267 Fed. 2d. 808. As events developed, no members were appointed to serve on the Macon County board of registrars from December 1958 to May 1960 (eighteen months). The efforts of the blacks to secure appointments are reported in my *Minority Politics in Black Belt Alabama*. Several times the TCA thought in terms of pursuing Judge Johnson's language and

son proceeded to say that he would not sanction "bad faith" resignations.

The Court of Appeals for the fifth circuit sustained each of the district court's holdings on June 16, 1959.[5] The Supreme Court then took the case on certiorari. In the interim, the Civil Rights Act of 1960 authorizing action against a state was passed. The Supreme Court vacated the judgments and remanded the case to the district court with instruction to reinstate the action against the state of Alabama. Thus, one of the immediate results of the 1960 law was to nullify what had been a rather effective tactic of registrars—resignation.

Macon County is adjacent to Bullock and Montgomery counties, and while the latter did not have the dramatic examples of college professors being denied the right to register, there were several instances of college-trained blacks being rejected. High concentrations of blacks characterized all three counties. Before examining the district court's activity, it is appropriate, for purposes of organized presentation, to examine the background of the three cases.

Although there were approximately 11,900 black people of voting age in Macon County, less than 10 per cent (approximately 1100) were registered. The court found this to be largely the result of the discriminatory administration of the registration tests. Judge Johnson said:

The evidence in this case is overwhelmingly to the effect that the State of Alabama, acting through its agents including former members

---

filing a mandamus action. Resignation of board members was nothing new for Macon County. There was no functioning board during the following periods: June 1946 to January 1958 (eighteen months); February 1956 to March 1957 (fourteen months); December 1958 to May 1960 (eighteen months); January 1961. The TCA sent weekly petitions and registered letters to the governor and the state appointing board from January 1959 to May 1960 requesting appointments. One registered letter was sent to the state representative of Macon County. It was returned marked: "Refused." The TCA was able to obtain seven blacks and one white citizen who wrote and offered to serve on the vacant board. Over the entire eighteen-month period, there was never a reply of any kind to these communications.
5. 267 Fed. 2d. 808.

of the Board of Registrars of Macon County, has deliberately engaged
in acts and practices designed to discriminate against qualified Negroes in their efforts to register to vote. Such acts and practices have
brought about and perpetuated the disparity between the relative per-
centages of Negroes and whites registered to vote.[6]

Essentially, the registrars relied on three tactics: resignations, use
of a double standard in receiving and approving applications for
registration from black and white applicants, and slow-downs. The
court found these practices to have existed for at least five years.
White applicants were always received before blacks, although the
whites arrived at the registration office after the black applicants.
The evidence in the case clearly indicated that at least twelve named
white applicants who had not finished elementary school were
registered, while several college-trained blacks failed the registration test. "The registrars . . . could not explain the standards that
permitted such to happen. It is quite obvious to this court that
[the named white applicants] had received assistance in completing
their forms. It is equally obvious that Negroes with high school and
college education who were rejected repeatedly for minor errors
have not been given assistance." [7] No applicant was entitled to assistance, but the court would not permit this kind of preferential
treatment. Further, the application forms of whites and blacks
showed that whites were frequently not required to write out a
section of the Constitution or that they had to write a section much
shorter than that required of all black applicants. Only black applicants were rejected for errors of a formal, technical, or inconsequential nature. Whites committing the same errors were passed.
Black applicants were frequently not notified whether they had
failed the registration test. Some black witnesses testified they had
applied as many as five times without ever having been notified of
their rejection. This was not a problem for whites, since none ever
failed. Inadequate registration facilities were maintained for black

6. 192 Fed. Supp., p. 629.
7. 192 Fed. Supp., p. 679.

citizens, but sufficient facilities prevailed for whites, and under state law, persons could apply for voter certificates only in the "beats" (districts) where they resided. In 1960, the registrars devoted two-thirds of the time allotted to receive applications outside Tuskegee in the rural areas where the black demand for registration was low.[8]

With these tactics operating in 1960, only fifty persons were able to complete applications over a seven-month period—thirty-two whites and eighteen blacks (the thirty-two whites passed; ten blacks were successful). The board would process only one black applicant at a time. In 1960 the largest number of applicants received by the board in any one day was five.

What was the attitude and response of the registrars? Judge Johnson asked the state of Alabama to call the registrars as witnesses. The state declined. In his opinion Johnson wrote:

The Court, in an effort to understand fully the attitude of the present members of the Board of Registrars in Macon County, called Johnson and Dyson [the two current registrars] as witnesses of the Court. Their lack of concern and their failure to take any action toward changing the pattern and practice of racial discrimination was fully evident from their testimony.[9]

The facts in the Bullock County case also dealt with the activity of the registrars. But here the focus was narrowed to two specific practices—requiring a voucher and requiring applications to be completed "with technical precision." In 1960 Bullock had a total population of 13,462 of which 9681 were black. There were 3781 whites. In 1960 there were 2200 whites registered, and only five blacks. Since 1951 the Bullock County board of registrars required each applicant to have a registered voter of the county appear before the board and swear to the bona fide residence and good character of the applicant. Another part of the rules established by the

8. Tuskegee is beat one, containing 60 per cent of the county population of which 65 per cent of that group was black.
9. 192 Fed. Supp., p. 681.

board limited each voucher to two applicants per year. The evidence showed that no white citizen had ever vouched for a black applicant. At the trial, one black witness was asked by the court if black applicants "made an effort from people of your own race to get them to vouch for you." The witness stated that this effort had been made several times without success. He replied:

Oh yes. Mr. Russell said his wife was teaching school and someone had passed the word to her that if he come back up there vouching for anyone else they would fire her from her job.[10]

The United States argued that the particular racial conditions and the minimal number of registered blacks made the voucher rule "constitutionally impermissible." Bullock County was a racially segregated community; blacks and whites did not attend the same public or private schools or the same churches. The voucher rule meant that black applicants had to "attain not only the consent but the active cooperation of members of the white community as a prerequisite to voting and thus whites hold the key to the registration door." [11] Because of the small number of registered blacks and the two-per-year voucher rule, in many instances blacks would have only white voters to approach to secure vouchers. On its face, this might not appear racially discriminatory, but the United States cited the language of *Gomillion* v. *Lightfoot* which struck down an Alabama gerrymander statute that had worked in a similar way. *Guinn* v. *U.S.*[12] was cited wherein the Supreme Court dealt with the grandfather clause. These "sophisticated" and "onerous" methods of evading the Fifteenth Amendment were the same as the voucher rule in the particular racial setting in Bullock County. If the county were sincerely interested in establishing the bona fide residence of an applicant, there were numerous other ways of doing so—tax records, real estate records, drivers' licenses, hunting licenses. And to

10. Trial record, *U.S.* v. *Alabama,* civil action No. 1677-N.
11. Government's Brief, *U.S.* v. *Alabama,* civ. no. 1677-N.
12. 238 U.S. 347.

require a black person to seek a white citizen to vouch for the black's "good character" under the racial circumstances prevailing in Bullock County was asking too much. In addition, the United States contended, the only possible reason for limiting a voucher to only two applicants per year was "to hold down Negro registration."

While the registrars in Macon County were found to apply double standards, the evidence in the Bullock County case revealed that after March 1960 the registrars proceeded to apply a "single standard." The United States attacked this as an unconstitutional "freezing device." The board adopted very strict standards which it applied to white and black applicants alike. This again was another sophisticated way of avoiding the Fifteenth Amendment. The government's brief argued, "Although a State may set registration standards, in a community like Bullock county, to require future applicants, white and Negro, to complete their applications with technical precision is constitutionally suspect. . . . This amounts to a freezing of the status quo. And the effect is the practical disfranchisement of almost 99 per cent of the unregistered Negroes, while only about 5 per cent of the whites remain unregistered."

The activity of the registrars came under scrutiny in Montgomery County in the third case handled by Judge Johnson. The evidence taken in that case dated back to January 1, 1956, and consisted of the testimony of 175 witnesses and 13,000 exhibits. During the five-year period from January 1, 1956, to November 14, 1961, according to the testimony of one board member, the board consistently gave assistance to white applicants in the completion of the application form, but such aid was never given to blacks. The court concluded from the evidence that the registration questionnaire was used as a "tricky examination or test" when applied to black applicants, but merely as a method for obtaining substantive information when applied to whites. In the five years from 1956 to 1961, 96 per cent of the whites applying were registered (1070 of these had applications which contained the same kinds of technical errors used to reject blacks), while 75 per cent of the blacks applying were rejected. Approximately 4522 black applications had been made. Of those rejected, 710 had twelve years or more of formal education, six had M.A. degrees, 152 had four years of college training, 222 had some college training, and 108 were public school teachers.

After February 1961 the board raised the standards to require a perfect application. Very strict requirements were put on white and black applicants alike. This was, of course, similar to the Bullock County "single standard," freezing tactic. Yet registrars continued to give assistance to whites. The court made a careful study of the applications of whites accepted and of the blacks rejected during the period involved in the case. In a two-year period from 1958 to 1960, approximately 600 black applications were rejected for failure to sign the oath on page three of the four-page questionnaire, although the oath was administered orally and was to be signed in the presence of the registrar. "Yet," Judge Johnson stated in his opinion, "the registrars let the Negroes walk out of the office without calling the omission to their attention. Such a practice by the Board evidences bad faith and leads to the inevitable conclusion that such a device was used by them for deception." Exhibits presented in the trial showed that hundreds of white applications had X's, check marks, dots, and dashes on the oath line of the application form. Judge Johnson argued from this that

This court would be naïve to the point of absurdity if this evidence such as the marks themselves, the contrasting shades in ink used in making them, the places where they occur, the fact that no marks appear on applications of Negroes and that all testimony concerning the marks did not compel the conclusion that they were made by the registrars and made for the purpose of showing the white applicants where to sign. The only witness offered by the defendants in an attempt to explain these marks was a clerk in the office of the Judge of Probate. Her explanation, which is totally inadequate, was that some marks were placed on the applications when they were processed by the office of the Judge of Probate. The marks which this witness demonstrated that she used are totally different from those made to indicate where the oath is to be signed. This is aside from the fact that applications of Negroes are processed at the same place and no such marks appear on them. Only on applications of whites.

The evidence also revealed that the Board did not notify blacks that they had failed; thus the black applicants did not know when their thirty-day period for appeal began to run.

Judge Johnson was not impressed that several whites were rejected after 1961. The fact that certain white applications were rejected "approached the ridiculous when the Board rejected the law partner of one of the defense attorneys [in the case before the court], a retired general and graduate of West Point, and the college graduate son of one of the State's attorneys general. . . . Such evidence has little or no probative value." Johnson's further comment on this was as follows:

The rejection of whites subsequent to June, 1960 and particularly since June, 1961 when it became apparent this case was to be filed impresses this court as being nothing more than a sham and an attempt to disguise past discriminatory practices.[13]

These were the practices that Judge Johnson was called upon to adjudicate under the Civil Rights Acts of 1957 and 1960. We now turn to his handling of these matters in terms of ordering the registration of specific black applicants, the standards he set for registrars in reviewing future applications, and the manner by which he sought to supervise this entire operation.

The Judge as Registrar

Judge Johnson first demonstrated his aggressive approach to these problems by ordering fifty-four[14] specific blacks registered immediately in Macon County without re-examination or voter referees. Johnson concluded that the evidence was so "abundantly clear" in the Macon case that a "decree mandatory in nature," not merely prohibitory, was warranted. He ordered certain blacks

13. Opinion in *U.S.* v. *Alabama*.
14. This figure was subsequently cut to fifty-four after ten were disqualified for various reasons.

placed "on the voting rolls immediately." The court had the power
to do this, he stated, under the power granted by Congress.[15] The
Macon County registrars were ordered to register and notify the
specific black citizens within ten days. Johnson felt that such a mandatory order was necessary "to correct the effect of the Board's past
discriminatory practices. . . . The entering and the enforcement
of such a decree will not have the effect of substituting federal administration of the registration processes for that of the state. The
decree is for the sole purpose of establishing a standard which requires the defendants to be fair and to apply the laws as they relate
to the registration to vote without racial discrimination."[16] While
Johnson made a finding of a pattern and practice of racial discrimination, he declined the power to appoint voter referees in order
to give the registrars time to register all applicants fairly themselves.

Such a declination is made with the idea that the defendants can act
fairly if the directions spelled out in this court's decree are followed
in good faith. If the defendants so act, they will have regained for
Macon county and for the State of Alabama the integrity that the
evidence in this case makes abundantly clear has been lost in this
field of voting rights.[17]

The defendants appealed the order to the court of Appeals for the
fifth circuit. They objected only to the specific order requiring
the immediate registration of fifty-four blacks on the grounds that
the court lacked the power to enter such an order and that the order
transcended the scope of issues at the trial and prejudiced the defendants because they were given no opportunity to test the qualifications of the individuals named in the order. The mandatory order
usurped the discretionary functions of the board of registrars, and
it was based on an examination of the applications alone. Alabama
argued that if the 1957 and 1960 Acts were constitutional, then

15. See *U.S.* v. *McElveen,* 180 Fed. Supp. 10.
16. 192 Fed. Supp., p. 683.
17. *Ibid.*

persons could be registered only in the manner prescribed by those acts. In addition, the application forms were only aids in determining qualifications of applicants. The questionnaire did not reveal good character. In support of its position, Alabama stated that since the issuance of its initial order, the court had ordered eighty-four more blacks placed on the rolls. Two more would have been ordered registered had not the state called the court's attention to the fact that these particular two black applicants had several illegitimate children. Finally, Alabama pointed out that it was clear from the original complaint as well as from an exchange between the court and the counsel for the government that the main issue in the case was whether a pattern and practice of racial discrimination existed in Macon County's registration of black voters. Judge Johnson's mandatory decree went beyond this main issue. The oral argument before the appellate court by counsel for Alabama ended with the following observation:

Qualified persons are entitled to vote, but it is well known that both political parties favor the abolition of state literacy tests. No good will come from this fishing for Negro votes by these political parties. The Federal courts should not sanction the use of a "throw net" to catch all regardless of their character, intelligence and criminal tendencies. Just one visit by federal judges to black belt towns in Alabama like Eutau, Union Town and Greensboro on a Saturday afternoon will convince reasonable minds that not one out of 25 Negroes is qualified to intelligently cast his vote. At one time, there were 190,000 Negro voters in Mississippi and only 69,000 whites. I for one do not wish the return of those days.

The government countered by arguing that the legislative histories of the 1957 and 1960 acts indicated congressional intent that the federal district courts use their full powers of equity as far as the right to vote was concerned.[18] A court of equity must fashion its

18. The government's brief cited the hearings on civil rights before the House Committee on the Judiciary, 84th Congress, 1st Session, incorporated into Hearings on Civil Rights Before Subcommittee No. 5 of the House Committee on the Judiciary, 85th Congress, 1st Session, pp. 571–72; also 103 *Congressional Record,* p. 12572, and 103 *Congressional Record,* 12460.

decree to accomplish the congressional purpose, and this was what
Judge Johnson did in his mandatory decree. As far as the specific
blacks named in the decree were concerned, to require them to re-
apply for registration would not have been consistent with the intent of Congress. The fifty-four blacks applied for voter certificates
and were denied, so the court found, solely because they were black.
They met all other standards then being applied to white applicants.

Nothing the present registrars could now do could alter the fact that
the Negroes met those standards. Thus, for the Court below to enter
a decree which was not mandatory in terms or in effect would not have
corrected the effect of past discriminatory practices and would have
required the individuals involved needlessly to repeat a process in
which they had already engaged. In such circumstances, the only
truly equitable remedy was the remedy selected by the Court.[19]

The United States met the state's argument regarding the remedies set out in the 1960 act by pointing out that the Civil Rights
Act of 1960 applied to future applicants. As to the complaining
witnesses at the original trial, they need not necessarily be required
to apply to voter referees. "As to these individuals, the judicial de-
terminations stipulated in subsection (e) [the voter referee section]
already have been made. . . . Subsection (e) has no bearing on
the court's power to direct the registration of specific individuals
who have made application where such proof has been made." [20]

Alabama had argued that Judge Johnson's mandatory order went
beyond the issue at trial. The United States countered with the contention that the complaint in the case sought an injunction enjoining
the registrars from "failing or refusing to register the persons listed
in 'Exhibit A' attached to this Complaint, and others similarly situated, and from permitting their names to remain off the current list
of qualified voters of Macon County, Alabama." The complaint also
asked the district court to "grant such additional relief as justice

19. Government's brief in fifth circuit Court of Appeals, p. 19.
20. *Ibid*. pp. 20–21.

may require . . . or as may be required in aid of the jurisdiction of this court." Thus, the defendants were well aware of the possibility that the district court would grant the relief which it did.

They also well knew that in order to avoid such relief it was incumbent upon them to show that the individuals named in Exhibit A, and others similarly situated, were not qualified to vote.
Beyond that, one of the central issues in the case was the question of whether registrars had applied more stringent standards. Necessarily subsumed in this issue was the question of the relative qualifications of the Negro and white applicants. All of the registration applications of the Negroes who were conditionally ordered to be registered were introduced in evidence.[21]

If the state had any evidence that any of those listed in the exhibit were not qualified, then it should have introduced such evidence in the trial. The state should have cross-examined the government's applicant-witnesses to show their disqualifications, if any. Finally, Judge Johnson's mandatory order provided Alabama full opportunity to demonstrate that any of the fifty-four named individuals had subsequently become disqualified.

The Court of Appeals for the fifth circuit agreed with the government's position and upheld Judge Johnson's mandatory decree.[22] The Supreme Court affirmed the lower courts' order in a brief, per curiam decision in October 1962.[23]

An attorney for the Department of Justice made the following observation:

The interesting thing to note about Judge Frank Johnson is his development from the Macon County case to Bullock County to Montgomery County. He registered 1000 recently in Montgomery. He is getting more experience in handling these cases and is getting tougher on the registrars—more able to see the subtleties in the discriminatory acts. He registered 1000 in Montgomery by a stroke of the pen,

21. *Ibid.* p. 35.
22. 304 Fed. 2d. 582.
23. See *Terry* v. *Adams,* 345 U.S. 462 (1953).

but he waited until the Fifth Circuit Court of Appeals said his Macon County action was all right.[24]

The Judge Sets Standards

As stated earlier, Judge Johnson did not appoint voter referees in any of the three cases, although he found a pattern and practice of discrimination in each instance. His approach was to permit the local registrars to remedy their own practices. Throughout his official opinions, statements in court and in private conference with the litigants, he constantly alluded to his preference not to appoint referees but to rely on the good faith and integrity of the local officials to do as he had decreed. This was his procedure in Bullock County. In his statement in open court on March 30, 1961, immediately following the trial of the case, he stated:

All right gentlemen, the court is, in this case impressed with the sworn statement of these registrars that they are ready and willing even to the point of eagerness to register all qualified Negro citizens in Bullock County who see fit to apply to this Board to vote. . . . This court is impressed by the declarations of good faith by these members of the Board of Registrars and by the several citizens—white citizens who have testified that they stand ready and willing to vouch for qualified Negroes, that this court is going to reserve judgment on most of the injunctive phase of this suit for the time being.

The court reserved judgment on all matters except the rule limiting the number of persons one could vouch for to two per year. It held this to be "patently unconstitutional." As to finding a pattern and practice of discrimination, the appointment of referees, and the constitutionality of the voucher rule per se, the court reserved ruling. Instead, on March 30, 1961, Judge Johnson ordered the board to report each month during April, May, and June on the progress of registration in the county. The board was to report the name,

24. Interview with Attorney David Norman of U.S. Department of Justice, Washington, D.C., January 21, 1963.

address, and race of each applicant, the date of application, the name, address, and race of the voucher, and the final action taken on the application by the board.

The Bullock County board went back to the county, met two days in April and two days in May. One hundred and forty black citizens had signed the priority list to make application for voter certificates since March 30, 1961. The first monthly report (for April) showed that on the first registration day, fifteen applications from blacks were processed, five were rejected and five were not acted upon. The report for May showed that in the "suspense file" from the previous month, ten were registered and ten rejected. The board met two days in May also. During that time, it processed fifty black applications and rejected fifteen.

In a hearing before Judge Johnson on June 29, 1961, the court again put off ruling for three months and ordered the Bullock County board to file more detailed monthly reports. At the June hearing, thirty-two applications of blacks were examined by the court, and Johnson found they had been rejected for technical errors and because the applicants had not signed the oath. He called this to the attention of the board, and shortly afterwards the thirty-two were registered.

Early in September 1961 the United States filed a motion to have the Bullock County board expedite the registration process. The court heard the motion and issued its findings on September 13. Here Johnson set forth very specific operational standards to guide the board. At first, however, he summarized the board's practices since his first order in March 1961. Over 700 blacks had signed the priority list as a first step in the registration process. Only 250 blacks on that list, however, had been able to make application, and half of those were rejected by the board. Four hundred black citizens were still waiting to apply. At that point (September 1961) there were approximately 4400 blacks of voting age in Bullock County and only 130 were registered. The court found that the board was receiving applications at the rate of twenty-four per day.

Johnson noted that on March 7, 1960, a day when all applicants were white, the board handled forty-five applications. On July 4, 1961, the board advised blacks that the board would not be open for business, and yet it did work on that day and received applications from white citizens—one of whom testified to that fact. Black applicants were handled in groups of eight, and the proceeding group had to wait until the slowest one of the previous group had finished. The court room, with a seating capacity of over 250, was used as a waiting room while the registration process took place in a small room. Some blacks waited all day and returned repeatedly until their numbers were called.

This evidence, according to Judge Johnson, indicated that his faith in the board had not been vindicated. He stated:

The defendants have been practicing token registration in the face of a large backlog of large groups of Negroes waiting to apply. The Court can do no less than conclude that the registrars have failed to live up to their sworn statements that they were ready and willing to register all qualified Negro citizens in Bullock county and would do so if given the opportunity.[25]

As a consequence of this failure of the board to perform without further prompting by the court, Johnson entered a finding of a pattern and practice of discrimination, but still did not appoint a referee. Instead, he issued very specific orders in the form of a mandatory decree spelling out how the board was to operate in the future.

We concluded that where the percentage of one race already registered was very large and that of the other race very small, the board could not maintain the existing imbalance by arbitrarily adopting stricter standards and procedures. He stated, as in his Macon opinion, that the evidence showing a history of racial discrimination in the county warranted the issuance not only of a prohibitory, but also of a mandatory decree. Complete relief would require the correction of past practices; the prohibition of dis-

25. *U.S.* v. *Alabama,* Civil Action No. 1677-N, September 13, 1961.

criminatory practices; the expeditious and non-discriminatory processing of future applications; and supervision of the entire process on a fair basis.

The board could not apply different standards for current applicants from standards applied to white applicants since 1954. Neither could a different form or questionnaire be used from that used prior to March 30, 1961, and applicants could not be rejected for "formal, technical or inconsequential errors."

The board was ordered to process all applications by persons who then appeared on the priority list within sixty days of that (September 13, 1961) decree. The board had to post in a conspicuous place in the courthouse or place of registration the number that would be called first on the next registration day. All persons who subsequently signed up to apply had to be received and processed within five registration days of the date of their signing. Each rejected applicant was to be notified of the specific reasons for his rejection within ten days after his application was processed. Johnson ordered the board to post in a conspicuous public place or publish in a county newspaper the exact times and places applications would be received in outlying "beats" or precincts.

In his order Johnson directed the Department of Justice to submit the names of six persons within thirty days to serve as voter referees "in the event the court found the use of such to be necessary at some later date."

It would be difficult to conclude that Judge Johnson had acted hastily in laying down specific operational standards for the Bullock County registrars. He issued his first ruling on March 30, 1961. Four months intervened before his next order. Then in January 1962 he called an informal conference in his chambers which was attended by the Bullock County registrars, the attorneys for the Department of Justice, and attorneys for the state. The purpose of the conference was to discuss the activity of the board during December 1961. Johnson was disturbed by the large number of rejections of black applications merely on the basis of minor, formal, or inconsequential errors. A seasoned attorney for the Department of Justice made the following observation:

This business of chamber-ruling is very important. Take Judge Johnson, for instance, in the Bullock case. That was one of the strongest sessions [the January 1962 informal conference] I had ever heard. It showed just what a judge can do if he wants to.[26]

Part of that session is reproduced to give a further illustration of the possibilities of judicial aggressiveness in these matters. Johnson had before him the December 1961 Bullock County report which showed that 377 blacks had made application and 324 had been rejected. He noted that the FBI had interviewed the twenty-two who reportedly had refused to sign the oath and they all denied that they had so refused. Applications were taken from eighty-two whites, of whom sixty-seven were accepted and fifteen rejected. Ten of the fifteen rejections were for errors, three for lack of legal residence, one for being under age, and one not noted. Johnson noted that 177 black applicants had been rejected according to board notations for the following reasons: "false statements about applying previously for registration"; "supporting witness gave no residence of applicant"; "conflicting answers about applying for registration"; "no residence date in precinct"; "no precinct number."

Judge Johnson proceeded to admonish the board members after citing these reasons for rejection:

All that means this: that the Board for December refused to register the majority of the Negro people for technical and inconsequential reasons, and it is in violation of my injunction. And all 3 of you members of the Board are guilty of contempt of court. You are enjoined not to do that and you have done it. And you have done it on a wholesale scale.
Now I have several alternatives and it doesn't make very much dif-

26. Interview at Justice Department, Washington, D.C., January 22, 1963.

ference to me which one we take. I can order specifically as I have done before that the bulk of these people that you have rejected for these technical and inconsequential reasons be registered and give you a certain number of days to register them.

Along with that I can direct or suggest or permit the attorneys for the Government to institute contempt proceedings against each of the 3 of you. I don't want to do that and I don't intend to do that if we can work it out.

It may be that I have reached the point in Bullock county that I need to appoint voting referees. I am ready to do that if that is what it takes to get these people registered down there. The only other alternative is for you members of the Board to go on back down there and call these people in that you have rejected for these technical and inconsequential reasons and register them. That is all I have to say about it.

One of the attorneys for the state, mindful of Johnson's Macon County "stroke of the pen" act, stated that he wanted the judge to see the applications before he gave specific orders to register any blacks. Johnson then stated his position more clearly; he was caught in the middle but had no intention of being trapped or torn between conflicting demands:

Well, I haven't reached the point . . . where I am going to give you any specific instructions. I am faced with some alternatives. I didn't create the position that I find myself in. According to my view of the case, I am going to offer the Board the alternative—and that is the reason I called you down here—of registering these people and filing a supplemental [report]. I don't mean every single one of them. I mean all those that were denied registration for these technical reasons that I just went over a few minutes ago. If the Board wants to do it, it will be the last you hear from me as far as this December report is concerned. If they don't, I'm going to have to do something because they are entitled to vote if they want to vote.

Johnson was of the opinion that if the applicants failed to give precinct numbers, then the board should fill that in. It was also the responsibility of the board clearly and specifically to call to the attention of the applicant that the oath had to be signed "before you let them walk out of there." The court hesitated in spelling out more fully its definition of a technical or inconsequential error, because it preferred the board to take that responsibility. But Johnson did indicate an example: where the entire application showed that an applicant had lived all his or her life in the county but the line pertaining to the date of bona fide residence was left blank, then to deny this person registration, as was done in several instances, was wrong. The necessary information could be obtained from the remainder of the application.

One of the attorneys for the state referred to the fact that there were many virtually illiterate blacks, especially in the rural areas, who obviously, judging from the entire application, were not qualified. Johnson replied, "I am sure of that. I am sure of that. I am not requiring the registration of illiterates." After getting a firm commitment from the board members (which he insisted on having that day before they left Montgomery to return to Bullock County) that they would review all 324 of the rejected black applications, notify those who were rejected for technical reasons, recall them for purposes of correcting the errors and being registered, and file a supplemental report for December with him—all of which was to be done within ten days, Judge Johnson concluded:

I can't and I am not going to permit these people to be denied registration because of some technical error or omission in their application. . . . Now once we can reach a meeting of the minds on that, we'll get along all right. But we haven't so far in the Bullock county.[27]

Were Judge Johnson the only Southern federal judge hearing voting cases, judicial action of the type would have completely vindicated proponents of the judicial approach. Johnson's refusal to appoint voter referees was based on his strong inclination to have the imperfections worked out by the local officials with only

27. From transcript of conference in official files of the Department of Justice.

that amount of federal intervention which was absolutely necessary. Throughout, he was solicitous of local feelings (he took pains to compliment the lady member of the Bullock board for her prompt preparation of the monthly reports) but he was firm in his insistence that the local officials abide by his orders. His orders were reluctantly given, but once issued, they were clear and unambiguous.

But there were limits to this role. He had to take care lest the credibility of his threat to bring in federal referees be undermined. On this point, one attorney for the Department of Justice believed that Johnson had protected himself. He said, "When Judge Johnson threatens to appoint voter referees, they [the board members] know he means business and he will do it if necessary." [28] Johnson was not finished with standard-setting in Bullock County, however, notwithstanding his strong admonishment in the informal conference in January 1962. On July 26, 1962, he issued an official order spelling out in greater detail the exact standards to be applied in registering blacks in the county. These standards were based on a comprehensive study by the Department of Justice of the standards applied to white applicants during the period from 1952 through 1960. These were compiled and attached to Johnson's order as exhibits one and two, consisting of notebooks containing photographic copies of records of the Bullock County registrars between 1952 and 1960. If the current registrars wanted standards, Johnson would provide them with those standards used by their predecessors in registering white applicants during this earlier period, during which 867 white applicants were registered to vote in Bullock County. This represented over 96 per cent of all white persons who applied for registration during this period. Of the 867 persons registered, 570—or 63 per cent—were registered between January 1, 1952, and August 14, 1954.

Question number 20 of the registration application (one fre-

28. Interview at Justice Department, Washington, D.C., January 1963.

quently used to disqualify black applicants) reads, "Name some of the duties and obligations of citizenship." In some instances, registrars in black-belt Alabama counties had rejected black applicants if they did not list specific duties and obligations. The first notebook attached to Johnson's order contained an extensive study of sixty-four applications accepted by the board during the 1952–54 period. All of the sixty-four were filled out for the applicants by board members. Ten applications answered question 20 by saying, "support the constitution of USA and the State of Alabama." Sixteen applications answered, "to vote, to uphold the constitution." Eighteen filled out by a board member named Chappell answered question 20 in the following manner: "to vote, to obey the law." On one application, Chappell signed his own name on the oath line. On two applications, question 20 was left blank altogether, but the applications were accepted. In fact, all of the sixty-four applications were accepted by the board. The notebook concluded, and Johnson agreed, "Even when the board members filled out the forms themselves only the barest of essential information was required of the applicant before he was registered to vote in Bullock County, Alabama."

The important portion of Johnson's order set out the following standards:

1. Applicants who possess these qualifications must be registered, and it is the duty of the board to determine whether the applicants possess these qualifications.

2. If from the information contained on the application form the registrars are unable to determine whether the applicant possesses the qualifications of citizenship, age, or residence as set forth above, or if they are unable to determine whether the applicant is disqualified by reason of bad character, conviction of a disqualifying crime, insanity, or idiocy, then the registrars should point out the deficiency to the applicant and permit him to supply the necessary information on this form. If information supplied by the applicant on his application form disqualifies him under any one of the above grounds, the registrar should call this fact to his attention to insure that the information is correct.

3. If the applicant is willing to take the oath he possesses the qualification that he embrace the duties and obligations of citizenship.
It is the duty of the board to administer the oath to the applicant
and to have the applicant sign it in the proper place if he is willing
to do so. An applicant who takes the oath cannot be denied registration for errors or omissions in his answers to the loyalty and
belief questions in the questionnaire which are inconsistent with
his sworn oath.

4. If the applicant is literate he possesses the qualification that he be
able to read and write. If the applicant's answers on the application form are legible and his answers on the application form
demonstrate that he read the questions, then he has satisfied the
requirement that he be able to read and write. This determination
must be one of reasonableness and fairness. The application form
cannot be used as a test for the purpose or to form the basis of
rejecting applicants. Instead it must be used as a means to obtain
essential information to facilitate the registration of applicants.
Rejection notices sent to applicants who are rejected for their inability to read and write shall specifically state that fact.

These standards and procedures were in accordance with those
used by the Bullock County board in registering white persons
during the period 1952 through 1960.

In following this procedure, Johnson was consistent with his
preference to give the particular board members every opportunity
possible to correct their own errors. Bullock County got two new
board members since the informal conference in January 1962.
Johnson stated in court in July 1962, before issuing the order referred to above, that because the two members were new, he was
going to proceed with them as he had with the Macon County
board and with the former members of the Bullock board. That is,
he was going to presume that if he set out specific standards to
guide the new members they would comply in good faith. Once
again, in his open court statement, Johnson referred to his ultimate
alternative, which he said he did not wish to exercise, of appointing voting referees.

The United States, in its motion, had requested that the court
order twenty-five named black citizens registered. Johnson re-

fused this request, but stated in his order that the persons named be notified "forthwith" and be permitted to make new application within fifteen days of the notice. "The qualifications of these applicants as well as all applicants for registration in Bullock County from this day on shall be judged and determined in accordance with this order." [29]

In the meantime, Judge Johnson had been pursuing a similar line of action in the Macon County case. He issued his first order there on March 17, 1961. In September 1961 he found that the board had slipped back into its former ways, so in that month he issued another order on a motion of the United States covering both operational and questionnaire standards. He found that for three months following the court's decree, about forty-four applicants were processed per registration day, but after that, only eighteen applicants per day were taken. This was done not withstanding the fact that the number of persons waiting to apply had been steadily increasing—in September 1961 there was a backlog of approximately 550, an increase of 150 over the 400 in March 1961. Likewise, for three months the board permitted applicants to correct formal, technical, and inconsequential errors. Then it stopped doing so. One frequent mistake of applicants was in listing the date residency began in the county. Some applicants listed 1961, while the rest of the application showed that the person had lived in the county all of his life. This was a technical error.

Johnson issued orders that a full three-man board be appointed within two weeks (one of the registrars had resigned on September 4, 1961), that each person in the backlog be permitted to make application within *at most* eight registration days beginning and including October 2, 1961. He also ordered eighty-four blacks named in the order placed upon the current and permanent registration rolls by October 16, 1961, unless they had died, moved from the county, or in some other way been disqualified. As far

29. *U.S.* v. *Alabama,* civil action no. 1677-N, p. 6.

as standards to be applied on the questionnaire were concerned, the order contained detailed evidence of standards applied to white applicants since 1957. "Said standards include assistance to white applicants in filling out the forms, as well as allowing white applicants to register whose forms contained errors or omission." [30]

The United States filed its case against the Montgomery County board members and the State of Alabama on August 3, 1961. By this time, the Department of Justice attorneys and Judge Johnson had come to know each other's thinking in these voting cases. They were in the midst of the Macon and Bullock cases, and the brief filed by the government and the subsequent decree entered by Johnson reflected a mutual familiarity that came from constant and close contact with a problem.

In early January 1962 a brief filed by the government had asked that the district court set up specific standards for the Montgomery board—standards based on past actions of the predecessor board in the county. The government's contention was that individual board members would change and new members should not be expected to cipher through "mountains of records" from earlier years to determine the standards used to register white applicants. This determination could best be done by the district court. What the Department of Justice obviously meant was that its own staff in the Civil Rights Division would do the job and present the findings to the court in a concise, yet comprehensive notebook as it did in Bullock County.

The United States argued that such standards were necessary because the black citizens should be required to qualify only under the same kind of standards used to register the white citizens in the county then on the rolls. In addition, should a referee be appointed in the future, he would need to know what those earlier standards were.

The government specifically set forth what should constitute a

30. *U.S.* v. *Alabama,* civil action no. 479-B.

formal, technical, and inconsequential error. It included all the errors Judge Johnson had previously overruled in the Macon and Bullock cases. The United States suggested the use of the local telephone book to obtain addresses of vouchers if necessary. The government brief pointed out that on one day, the Montgomery County board had processed 227 applications, and there was no reason why that kind of diligent effort could not be emulated in 1962. As was done in Macon and Bullock, the United States asked the court to spell out the maximum time allotted to process an application. It is interesting to note in this connection that the government did not ask the court to appoint voter referees. Instead, it stated that the kind of decree it sought would facilitate the work of a referee if the appointment of one became necessary. The government had studied Judge Johnson and knew the type of decrees he would issue.[31]

The Assistant Attorney General of the Civil Rights Division summarized the effects of a voting case on the participants:

Clearly the first case in a judicial district is educational for all concerned. The courts, we, and defense counsel know better the materials that will be subject matter of any subsequent controversies. We know each other, too.[32]

Judge Johnson issued his order on November 20, 1962. At the outset, he adopted the government's theory:

In determining whether the Negroes are qualified, the court must apply the same standards used by the Board of Registrars in qualifying white applicants during the period in which the pattern of discrimination is found to exist.[33]

31. It should be noted that the government's brief in the Montgomery case was filed on January 20, 1962, nine days after the important informal conference between Judge Johnson, the Bullock board members, and the U.S. attorneys.
32. Burke Marshall, *op. cit.*, p. 467.
33. *U.S.* v. *Alabama.*

The period under consideration was 1956 to 1962. The court examined the exhibits presented by the United States pertaining to standards during that time and found that certain black applicants who had applied and been rejected for that period were, in fact, qualified. Consequently, he ordered the registration of 1076 blacks. Aside from race, they possessed the same qualifications as the whites registered during the six-year period.

Judge Johnson then proceeded to set up specific standards for future operation of the board. The length of residency in the county was to be determined by oral examination or any other methods and the residency line on the application was to be filled in by the board. Prior to that time, blacks were required in many instances to calculate the exact number of years, months, and days they had resided in the county since their birth. No applications were to be rejected for failure to sign the oath. Only a flat refusal by the applicant would suffice. No technical, formal, or inconsequential errors were to serve as basis for rejection. Attached to the decree were exhibits that showed what constituted such errors. The board had to process all future applicants within a stipulated time and those rejected were to be notified within ten days with specific reasons for the rejection. A maximum time was specified for mailing certificates to those who had been accepted. Judge Johnson cited as a precedent the Macon County case. He also agreed that such a decree would facilitate the work of a voter referee if subsequent action by the board made such an appointment necessary. He directed the Department of Justice to submit to the court within thirty days the names of three qualified persons who might be able to serve as voter referees if they became necessary.

Johnson concluded his decree by noting that this was the third such case before his court. He spoke as one who had become familiar with the manifestations of these kinds of cases. He said:

The State of Alabama through some of its agents and officers continues in the belief that some contrivance may be successfully

adopted and practiced for the purpose of thwarting equality of the
right to vote of citizens of the United States.

Such an attitude ignores the principle that the only true basis for a
representative government is equality in the right to select those representatives. No such equality can exist when a class of our citizens is
deprived of its right to vote because of its color. This right to vote is
a personal right that is vested in qualified individuals by virtue of
their citizenship. It is not a privilege to be granted or denied at the
whim or caprice of state officers or state governments.[34]

Judge Johnson had heard the evidence, entered his orders, set
the standards, and stated the philosophical framework underlying
his action. He was more than considerate of local sentiments in
not appointing federal voter referees. But he had made it clear
that the local officials had the burden of exercising their responsibilities.

The Judge as Overseer

In all three cases, Johnson retained jurisdiction for purposes of
enforcing, modifying, or extending his orders. Each decree ended
with specific directions to all litigants in the case. The registrars
were to submit a report of the progress of the board in its respective county each month to the clerk of the court on a specified
day. This report was to contain the number and dates of applications received during the reporting period—prospective applicants
were to sign a priority list at the place of registration and be given
a number; the name, address, and race of each applicant; the name,
address, and race of each voucher and the specific identity of the
applicant for whom he vouched; and the action taken during the
reporting period. The report was to contain the names, addresses,
and race of those accepted and the date the voter certificate was
mailed to the new registrant. The names, addresses, and race of
those rejected were to be submitted along with the exact reasons
for the rejection.

34. *Ibid.*

The judge ordered that the United States, acting through the Department of Justice, be given the opportunity at all reasonable times to inspect voting records in the respective counties and to submit monthly reports containing the same information given by the county boards. In addition, the Department of Justice was to furnish information to the court periodically to assist the court in determining if the decree was being fully complied with or if contempt proceedings should be instituted. Likewise, if vacancies occurred on the boards, the Department of Justice was to ascertain and report to the court if such vacancies could be filled by the state appointing board (consisting of the governor, the auditor, and the commissioner of agriculture and industries) within a reasonable time. Finally, the Department of Justice was to assist the court in determining if resignations were made in good faith or were efforts to frustrate the orders of the court.

Judge Johnson's orders erased many of the obstacles besetting some blacks attempting to conduct voter registration drives in the three black-belt counties. In addition to overcoming the frustrations connected with the resignation of board members, black civil rights groups no longer had to worry about instructing their recruits in the art of completing letter-perfect applications. Voting clinics were prolific in the three counties in the late 1950s and early 1960s. Much of the time spent in these classes was devoted to checking and rechecking to make sure the prospective applicants had dotted all i's, crossed all t's, and placed periods at the end of each sentence. Before Judge Johnson issued his orders, the application form to be filled out by blacks was a test that they could pass or fail like an examination in school. As a result of these cases, it was no longer necessary for organizations like the TCA to check on the work of the boards. No private person needed to be stationed at the courthouse as the TCA had done for more than eight years. This time-consuming and tedious police work was now taken over by the board members and the Department of Justice. Whatever other effects the 1957 and 1960 Acts had, it is important not to overlook these factors. Southern blacks who had been working for decades on voter registration now found they could shift their efforts to more important aspects of the over-all problem—aspects to which only they could attend. "Now," one black leader said, "we can spend our time getting our people to go down. And man, I'll tell you, that is tough enough itself." Thus, even if the registration rolls did not increase by leaps and bounds, some black leaders were greatly impressed by these major modifications. Another black activist in Montgomery stated, "At least we don't have to fight that board as much and all alone, and that's a talking point right there to get folks to go down."

One of the major objections to utilizing the judicial approach had been that the prestige and consequent effectiveness of the federal court would suffer. To inject the court into such politically explosive controversies, the objection went, was not sound policy from the standpoint of protecting the judiciary. The following editorial appeared with a picture of Judge Johnson in the *Birmingham News* three days after Judge Johnson issued his Montgomery decree:

Judge Frank M. Johnson, Jr., has ordered the Montgomery County board of registrars to enroll 1100 Negroes. He had been considering evidence on the case for months.

The ruling is not surprising. Judge Johnson's position as a jurist consistently has been clear on this issue, when evidence was substantial. Through his court it previously had been determined that the federal bench may direct such registration. This had been done in Macon County.

Judge Johnson also asked the Justice Department to provide him with a list of three qualified persons to serve as federal voter registration referees should Montgomery County registrars refuse to obey his instructions—or should they resign. Courts have power to enforce Negro registration. Naturally many in Montgomery County and in much of the rest of Alabama will resent such direct federal action. Common consensus in the state is that voter registration is a state matter.

But as the **News** has said ever since this issue first came up in Alabama, it is not realistic to assume that the federal government, under either GOP or Democratic administration, will fail to act to guarantee Negroes' right to vote in federal elections.

Whether one likes federal intervention or not, the record is clear that in some such cases, at least, obviously qualified citizens have been denied the vote. In the Montgomery case, evidence as reported indicated that vastly more Negroes proportionately than whites had been refused registration. Among those refused: six holders of master's degrees obtained through advanced college work beyond a normal four years; 152 persons with four years of undergraduate work in college; 222 with some college work; 710 applicants with at least a high school educational equivalent, and 108 Negroes teaching public school in the county.

There is no logic in argument that such citizens, regardless of their color, could be denied the vote.

Apparently it still needs saying in this state that it is the opposite of wisdom to invite federal intervention through wholesale failures to grant the privilege of voting to qualified persons. Negroes are citizens. If any whites turn their backs on that hard fact, then the federal government will certainly intervene.[35]

It would be difficult to conclude that Judge Johnson or the federal court system suffered from that type of editorial comment coming from such an influential newspaper in the state. At least in Alabama, the right to vote free of racial obstructions when aggressively enforced by the federal judiciary received the sanction and even the support of important elements in the local community.

35. The Birmingham *News* had never been noted for a pro-civil rights attitude or even moderate approach on race relations. It was staunchly pro-segregation.

6 Judicial Resistance

The judicial behavior reviewed in this chapter is a study in contrast to that of Judge Johnson. Federal judges Harold Cox and Claude Clayton in Mississippi added the force and effect of their positions to that of local Mississippi registrars to erect additional obstacles to registration of black citizens in at least the three counties examined here. The federal government encountered barriers from the outset in inspecting local voting records, in obtaining a speedy hearing on its complaints, and in receiving court rulings that dealt with the essence of the alleged discriminations. Many of the objections to utilizing the Southern federal courts were rather completely vindicated when the actions of these two judges are considered.

The Fight To Inspect Records

On August 11, 1960, the Attorney General, then William P. Rogers, requested that the registrar of elections of Forrest County, Mississippi, Theron C. Lynd, make available to the Department of Justice for inspection and copying various records and papers pertaining to registration and voting. The legal basis for this request, as we have noted, was Section 303 of the Civil Rights Act of 1960. On August 23, 1960, Lynd, through his counsel, requested a ninety-day extension in which to reply. The government agreed to a twenty-one-day extension until September 16, 1960. On September 15, 1960, Lynd repeated the request for the full ninety days. On October 10 he declined to turn over the records, but some indication was given that he might comply. When negotiations failed, the United States filed a suit on January 19, 1961, under Title III of the Civil Rights Act of 1960 seeking a court order to inspect the registration and voting records. The case was filed before Federal District Judge Mize, who set March 13 as the date for hearing.[1]

On March 13, moments before the hearing was to begin, Lynd's attorneys moved that the action be dismissed unless the newly appointed Attorney General, Robert F. Kennedy, be properly substituted in place of former Attorney General Rogers. This was, at best, a highly technical and inconsequential point, but the court so ordered. A motion was submitted on March 21 to substitute Kennedy for Rogers, and on April 4 the requested substitution was ordered by the court. Following this substitution, Lynd requested an additional sixty-day extension in which to plead. The government objected strenuously on the grounds that the defendant should have been prepared on March 13 and that the issue in the case did not involve any complex legal or constitutional issues. This last point was especially stressed in light of federal court rulings in 1960 and 1961 [2] on this identical point—demand for inspection of records. This information notwithstanding, the district court granted the defendant thirty days in which to file all preliminary motions and an additional ten days in which to file an answer and any other motions not previously filed. After this period, the court, again over strenuous objection of the government and for the

1. At this point, for purposes of this study, dates and intervening lapses of time become significant. This was not important in the Alabama cases because of Judge Johnson's approach to these cases.
2. *In re Crum Dinkens,* 187 Fed. Supp. 848 (1960), affirmed 285 Fed. 2d. 430 (1961), certiorari denied, 366 U.S. 913 (1961).

same reasons listed before, permitted the defendant forty days to prepare a legal brief contesting the constitutionality of Title III, although its constitutionality had been upheld by the federal courts. On this point Judge Mize stated:

You can brief the constitutionality of the Act if you want to. We can argue that, because, of course, the court sometimes changes its mind about what act is constitutional or is not. So you can brief all those questions [certain other procedural matters raised by the defendants].[3]

The government, given fifteen days to reply, filed its response on July 18.

Apparently frustrated in their almost year-long effort merely to examine the records in Forrest County, the United States proceeded to file a suit against Lynd and the state of Mississippi alleging racial discrimination in the registration process. The complaint was filed on July 6, 1961. At the same time it sought to inspect the county records under another federal procedure, known as Rule 34. This case was filed before Judge Cox.

Six months later, in January 1962, Judge Cox announced that Judge Mize had transferred the original Title III case to him. On January 15, 1962, Judge Cox rendered an opinion in which he held that by filing the second case, the government abandoned its Title III proceeding:

The issues to be decided in the latter case have been rendered and are academic and moot by reason of the abandonment of said former suit by the subsequent suit in this court embracing the same subject matter and other relief therein requested.[4]

Shortly thereafter, on January 26, 1962, Judge Cox entered an order striking from the complaint all incidents pre-dating February 26, 1959—the beginning of Lynd's tenure. On March 7 he

3. Trial record, *Kennedy* v. *Lynd*, civil action no. 19636.
4. Trial record, *In re Theron C. Lynd*, civ. no. 1604, p. 149.

granted the government's motion for discovery under Rule 34 but restricted it to records made during Lynd's tenure in office.

The order dismissing the Title III suit was entered on February 16, 1962. The government appealed to the Court of Appeals for the fifth circuit on March 16. The United States' appeal was simply stated and bolstered by recent decisions. *In re Crum Dinkens* clearly stated that the Attorney General was entitled to inspect state voting records. That case was soon followed by a 1962 decision in the Court of Appeals for the fifth circuit, *Kennedy* v. *Bruce,*[5] in which that court held "the procedure established under Title III of the Civil Rights Act, under which the Attorney General proceeded in the District Court, does not amount to the filing of a suit of any kind." That court further stated that an enforcement order should be granted "as a matter of course." [6]

The only possible justification for Judge Cox's action, according to the United States, was the fact, which was not present in the *Dinkens* or *Bruce* cases, that other actions had been filed pending the ruling on Title III. But, the government argued, the subsequent suit should not overrule the first. The standard for obtaining discovery under Rule 34—the showing of good cause—was far more stringent than the applicable criteria under Title III. In a Title III case, the Attorney General need only make a request of the registrar and have that request refused to be entitled to an order from the court. But under Rule 34 the Attorney General had a greater burden:

In a proceeding under Rule 34, the range of discovery depends upon the factual issues in dispute and is subject to limitations within the discretion of the trial judge. On the other hand, the area of inquiry available in a Title III proceeding is specifically prescribed by statute and might encompass considerably more than would be accessible under Rule 34.[7]

5.   298 Fed. 2d. 860.
6.   *Ibid.,* p. 864.
7.   Government's Brief in *Kennedy* v. *Lynd* (no. 19636) before Fifth Circuit Court of Appeals, p. 10.

Under Title III, the Attorney General would have been entitled to inspect and copy all records prior and subsequent to February 26, 1959. But now the government was severely restricted in the material it could inspect and in properly preparing its case to prove a "pattern and practice" of discrimination in Forrest County. So the abandonment of one action by the institution of another could only occur where the second action was coterminous with the first. Such was not the situation in the Lynd case. The abandoned remedy exceeded greatly the scope of relief provided by the surviving remedy.

The Court of Appeals agreed with the government's position, reversed Judge Cox's ruling on Title III, and ordered the Forrest County records opened to the Department of Justice for inspection. The appellate court began its opinion in a tone of impatience with the number of such cases still coming before it on appeal:[8] "As this is a matter of recurring importance, we think it appropriate to make plain again that which we have tried so painstakingly to make plain before." [9]

While a Title III demand was, to be sure, a situation involving a "case or controversy," it was not to be considered an ordinary civil action. While there were adversaries and it sought "appropriate process" calling for the exercise of judicial judgment, it nonetheless was a "special statutory proceeding in which the courts play a limited, albeit vital, role." When the Attorney General filed a simple demand statement, "the court is required to treat it as a summary proceeding."

The Court, with expedition, should grant the relief sought or, if the respondent-custodian opposes the grant of such relief, the matter should be set down without delay for suitable hearing on the matters open for determination. These are, of course, severely limited. In the event of a genuine dispute thereon, it would be in order for the Court

8. The Lynd case was combined with four other Title III cases coming out of four Louisiana parishes.
9. 306 Fed. 2d. 225.

to determine whether the written demand has been made, Section 1974(b), or whether the custodians against whom orders are sought have been given reasonable notice of the pendency of the proceeding. On the other hand, the factual foundation for, or the sufficiency of, the Attorney General's "statement of the basis and the purpose" contained in the written demand, Section 1974(b) is not open to judicial review or ascertainment.[10]

The district court was also in error in limiting the scope of inspection to Lynd's tenure in office. The Congress, by statute, had determined what records could be inspected. Since the statute specified "all records and papers" in the officer's custody "relating to any application . . . or other act requisite to voting" in such elections held within twenty-two months, the registrar's (custodian's) duty to retain and preserve, and the Attorney General's right of inspection and copying extended as far back as the earliest date of any such record or paper which bore on the eligibility of any currently listed voter:

The cutoff date is in no way related to the identity or status of "the person having custody, possession, or control," or the time at which any such person acceded to or terminated such office.[11]

The appellate court's view was that the Title III proceeding was investigative in nature. Its purpose was to find out if a suit should be filed and then to enable the government to use the evidence once a suit was filed. When the subsequent action was filed along with the Rule 34 motion, this did not exhaust the mechanisms of discovery. Rule 34 was concerned with relevancy and good cause as these pertained to the particular suit filed. Such questions "are completely foreign to the summary proceeding under Title III."

10. *Ibid.*, p. 226.
11. *Ibid.*, p. 227.

"An Interminable Pleading Duel": Forrest County, Mississippi

The Section 1971 action filed by the United States on July 6, 1961, against the state of Mississippi and the registrar in Forrest County, Theron C. Lynd, provided a good example of the possible delays and frustrations connected with a law suit of this kind when the judge seemed intent on accomplishing those goals. The complaint charged that the defendants applied different and more stringent standards to blacks than to whites in determining their qualifications to vote; that they refused to afford black citizens an opportunity to register equal to that afforded white citizens; that they unreasonably delayed the receipt of black applications; and that they arbitrarily refused to give blacks an opportunity to apply for registration. It was further claimed that a substantial majority of the 22,431 white voting-age residents of Forrest County were registered to vote whereas only about twenty-five of 7495 blacks of voting age in Forrest County were registered. The government asked for a preliminary and permanent injunction. The plaintiff also moved, as noted earlier, for discovery of the official registration records of Forrest County under Rule 34. A hearing was set on the Rule 34 motion for August 7, then reset for August 14. On July 24, 1961, the defendants moved for an extension of time in which to plead, and were given until August 21.

A hearing was had on August 14 on the Rule 34 motion. The hearing was adjourned without decision, however, and on August 29 the court held that it would not resume the hearing unless the government amended its complaint to comply with Rule 9 of the federal rules of civil procedure. This rule provided that the circumstances constituting fraud should be stated with particularity. It was the government's contention, that it was not alleging fraud, but the court refused to grant a certification permitting the government to appeal this decision.

On September 5 the parties argued a motion by the defendants to require the plaintiff to make a more definite statement, and on September 25 Judge Cox required the government to amend its complaint to state specifically:

1. The date of each application or attempt to register;
2. The name of each Negro denied the right to vote;
3. The name of each Negro refused registration who applied therefor;
4. The dates involved in any discriminatory mishandling of Negro registration applications;
5. The names of white people allowed to register who possessed no better qualifications than such Negroes denied the same privilege;
6. The facts and circumstances in necessary detail showing such discrimination in each of said instances and respects so as to reveal with fair and reasonable particularity the factual background for all of plaintiff's conclusions in the eighth paragraph (wherein allegation was made of discriminatory acts and practices) of the complaint.[12]

On October 10, in compliance with the court's order, the government filed an amended complaint, naming sixty-three blacks and detailing the circumstances of their attempts to register and their rejection by the defendant Lynd. No white persons who had been given preferential treatment were listed in the amended complaint because, due to the inability of the government to obtain access to the Forrest County registration records, no information then within the knowledge of the plaintiff concerning specific white applicants was available.

On January 4, 1962, the government's motion for a preliminary injunction and the motion for discovery under Rule 34 were set for hearing on January 12, but on that date the hearing was postponed again until March 1. On January 26 the court granted defense motions to strike from the amended complaint all incidents of discrimination predating February 26, 1959, the date Lynd

12. Trial record, p. 247.

took office. The complaint, amended a second time in compliance with the court's orders, was filed on February 5.

Finally, between March 5 and March 7, arguments were heard for a preliminary injunction and on the Rule 34 motion. At this hearing, the court refused to permit the government to introduce the testimony of witnesses where the details concerning such witnesses were not specifically set out in the complaint. In view of this ruling, the government orally amended its complaint—the third amendment—and introduced its evidence. The defendants offered no proof at this hearing, but nevertheless the court refused to grant or deny the motion for a preliminary injunction. Instead, the court granted the defendants thirty days in which to answer the complaint as amended at the hearing—the government's request that defendants be allowed a five-day rather than a thirty-day delay was rejected—and the right to reserve cross-examination of witnesses who were not specifically mentioned in the complaint prior to the last amendment. The court indicated that it would resume the hearing fifteen days after the defendants' answer was filed.[13]

When counsel for the government was examining black witnesses, it became apparent that defendant Lynd had with him the application cards of the thirteen black witnesses who had been permitted to apply, and the court ordered them to be given to the plaintiff as each witness was questioned during the hearing, but not before. During the hearing the court ordered the defendants to produce the application forms of the white witnesses. Six of these were produced and the court permitted their introduction at the close of the testimony. Not until after the hearing on March 8 did the court order production of certain other records requested by the government. This order was limited to records made during Lynd's tenure in office.

13. The reason for the postponement was that the defendant, Lynd, and his counsel were unable to appear on account of a storm in Mississippi. Nineteen of the twenty Government witnesses were present, however.

On March 21 the government appealed the failure of Judge Cox to render a preliminary injunction. On April 10 the Court of Appeals issued an injunction pending the appeal.[14] On its appeal, the United States attacked four specific rulings of the lower court: its refusal to grant the request for a preliminary injunction notwithstanding the evidence showing that distinctions on account of race or color had been made in the registration procedures of Forrest County; its characterizing the government's action as one in fraud and requiring the government to plead in accordance with Rule 9 of the federal rules of civil procedure; its repeatedly frustrating the government's access to the voting registration records in the possession of the registrar; and its excluding evidence of racially discriminatory acts occurring prior to the incumbency of Lynd as registrar.

The government contended it was entitled to a preliminary injunction because the evidence showed that discriminations were being practiced on account of race. Forty blacks were named in the amended complaint as having attempted to register since the beginning of Lynd's term of office. Prior to January 31, 1961, no black person was permitted to apply for registration. Sixteen black witnesses testified that from March 3, 1959, to January 1961 they were "told by a lady at the office to see Mr. Lynd"; that "Mr. Lynd said he was not set up for registration and did not know when he would be"; that "Mr. Lynd told me I would have to come back because he did not have his feet on the ground"; that they were "told by Mr. Lynd he did not have time and did not know when he would have the time."

While some blacks were permitted to make application after January 31, 1961, no black citizen had been registered. Those rejected were high school teachers, an elementary school principal, and two were ministers. The trial record listed the educational level of each. There were college degrees, twenty-seven credits toward a master's degree at N.Y.U.; a master's degree from Oregon State;

14. *U.S.* v. *Lynd*, 301 Fed. 2d. 818 (1962).

another in theology; the recent recipient of a National Science Foundation grant at Columbia. Even Judge Cox questioned the grounds for rejecting eight of these black applicants and he required the defendants to file within twenty days the reasons for such rejections. But he did not order affirmative relief for these eight persons, which was in sharp contrast with Judge Johnson in Alabama. No named white person had been rejected for registration during Lynd's entire term of office.

The undisputed evidence showed that white applicants were being registered by Lynd's deputies while every black applicant was referred to Lynd. This difference in treatment was admitted by Lynd and by his deputies. The explanations given were that the procedure was followed for "political" reasons and that deputy registrars had become apprehensive about processing black applicants. The only testimony as to the cause of the apprehension, however, was that on one unspecified occasion an unidentified black man had asked the lady deputy a "personal question," [15] and that on another occasion a black woman fumbled around in her handbag while waiting for the registrar, left the office, and returned with a black man. When the government asked Judge Cox to end this practice, the judge refused and said:

I think the colored people brought that on themselves. I am thoroughly familiar with some of the conduct of some of our colored gentry, and I am not surprised at Mr. Lynd's reaction to what he stated into the record. I think that is a clear justification of what he did. You people up north don't understand what he was talking about. I don't expect you to. But I do, I know exactly what he was talking about and I think he did just exactly right in taking those things on himself. He said he couldn't afford any male help and he used girls in there and those girls didn't want to be subjected to that kind of influence and that is understandable. Otherwise I think that he certainly did need a good explanation.[16]

15. The deputy testified that the black man had asked her, "How long I had been there and didn't he know me and didn't I remember him and one thing and another."
16. Trial record, p. 1192.

Ten white witnesses testified that prior to January 31, 1961, they were registered in the following ways: registered by a woman and remembered signing only the registration book; registered by a woman upon telling her his name and showing his identification; registered immediately and did not recall filling out a form or interpreting the Constitution; registered by a deputy clerk and re-called only signing the registration book.

After January 31, 1961, when blacks were permitted to apply for registration, the registrar initiated the practice of requiring all applicants to fill out a form. The evidence showed that blacks were given long and difficult passages of the Mississippi constitution to interpret, while white applicants, if given the constitutional inter-pretation test at all, were given shorter and less difficult passages. The trial record included examples of constitutional passages asked of blacks and their answers, as well as those put to whites. One passage frequently given to black, but never to white applicants read:

Taxation shall be uniform and equal throughout the state. Property shall be taxed in proportion to its value. The legislature may, how-ever, impose a tax per capita upon such domestic animals as from their nature and habits are destructive of other property. Property shall be assessed for taxes under general laws, and by uniform rules, according to its true value. But the legislature may provide for a special mode of valuation and assessment for railroads and other corporate property, or for particular species of property belonging to persons, corporations, or associations not situated wholly in one county. But all such property shall be assessed at its true value, and no county shall be denied the right to levy county and special taxes upon such assessment as in other cases of property situated and assessed in the county.[17]

The court expressed an interest in the interpretation given this passage by one black witness, stating that "The Supreme Court of Mississippi has had some trouble with this Section."

In one situation a white applicant was given Section 14 of the

17. Trial record, pp. 639 and 652.

Mississippi constitution to interpret, which reads, "No person shall be deprived of life, liberty or property except by due process of law." The interpretation which she gave to the section was that "Every citizen has equal rights." This applicant was found to be qualified and was registered to vote.

Judge Cox was not convinced that racial discrimination was practiced in selecting questions. He observed:

> I think the record clearly shows that they've got a bunch of cards down there that have sections of the Constitution on them and the record here clearly shows that they have just got one bunch of cards on white people and colored people alike and they pull them out according to the first one that is closest to them and use it, and I don't think that they make any distinction in whether the section of the Constitution was easy or hard. . . . I don't believe you could make a statement like that and be supported by the record.[18]

White applicants were assisted consistently in filling out their application forms; black applicants never were. In this connection, it is interesting to compare Judge Cox's reaction to conspicuous marks on white applications to Judge Johnson's response noted earlier. Several white witnesses testified that they were told their election district. All six white witnesses whose forms were produced in court signed the last line for the signature. The United States attorneys were not permitted to see these forms until after they had finished presenting their witnesses. On four of these forms there were checks or cross marks on the signature line. Judge Johnson had concluded that these were put there to show the applicant where to sign. When this was called to the attention of Judge Cox, his initial response was to inquire if the government attorneys knew how the check marks got there. Lynd also refused to tell black applicants the reason for their rejection and required such blacks to wait six months before reapplying for registration.

In light of all this, the government felt that Judge Cox should

18. Trial record, p. 1194.

have ordered a preliminary injunction restraining these practices.

Another point of comparison between Cox and Johnson was in what each judge judicially noticed. Johnson felt that the government's evidence was "overwhelming" in the Macon and Montgomery cases and that the court would be "absurd" and "naïve" to overlook some obvious discriminatory practices. Cox, on the other hand, took judicial notice of the high illiteracy rate among blacks. The government produced statistics showing that there were approximately 7495 blacks and 22,431 whites of voting age in Forrest County and of these about twenty-five blacks and a substantial majority of the whites were registered to vote. The government's intent, of course, was to offer evidence tending to prove that the great disproportion was due in large measure to the discriminatory practices of the registrar. The Court of Appeals had stated in another case, *Alabama* v. *U.S.,* that "in the problem of racial discrimination, statistics often tell much, and courts listen." But Judge Cox chose to listen to different facts. He had this to say:

I think that the Court could take judicial notice of the illiteracy that is prevalent among the colored people, and I do know that of my own knowledge, and the intelligence of the colored people don't compare ratio-wise to white people. I mean, that is just a matter of common sense and common knowledge. . . . Mentioning figures like that to me wouldn't mean a thing in the world without something to go along with it.[19]

One might suggest that the government's case did have, in fact, "something to go along with it," but the judge apparently overlooked it.

The government objected strenuously to the district court's requirement to plead the case as one of fraud. Because of this requirement, the United States had to plead the specific dates, names, and full circumstances of each incident of discrimination. Judge Cox limited the testimony to witnesses who were actually named in the

19. Trial record, p. 405.

complaint, and limited the testimony of witnesses who were named to the precise allegations of the complaint. The government argued that the 1957 and the 1960 Civil Rights Acts were remedial in character and were proposed and adopted not for purposes of prosecuting for fraud but in order to afford the government a speedy and effective means of dealing with discrimination in voting. To require the application of fraud rules would frustrate the purposes of the Acts. Specificity is required in fraud cases because by its nature fraudulent conduct can consist of an infinite number of widely diversified specific acts. It is therefore incumbent upon the pleader to inform his adversary of the particular claim which he must meet. But in the Forrest County case, the government was hindered in specifically pleading and proving because the records were in the possession of the defendants and unavailable to the United States attorneys.

The technical pleading of fraud had never been required in civil rights cases. In a Supreme Court opinion in 1957,[20] a case involving a charge of racial discrimination by a labor union, the court held that the pleading need not cite specific facts to support the general allegations. The earlier cases under the 1967 Act did not require fraud pleading.[21]

Even in fraud cases, Rule 9 required only that the circumstances constituting fraud "shall be stated with particularity." It is not necessary to plead the evidence. But Judge Cox demanded that the government not only plead the circumstances "with particularity" but that it plead all its evidence, down to the detailed circumstances of the handling of each application for registration to which the government might want to refer in its proof.

It was the accumulation of rulings by Judge Cox on the fraud motion and Rule 34 which brought about the several amended

---

20. *Conley* v. *Gibson,* 355 U.S. 41.
21. See *U.S.* v. *Alabama,* 362 U.S. 602 (1960); *U.S.* v. *Thomas,* 362 U.S. 58 (1960); *U.S.* v. *Raines,* 362 U.S. 17 (1960).

complaints and continuous delays. At one point in March 1962
Cox himself characterized the entire proceeding as an "interminable
pleading duel."

The government sought to introduce evidence of discrimination
predating Lynd's assumption of office because it felt such revela-
tions would throw light on what patterns of discrimination had become fixed and it would also have served to explain why many
black citizens might have thought it futile even to try to register to
vote. Past practices of discrimination could conceivably lead to
widespread discouragement and a what's-the-use attitude, the government argued. Judge Cox's position on this was that Lynd should
not be held accountable for the actions of his predecessors. But this
overlooked the fact that the Civil Rights Act of 1960 provided for
adding the state as a party defendant, and if the registrar resigned
prior to the institution of proceedings, the case could proceed
against the state.

Judge Cox did not say why the pre-Lynd evidence was inad-
missible against the state, but the following colloquy is in the trial
records:

By the Court: The bad part about that is that the State don't have a
thing in the world to do with registration.

By Mr. Doar [Department of Justice attorney]: Yes, but the State is
made a defendant under the provision of Congress.

By the Court: I know, but you might as well have made me a defendant in there. I don't have anything to do with it and the
state don't either. I know from many, many years of experience and familiarity with the situation that it's a very trouble-
some question.[22]

Only a verbatim account could attest to the almost incredible position taken by Judge Cox. His views were directly contradictory to
a host of authorities, including the Fourteenth and Fifteenth

22. Trial record, p. 426.

Amendments to the Constitution, as well as Supreme Court opinions.[23] It is virtually impossible, by any stretch of the concepts of judicial review or judicial policy-making, to defend him in this ruling.

In addition, the government had urged that pre-Lynd evidence was needed and relevant in showing a "pattern and practice" of discrimination. The defendants objected on the grounds that the district court should not consider evidence on the question of whether a pattern and practice of discrimination existed until it had determined that there was racial discrimination. They urged the view that evidence on the pattern and practice question must be introduced in a second, separate proceeding and was irrelevant during the first proceeding and its preliminaries. The court did not explicitly rule on this objection, but since it did not allow the pre-Lynd evidence, one might assume that Judge Cox was persuaded in this respect.[24]

Delay, Inaction, and a Suit Against the Judge: Bolivar County, Mississippi

Another example of the extreme resistance on the part of a Southern federal judge to the efforts of the Department of Justice was illustrated in Bolivar County, Mississippi, by district court judge Claude F. Clayton. The case developed there merely involved the request to inspect the voting records of the registrar, Mrs. Walter Lewis. A total of twenty-eight months elapsed between the first routine request by the Attorney General and the order entered by

---

23. See *Screws* v. *U.S.*, 325 U.S. 91 (1945); *Cooper* v. *Aaron*, 358 U.S. 1 (1958) wherein the Supreme Court stated: "A state acts by its legislative, its executive or its judicial authorities. It can act in no other way;" *Ex parte Virginia*, 100 U.S. 339 (1879), as well as a recent decision by the 5th Circuit Court of Appeals in *Kennedy* v. *Lynd* which expressly said: "Relief under Section 1971(c) is not confined to named individual voter officials but extends as far as the sovereign State itself."
24. But again no other voting rights cases tried under the Civil Rights Acts of 1957 and 1960 and ultimately decided made such a requirement.

Judge Clayton. This was an order that was very incomplete in terms of providing the government the records it needed.

The United States first requested Mrs. Lewis to make the voting records available on August 11, 1960. On August 22 she requested an extension of thirty-one days to enable her counsel to study the request and to advise her. The government notified her by telegram that she would be given twenty-one days. On September 15 she wrote the government that she was denying the request. A period of three months followed during which time discussions were held between Mississippi officials and officials of the Department of Justice in an attempt to persuade the state authorities to produce the records. These negotiations were to no avail.

On January 11, 1961, the Government filed a Title III action against Mrs. Lewis in the federal district court to compel the production of the voting records. Judge Clayton was to hear the action. In the interim, Robert Kennedy was appointed Attorney General to replace William Rogers. Normally, parties to the suit would consent to the substitution of the new Attorney General. Attorneys for Mrs. Lewis, however, refused to consent to the substitution, and on May 18 Judge Clayton gave the defendant twenty days to file a brief supporting her position against substitution, then the government twenty days to reply, and finally an additional twenty days for the defendant to rejoin. On July 6 Clayton entered an order sustaining the government's motion to substitute Kennedy for Rogers.

On July 26 the defendant filed a motion to have the United States make a more definite statement of the matters contained in its request. The plaintiff should be required to substantiate charges of discrimination in registration and voting. The defendants contended that the allegations in the plaintiff's demand on Mrs. Lewis were "broad, indefinite, loose, vague, general, ambiguous and all-inclusive." The plaintiff's statement was that the demand was based on information in the Attorney General's possession that tended to show that discrimination based on race was being practiced in

Bolivar County. In view of this, the defendant moved that the plaintiff specifically supply the name and address of each person against whom the plaintiff said distinction as to race or color was made; who made such distinctions as to registration and voting; where such distinctions were made; and the race of such persons against whom such distinctions were alleged to have been made. The defendant also wanted to know what the defendant had done to cause the plaintiff to say that racial distinctions were made and the names and addresses of persons who were present when the alleged distinctions were made.

The government filed a memo on July 26 against the defendant's motion for a more definite statement. It stated that there was no basis whatsoever for requiring a more definite statement, and the memo cited relevant authorities, namely *In re Dinkens*. The memo stated that there was nothing in the legislative scheme to indicate that more need be done than that the demand itself inform the registrar of the legal authority under which the demand was made.

The court, over government objection, granted the parties twenty days to file supporting briefs on the matter of a more definite statement and the constitutionality of Title III. At this point, the government pointed out to Judge Clayton—to no avail —that the same matters had been briefed recently by the same attorneys for both parties in the Lynd case and that twenty days were not necessary. On August 21 the defendant indeed filed a thirty-five-page brief—identical with the brief filed on behalf of the registrar in the Lynd case.

On September 6 the court granted the defendant twenty more days to file a supplemental brief on the motion to make a more definite statement and on the constitutionality of Title III. Clayton gave the United States twenty days to reply, but the Government waived the privilege inasmuch as there was nothing new in the defendant's brief.

Judge Clayton entered his order on November 28 requiring the government to give a more definite statement. He distinguished

In re Dinkens. Title III, Clayton said, provided that the demand of the Attorney General should contain a statement of the basis and purpose of the demand. He then said, repeating the language in the Attorney General's demand, "This demand is based upon information in the possession of the Attorney General tending to show that distinctions on the basis of race and color have been made with respect to registration and voting within your juris-diction. The purpose of this demand is to examine the aforesaid records in order to ascertain if violations of federal law have occurred." Clayton then added:

The Attorney General didn't have to couch his language this way, but it is obvious he has information in his possession that would show violations of federal law—which in turn would lead to prosecution of Mrs. Lewis. . . . **Dinkens** is not controlling. It decided that the de-fendant was not entitled to get at what evidence the plaintiff had, but here we are not concerned with evidence but with pleading. . ..
Congress intended to safeguard the rights of all persons by judicial proceedings. . . . From the Attorney General's language it is clear that the Attorney General believes Mrs. Lewis is now violating laws.[25]

Clayton held that the government should plead the facts which it expected to prove in order that Mrs. Lewis might reasonably be informed as to the course a hearing would take. He proceeded to say:

It could be that when this is done, the answer which Mrs. Lewis makes to the amended application and her evidence will reveal that the information in the possession of the Attorney General is in fact not correct, or it may be that a real need exists to investigate further. Facts of fraud may not be plead in general terms. These allegations of plaintiff if proven would amount to fraud.[26]

The court then proceeded to order not only the more definite statement as set out in the defendant's motion, but also the names

25. Judge Clayton's Order for a More Definite Statement in *In re Mrs. Walter Lewis* of November 28, 1961.
26. *Ibid.*

and addresses of persons *in whose favor* the alleged distinctions based on race were claimed to have been made. Judge Clayton also ordered the government to plead the *methods* by which such distinctions were made, and he gave the defendant thirty days to respond after this more definite statement was filed.

But the United States had had enough. Instead of filing a more definite statement in compliance with the court's order, on December 26 it filed a notice reiterating that it declined to make a more definite statement. The notice stated that the government's demand to inspect the records was adequate in itself. The government then stated that in order to expedite the case, it was attaching an order of dismissal to the notice for appropriate court action. The United States wanted the case dismissed so it could proceed to appeal Judge Clayton's ruling.[27] The court took no action on this latest development.

On February 15, 1962, the United States filed a motion before Judge Clayton asking him to reconsider his order of November 28 to have the government make a more definite statement. This motion to reconsider was possible because the court had not, in fact, dismissed the case. And the request for reconsideration was made in light of a recent fifth circuit Court of Appeals ruling in *Kennedy* v. *Bruce* made on February 5, 1962. There, the appellate court, in a Title III case, stated that the demand need not be specific: "It was not a suit of any kind." The court had cited *In re Dinkens*. The demand in the Bruce case was couched in language identical to that of the demand made on Mrs. Lewis back in August 1960. A copy of the Bruce opinion was attached to the motion to reconsider.

Judge Clayton still took no action. On April 11 Burke Marshall of the Department of Justice wrote to Judge Clayton calling the judge's attention to a recent opinion of the fifth circuit Court of Appeals handed down on April 4, 1962, in *U.S.* v. *Lynd*. Mar-

---

27. Information in Justice Department files indicated that this maneuver was discussed previously with the court and with defendant's attorneys.

shall was attempting to stress the government's view that a hearing was not required in a Title III proceeding. His letter read, in part:

I particularly want to call your attention to the reiteration by the Court of Appeals of the Government's right to an order for the production of records "as a matter of course." In view of this, I do not believe a hearing is necessary.[28]

This correspondence was followed by a letter, dated April 16, 1962, to Judge Clayton from Dugas Shands, Assistant Attorney General of Mississippi, stating that he had just received a copy of Marshall's letter. The defendant, Shands's letter stated, felt that the Bruce case was not controlling and therefore neither was the Lynd case. Consequently, the defendant wanted to be heard before an order was entered on the matter.

The letter-writing activity continued. Burke Marshall wrote to Judge Clayton on April 28:

Following my letter of April 11, 1962, I feel that I must write you again regarding the above matter. [**In re Mrs. Walter Lewis.**] I am strongly of the view that the Government is entitled to an immediate order requiring the production of records in the above case. The **Lynd** case to which my letter of April 11 made reference clearly establishes as the rule of the 5th Circuit that in the event of refusal to comply with formal demand for records under Title III of the Civil Rights Act of 1960 the Government is clearly entitled to an order requiring production of records as a matter of course. . . . If the Court should disagree, however, I think the Government is at the least entitled to an immediate order dismissing its application for an order permitting the inspection of voting records in Bolivar county in order that the matter may be appealed.[29]

The United States found itself in the position of not being able to inspect the voting records of Bolivar County unless it filed a statement more specific than its original demand, and not being

28. Letter in files of Justice Department.
29. Letter in files of Justice Department.

able to appeal a decision by the district court because that court simply would not enter such a decision.

At that point, the government resorted to another alternative. Early in June 1962 it filed a petition for a writ of mandamus before the Court of Appeals for the fifth circuit. It asked that the appellate court direct Judge Clayton to show cause why a writ of mandamus should not issue against him compelling him to issue an order in the Lewis case. The government's brief set forth the frustrations encountered, including the several requests for an order. The brief concluded, "Judge Clayton has taken no action of any kind in response to these requests. . . . It is in view of this complete frustration that petitioner seeks relief of writ of mandamus as the only available remedy." [30]

Judge Clayton received a copy of the petition for a writ of mandamus and immediately wrote to Burke Marshall. His letter read, in part, "I was very much surprised to say the least at your taking this action in this case." He said he had discussed with the U.S. Attorney, in Mississippi (H. M. Ray), the status of his calendar to see when he could set a hearing. His calendar was very crowded; he mentioned a lengthy case involving the "ownership of a very valuable patent." His letter continued:

Mr. Ray had to go on two weeks active duty with the Active Reserves, and I was scheduled starting June 24, 1962, for 15 days duty with the National Guard. I had tentatively agreed with the U.S. Attorney that the matter would be set for mid-July. I understand that he had talked to you about it in Washington, and I got the impression from him that this seemed satisfactory to you. Now maybe I misunderstood him or he misunderstood you, at any rate let it be said that no one ever informed me that there was particular urgency of any sort about a hearing on this matter. It is probable that I could have arranged such a hearing at an earlier date than the one tentatively fixed in conference with Mr. Ray. This I would have been glad to consider if request therefor had been made to me. Again let me say that I have no objection to your application for mandamus to the Court of Appeals. I

30. Government's Petition, *Kennedy* v. *Clayton*, No. 19732, p. 9.

simply wanted you—as apparently you have not had until now—the picture from my viewpoint.[31]

Of course, the hearing Judge Clayton referred to was on the motion to reconsider his November 28, 1961, order for a more definite statement. Ostensibly, this would not lead directly to an order to produce the records. Further, Clayton focused in his letter on his busy calendar and schedule over the last two months. The government had first come into his court in January 1961 —eighteen months before.

The judge proceeded to file a thirty-five-page brief opposing the issuance of a writ of mandamus. On page four of his brief he said, "The true and only question presented to this court in this mandamus proceeding is a procedural one whether the writ of mandamus should issue when prior to the filing of the petition for mandamus, the respondent had set the hearing on plaintiff's motion for mid-July, 1962." The gist of Clayton's opposition was that a writ of mandamus was for the purpose of causing one to act and he had acted in the case. He had set the hearing tentatively for mid-July. His brief stated, "Respondent says further that he is merely trying to give the parties in this cause their 'day in court' and that such had been provided for by agreement and understanding."

On June 22, 1962, Mr. Marshall appeared before the Court of Appeals and read a statement moving to defer argument and action on the petition for mandamus.[32]

31. Letter in files of Justice Department.
32. Burke Marshall's statement read as follows: "The Attorney General of the United States moves the Court to defer argument and action on the mandamus petition, *Kennedy* v. *Clayton,* No. 19732, in view of Judge Clayton's action in agreeing to set a hearing on the matter during the Grand Jury session convening in Aberdeen on July 18. In doing so, the Government wants to be clear on the record that it is not abandoning the petition, and that we believe we are entitled to the writ on the present record. We wish to point out that on the answer to the petition for mandamus, all that is clearly involved in the hearing set for mid-July is a hearing on a motion,

On July 28 Mrs. Lewis filed an answer to the government's initial action begun eighteen months earlier (and twenty-three months after the original demand was made on her). A hearing was set for August 21 at Oxford, Mississippi. Three months later, on November 27, Judge Clayton issued an order directing the registrar to permit the United States to examine certain records. Exactly what records the court was going to permit the government to inspect was important. It confined the inspection to those records pertaining to currently listed registrants. Clayton, citing the Lynd case, held that the Attorney General was entitled to inspect all records held by the registrar relating to any application or other act requisite to voting in federal elections held within the twenty-two-month period preceding the filing of the application for inspection. The application was filed on January 11, 1961, in the district court, so the twenty-two-month period extended back to March 11, 1959. And the inspection could relate to the earliest date of any record or paper which bore on the eligibility of any listed voter who was eligible in a federal election held during that twenty-two-month period. The court then proceeded to issue the order covering the following records:

1. All poll book sheets used in aforesaid primary and general elections during the year, 1960;

2. Duplicate poll tax receipts for 1958 and 1959, being those re-

---

filed February 15, 1962, to reconsider in the light of the *Bruce* case the court's order of November 28, 1961, granting a motion for a more definite statement. The Government believes that it is now entitled, under the *Dinkens, Bruce,* and *Lynd* cases, to a prompt order granting the demand for inspection of the records in Bolivar county made on August 11, 1960. Accordingly, we wish to reserve the right to ask again for a prompt hearing on the petition for mandamus depending not only on the holding, but on the outcome, of the hearing scheduled for mid-July.

The Respondent wishes to make it clear to this Court that he considers that his answer and brief filed in Opposition to the petition for mandamus constitutes a total and complete answer thereto, but nevertheless respondent is agreeable to deferring argument and action on the petition for mandamus. Respondent has no comment upon the remainder of the matter contained in the Government's statement."

quired by law to have been paid for one to vote in said primary and general election of 1960;

3. All pages in all registration books from January 1, 1943 (date when the last registration in Bolivar county was begun) up to July 8, 1960 (being 4 months prior to said general election on November 8, 1960);

4. All applications for registration from January 1, 1943, to July 8, 1960, made by persons who have been registered or listed as qualified to register;

5. All lists of poll tax payments showing persons who paid poll tax for 1958 and 1959;

6. All records of military voting certificates issued for 1958 and 1959;

7. All certificates of transfer or registration from January 1, 1943, to July 8, 1960;

8. All exemptions certificates exempting persons named from payment of poll tax for 1958 and 1959;

9. Any record used by Mrs. Lewis in determining whether an applicant to register was disqualified to vote in said 1960 primary election and general election because of convictions for certain crimes.

Thus the government could inspect only the records of persons who had been registered and not of those, as in Alabama, who had been rejected. This was a very limited order at best. It would facilitate the proving of a pattern and practice of discrimination if the government could compare the registration forms of rejected blacks with those of accepted white citizens as was done in Alabama.

How did Judge Clayton react, aside from his letter, to the mandamus maneuver? One reporter interviewed government attorney John Doar and wrote an article in which she quoted him as saying, " 'We really bulled through on that one,' John Doar recalled happily." (The reference was to the mandamus action against Clayton.)[33] Doar later denied having made such a statement and gave this account to this writer:

33. See Barbara Carter, "The Fifteenth Amendment Comes to Mississippi," *The Reporter*, January 17, 1963, p. 24.

Oh, there's no question that the **Reporter** article hurt. I never said we "bulled our way" through on the Bolivar case. We worked hard on that case. I'm sure there must have been a hundred people around the Department who said it offhand, but I'd never make a public statement like that. Why, the judge stood me before that court room for one-half hour and really bawled me out before a packed court and hundreds of lawyers for taking the case away from him to the Circuit Court. Later he said he wasn't mad at us but rather at the Court of Appeals. And so you just have to try to win these cases before some judges who are not altogether favorable or friendly and with Judges Cox and Clayton it's a slow process but we're making progress.[34]

A "slow process" would seem to be an understatement—some would call it "all process and no progress" in Bolivar County—but the obstacles available to a resistant judge were numerous.

Delay, Details, and a Pyrrhic Victory: Jefferson Davis County, Mississippi

The last case reported in this chapter is equally vivid in demonstrating the tactics and techniques of a judicial resistor—Judge Cox, again. In this case, the Department of Justice, after being required to plead very specific details, was able to prosecute to a final judgment after seventeen months in court, but the order entered by Judge Cox left much to be desired. This case was filed on the same day, August 3, 1961, as the case before Judge Johnson involving Montgomery County; Cox took longer to reach a final order, and the decree ultimately entered was much weaker from the government's point of view. Both cases were Section 1971(a) actions.

In February 1956 the board of supervisors of Jefferson Davis County, Mississippi, passed a resolution requiring a new registration for all persons in the county. Prior to 1955 applicants for registration had to read or understand when read to them or

---

34. Interview with John Doar, Department of Justice, Washington, D.C.

reasonably interpret any section of the Mississippi constitution. In 1955 an amendment was passed providing that an applicant must be able to read and write any section of the Mississippi constitution or give a reasonable interpretation of any section thereof and demonstrate to the registrar a reasonable understanding of the duties and obligations of citizenship. This new requirement was not to apply to persons registered prior to January 1, 1954.

At the time of the filing the suit, there were 3222 blacks and 3629 whites of voting age in the county. From 1954 to 1955, some 1200 blacks and more than 50 per cent of the whites of voting age were registered. But in 1960, four years after re-registration had been in effect, there were only 130 blacks registered and still more than 50 per cent of the voting-age whites.

The United States alleged in its complaint that the registrar, Jack Daniel, had discriminated against black citizens by applying different and more stringent standards to them than to whites in registration or re-registration; by failing to register blacks who possessed the same or similar qualifications as whites who were registered; by arbitrarily denying blacks the opportunity to register; and by unreasonably delaying the registration of blacks who sought to apply to register or re-register. All these acts constituted a pattern and practice of racial discrimination, and the government asked the court to issue a preliminary and permanent injunction enjoining such acts. With some of Judge Johnson's orders in mind, the government asked Judge Cox to direct the registrar to place upon the current voter registration rolls and otherwise register all black applicants in Jefferson Davis County who had applied for registration and who possessed at the time of their application the same or similar qualifications as the least qualified white person who was registered.

At the same time that it filed its complaint, the government also filed a Rule 34 motion to enable it to inspect the voter registration records of the county. It is necessary to set forth the specific items requested by the Rule 34 motion in order to compare them with Cox's order allowing the inspection. The government sought the following records:

1. All primary election poll books for each precinct or ward of each election district within the county;

2. All county poll books;

3. County books of duplicate poll tax receipts;

4. All records of poll tax exemption certificates;

5. All records of military exemption certificates issued by the registrar;

6. All records of voter certificates issued by the registrar;

7. All applications for registration and absentee registration accepted and rejected;

8. All books, documents and papers used to administer the constitutional interpretation test; the applicant's written interpretation or notations made by the registrar or his agents if the test was administered orally;

9. All books, documents and papers used in administering the duties and obligations of citizenship requirement and in testing the good moral character of the applicants;

10. All affidavits of applicants showing physical disability and the nature thereof;

11. The registration books of each election district in the county;

12. The list of individuals convicted of certain crimes which made them ineligible to register;

13. All books, documents, papers, and resolutions relating to the re-registration ordered by the county board of supervisors in February 1956;

14. All papers, registration books, and correspondence containing the names and matters relating to registration of any and all persons who had been registered or rejected for registration.[35]

The United States justified its request for the above items on the grounds that records before 1956 might serve to reveal the reason

35. Government's Motion for Rule 34 in files of Justice Department.

for re-registration in 1956. Likewise, a comparison of the pre-1956 and post-1956 records might reveal different standards on a racial basis used by the registrar in determining the qualifications of those who had registered or re-registered. And it might reveal that the registrar re-registered white voters who were no more qualified than black applicants who were not re-registered. Since 1956 at least forty-one black citizens had made one or more unsuccessful attempts to register in the county. All these blacks were registered prior to 1956, but none had been registered since 1956.

On August 28, 1961, the defendants, James Daniel and the state of Mississippi, filed a twenty-four-page motion before Judge Cox asking that the government be ordered to make a more definite statement of the allegations in the complaint. The charges as set out were "vague, broad, general, nebulous, all-inclusive and ambiguous" and did not tender specific issues to which the defendants could make responsive answers. The plaintiff should have stated each and every alleged act, by whom each was committed, what method was used, dates, places, and against whom —white or black. The government alleged that different and more stringent standards were applied to black applicants. Daniel and the state contended that the plaintiff should have specifically stated when, where, what the facts were surrounding this, and who the blacks were and their addresses, as well as, who the white applicants were who benefited by the application of different standards. The government should also have stated the particular details accompanying the acts of failing to register black citizens, who was present when such alleged acts were committed, when, where, the names and addresses of blacks rejected, and the names and addresses of whites who were alleged to possess no more qualifications than rejected blacks.

On September 5, 1961, Judge Cox stated that he would deny the government's motion for Rule 34 unless it was plead with particularity. The following week a hearing was held on the defendant's motion for a more definite statement. Two months later, on December 12, Judge Cox ordered the government to file a more definite statement. Six days later, the United States filed a five-page amended complaint with a twenty-seven-page appendix giving the names and dates of black applicants' attempts to register. At the same time, it again filed a motion for Rule 34. On December 30 the defendants filed a seventy-page motion to require the government to make still another more definite statement of the allegations in the amended complaint. The defendants filed a motion to strike the complaint along with this.

The defendants were not satisfied with the plaintiff's amended complaint in a number of instances. The appendix to that complaint set forth names and dates, but these were insufficient. The defendants wanted more detail. The complaint stated that Mr. and Mrs. Gaston Holloway (two blacks) attempted to register "in January or February of 1959." The defendants asserted this was not specific enough as to dates. The government's complaint also said that the Holloways "were told by a white lady in defendant's office. . . ." This was too vague. Who was the lady? What was her relationship to the registrar? At one place the complaint read, "About a week after. . . ." The Mississippi officials objected to this as not specific enough.

On February 2, 1962, John Doar of the Justice Department wrote to Judge Cox asking for a hearing on the government's motion for Rule 34. On March 15 the United States filed a motion for a preliminary injunction. On April 13 the parties appeared before Judge Cox and argued the defendants' motions for a more definite statement and to strike. At that time, John Doar again asked that the court set a hearing date on the government's pending motion for a preliminary injunction.

On May 3 the defendants filed interrogatories to have the United States:

1. State the names and addresses of whites named in the amended

complaint to whom the registrar allegedly applied a lower standard;

2. State names and addresses of whites who had been registered by the registrar who were alleged to have the same qualifications of Negroes who had not been registered;

3. State the dates and names of those registered and the conditions and facts surrounding such registration or re-registration;

4. State the names and addresses and dates of the clerks and the registrar who allegedly committed the racially discriminatory acts and the facts surrounding the acts;

5. State the dates, number of times, and names and addresses of persons (white and Negro) interviewed by the FBI within the last six months in connection with the case.[36]

The United States objected to the fifth interrogatory on the grounds that it sought information that was privileged and part of the "work product" of the plaintiff.

On May 15 Judge Cox denied the defendants' motions for a more definite statement and to strike and also rejected the government's objections to the interrogatories. The court had previously set May 11 as the date to hear the motions for preliminary injunction and Rule 34, but this hearing was postponed because Judge Cox was involved in matters relating to the judicial conference of the fifth circuit. Hearing was reset for June 8. He ordered the United States to answer all the interrogatories within five days after the hearing on the Rule 34 motion.

On May 29, nine months after the filing of the original complaint, the defendants, Daniel and the state of Mississippi, filed separate answers to the complaint. Registrar Daniel denied that after October 1956 he required any person named in the amended complaint who was registered in 1954 to file written application forms or to take a written test. He denied using discriminatory practices against the thirty-eight blacks named in the appendix to the amended complaint, and he asserted that he acted in good faith and

36. Interrogatory filed by Mississippi in files of Justice Department.

sought at all times to apply the laws of the state of Mississippi as written.

The state of Mississippi declared in its answer that in those instances when Daniel told blacks that he was busy and could not take their applications this was in fact true, and the blacks "gladly agreed to return at a later date." The answer further contended that the state was not a proper party to the suit.

On June 8 Judge Cox issued an order permitting the government to inspect, copy, and photograph certain records in Jefferson Davis County. The following items were covered:

1. All registration books of Jefferson Davis County in Daniel's possession, current or otherwise;

2. All county and primary poll books presently in use for each precinct in Jefferson Davis county;

3. All copies of poll tax exemption certificates issued since January 1956;

4. All duplicate poll tax receipts issued since January 1, 1956;

5. All lists of poll tax payers received in Daniel's office since January 1, 1956;

6. All records of military voting certificates issued since January 1, 1956;

7. All applications for registration including absentee registration accepted and rejected since January 1, 1956;

8. All books, documents, and papers used in administering the constitutional interpretation test, the applicant's written interpretation or notations made by Daniel or his agents if the tests were administered orally;

9. All books, documents, and papers used in administering the duties and obligations of citizenship requirement and in testing the good moral character of applicants;

10. All affidavits of applicants showing physical disabilities and the nature of such disabilities;

11. All books, documents, and papers used in determining if an applicant is disqualified for reason of conviction of crimes;

12. All books, documents, and papers relating to re-registration ordered by the county board of supervisors in February 1956;

13. All official documents and correspondence relating to registration or voting of any person since January 1, 1956;

14. All certificates of transfer of registration coming into Daniel's possession since January 1, 1956;

15. All copies of affidavits and certificates to vote issued since January 1, 1956.[37]

(James Daniel was elected circuit court clerk and registrar in January 1956.)

Finally, on January 4, 1963, Judge Cox issued his order on the merits of the case. He decided to reserve final judgment and to see if the local registrar would take the opportunity to follow the court's instructions. At the trial, Daniel testified that he would welcome instructions from the court and would do his best to abide by those instructions. Cox's order was characteristic of the effort made by other Southern federal judges—in his strong inclination to permit the registrar to correct his own errors without resort to federal voter referees. He felt

that a more efficient administration of the law would most probably be effected by instructing the registrar more specifically as to his duty in view of the sincere and conscientious statement by the registrar to the court while on the stand to the effect that he invited such instructions from the court and that he would immediately and voluntarily comply with such instructions in every detail and to avoid the stigma of any appearance of government by injunction and the court being impressed with the good faith of the registrar in such respect and his need for instructions as to his official duties with respect to both races in the administration of said laws.[38]

Cox instructed Daniel to register any citizen who was registered to vote prior to January 1, 1954, who was able to read or understand when read to him or able to give a reasonable interpretation of any of several sections of Mississippi's constitution of 1890—nothing more. Those registered prior to January 1954 were not to be required to pass any other test. The judge further ordered Daniel

37. Order in files of Justice Department.
38. Judge Cox's Order in *U.S.* v. *Daniel.*

to register fairly and impartially all applicants deemed by him reasonably qualified and found to possess the statutory and constitutional qualifications to register, and who successfully passed a fair and reasonable test which should be governed and controlled in its entirety by a single standard. This standard should be in common use for all citizens without any discrimination. Cox instructed Daniel to handle and process all applications alike without favoritism "or any courtesy or without any favor or assistance accorded a member of one race which is not generally accorded a member of another race in registering or re-registering as a voter in Jefferson Davis County." All applications were to be processed and decided upon within thirty days with notice to the applicant of the results. If the citizen rejected was a black, then the entire proceeding was to "be immediately processed for a statutory appeal" and all the facts and information used by the registrar in reaching his decision were to be certified to the clerk of Cox's court for examination. The court would make a determination of the "propriety of his [the registrar's] decision and as to its compliance with the court's instructions."

The final instruction to the registrar dealt with the method of selecting certain constitutional provisions for interpretation. This portion of the order read as follows:

In keeping with the spirit of this order, defendant-Daniel shall carefully select 50 more or less sections of the State Constitution having some reasonable interest to citizens who are not lawyers and number the cards bearing each section and deposit separate slips of paper bearing the correspondence number of each card in a container from which each applicant shall draw such slip without seeing which number is being selected and without knowing which number is on any such card bearing such section of the constitution. And the number so selected by the applicant shall be the section used by the registrar in the test given that applicant.[39]

The court made no finding of a pattern or practice of discrimination, which was the legal trigger necessary to provide for future ap-

39. *Ibid.*

pointment of referees. While applications of rejected blacks were to be forwarded to the court for examination, the order did not provide the Department of Justice with powers to assist in overseeing this compliance. Neither did the court set out what it considered to be—as it did in Bullock and Montgomery counties in Alabama— reasonable interpretations of the Mississippi constitution. In fact, the registrar was to register persons "deemed by him" to be reasonably qualified.

Another important point of comparison between judges Johnson and Cox is the way in which the two issued their orders. Both reserved final judgment, but Johnson did so in the Bullock County case in open court immediately after the trial and before a courtroom filled with black spectators. Both expressed faith in the local registrars, but Johnson employed a method more likely to gain results. Johnson, from the bench in front of a courtroom filled with blacks, announced that he believed the registrar would perform in good faith. One lawyer for the Department of Justice who had just finished arguing the case before Johnson, and who was present in the courtroom at the time, made this observation:

What Johnson was really doing was he was talking really directly at the Negroes in the audience—looking straight at them. He was telling them in so many words, "OK, now you've heard the registrars. I've heard them. They've said they would do the right thing. Now let's see. Go out there and register." And those guys went out and got a lot of people to register. This was Johnson's way of trying to let the local authorities do it rather than himself.[40]

This was an important technique that impressed some Justice Department lawyers and served as the basis for their differentiating between the two judges. One government attorney stated:

There is a big difference in reserving ruling in the manner done by Judge Johnson and reserving it in the way Judge Cox did in Mississippi. In the latter instance [Jefferson Davis county case] Cox waited until the trial was ended—2 or 3 months later—and he made a similar statement to the one made by Johnson, but not in court

40. Interview at Justice Department.

and not in front of any Negroes. And only in the form of a written order which few Negroes would see.

I think Judge Johnson wanted the Negroes registered but he wanted the local registrars to do it. I believe Judge Cox wanted to simply create another delaying device. It's hard to appeal from a ruling when it's like that [Cox's order in Jefferson Davis County]. There's really nothing to appeal from.[41]

Finally, the defendant's practice of filing motions to require the plaintiff to make a more definite statement was certainly used to delay proceedings. When a judge concurred in the motions, there was little the government could practically do. Comparing Judge Johnson and Judge Cox on this point, one lawyer for the Department of Justice summed up in this fashion:

Now, of course, as far as Judge Johnson is concerned, he really expedites those cases. In the Bullock case we filed that one in January 1961 just before the change of administration and went to trial on about March 29th—just two and one-half months. This is exceptionally fast. And this business of motions to make more definite statement that you find in Mississippi, this really delays things. It means usually an amended complaint and more motions and answers, etc. But Judge Johnson informally tells the lawyers: "Look, if you want more information, you can file interrogatories and that's what you should do." This is faster and gets the same thing, and that's what you see in the Johnson-tried cases.[42]

And then this same lawyer proceeded to discuss the futile and the self-defeating practice of appealing a judge's order to make a more definite statement. He pointed out:

You see, this business of ruling on a motion to make more definite is really—in a sense—not appealable. That is, a judge can rule on it and say you have to make more definite which really might get into the work product. And if you don't accept it, you can refuse and appeal that ruling, but you don't want to because that's another year and then you have to come back and try the merits, and so you just go along with the judge.[43]

41. Interview at Justice Department.
42. Interview at Justice Department.
43. Interview at Justice Department.

7 "Training the Judge": Judicial Gradualism

Department of Justice attorneys would frequently say that many Southern federal judges were segregationists. But in the same sentence, or shortly afterwards, the lawyers would add that the judges had a profound respect for the law. This had important meaning for those government lawyers who filed and argued voting rights cases before these judges. Most of the attorneys were not as frank or candid as the one who singled out Judge Ben C. Dawkins, Jr., of Louisiana as a segregationist, but a segregationist highly sensitive to the "injustices" and "gross inequalities we present to him." What this meant in a practical sense was that the Department of Justice worked with these judges—"We help them along." The department was in the business of training the judges to the department's point of view. "You shouldn't overlook this aspect of our job," one lawyer stated. This was not an aspect that federal officials could or would discuss publicly, but Burke Marshall alluded to it when he wrote about the effects of the trial situation: the Justice Department, the court, the defense counsel, all came to know each other better, he said.

One of the most promising pupils was Judge Dawkins. The department "started his training off with the case in Bienville

Parish." This chapter examines the work of Judge Dawkins. "One can't expect overnight results, of course," one Justice attorney said. "It's a long, slow matter. Oh yes, it's gradual enough." We will examine three cases handled by Dawkins before taking a look at two voter discrimination cases filed in his court and heard by him to a decision.

The state of Louisiana had a law[1] that permitted two registered voters in a parish to challenge the legality of another voter's registration. When this was done, it became the duty of the parish registrar to notify the person challenged, giving him time to answer. If the latter did not respond within the stated period, his registration would be cancelled. In April 1956 a challenge was filed against Dr. John I. Reddix, a black voter in Ouachita Parish, by two white voters named Burdine and Feeback. Dr. Reddix failed to appear, but instead filed a suit in the federal district court against Mrs. Mae Lucky, the registrar, alleging that his name was removed solely because of his race. He sought an injunction and money damages.[2] Judge Dawkins denied this contention. He stated that the registrar was not the proper person to sue if the plaintiff had a cause of action at all. Mrs. Lucky was merely the registrar who had to abide by the state statute in receiving the affidavits of the two challengers and in notifying the plaintiff. She was simply doing her duty under the law, and the plaintiff did not allege that the law itself was discriminatory. In fact, Dawkins stated, the statute was not unfair on its face. He then proceeded to admonish the plaintiff and to question Dr. Reddix's motives for bringing the suit:

Plaintiff's lack of good faith, in applying here for a declaratory judgment and an injunction—equitable and discretionary remedies—is shown plainly by his deliberate failure to seek reregistration since May 15, 1956, although he could have done so at any of the times the registration rolls have been open. His bad faith—his sheer stub-

1. Louisiana Revised Statutes, 1950, Title 18, Section 133.
2. *Redix* v. *Lucky,* 148 Fed. Supp. 108 (1957).

born vindictiveness—is doubly demonstrated by the fact that his wife applied for and actually was granted registration, as did a large number of other Negroes, but he willfully has refused to do so. He apparently prefers litigation to registration.[3]

Judge Dawkins suggested that Dr. Reddix should have exhausted the administrative remedy available to him. The judge took notice of an appellate court decision in the fifth circuit, *Hall* v. *Nagel,*[4] which held that the denial by a registrar of voter registration was sufficient cause to appeal to the federal courts on grounds of racial discrimination. But that case was distinguished inasmuch as "that decision does not hold . . . that a person who wishes to register is exempt, simply because he is a Negro, from taking the first and only administrative step, namely, requesting the Registrar to permit him to register at a time when such legally may be done." [5] The court further advised that if Dr. Reddix felt that Burdine and Feeback had wrongfully challenged his registration, then he should have proceeded against them in a state court.

Judge Dawkins was impressed, however, by several circumstances in the case. While he found no unfair or discriminatory act on the part of the registrar, he felt it was possible to conclude that the two challengers or others had so used the law that it operated unfairly against blacks in the parish.

This statement is based particularly upon the timing of the challenges, just prior to an election, when the books were closed for new registrations. We also are impressed with the fact that, although defendant had no alternative under the State law but to accept the challenges and proceed exactly as she did, such a large number of challenges were made that many of the persons whose registrations were challenged were unable to be served properly by defendant's staff before the legal delays expired.

. . .

3. 2 *RRLR* 426, p. 429.
4. 154 Fed. 2d. 931.
5. *Ibid.*

This is not to say that the Statute, as presently written, is unfair, for it is not. This is to say, however, that it can be used unfairly by challengers as it seems to have been done here.[6]

In line with this, Dawkins stated he would not dismiss the case but would give Dr. Reddix sixty days in which to file an amended and supplemental complaint if he chose to do so. Such a complaint would have to allege that the plaintiff had attempted to register but had been denied the right to do so by the registrar solely on account of his race.

Dr. Reddix was not satisfied with this disposition so he asked that a final judgment be entered to permit an immediate appeal. This was done on February 25, 1957.

Exactly one year later the Court of Appeals for the fifth circuit, by a two-to-one vote, disagreed with Judge Dawkins's ruling. The trial record indicated that the registrar had not conformed to some of the state laws in processing the challenge. There was conflicting testimony that Mrs. Lucky mailed notices of challenges within the prescribed time; there was no conflict, however, in ascertaining that she was delinquent by five days in having the challenges published. The defendant, by state law, was to hear protests from persons challenged within three days after publication. The appellate court made the following observation:

All normal rules for the construction of statutes aside, it does not appeal to an acute sense of justice to hear argument that Mrs. Lucky was legally prevented from hearing plaintiff's protest on the fourth day after publication (Sunday included) because she was powerless to act after three days, but that she had the power to make a valid publication of plaintiff's notice 10 or 11 days after the mailed notice when the statute required such publication "not more than 5 days" thereafter. If defendant relies on her lack of authority to serve plaintiff in protesting his being dropped from the voter's list because he was one day late, then he can certainly question her legal authority to make a valid publication because she was 5 days late. We think

6. *Ibid.*

Mrs. Lucky's failure to comply with the statute as to the time of publishing the notice as to plaintiff made her subsequent action in striking his name from the rolls a nullity.[7]

Was the cancellation an act that could be remedied in the federal courts? The plaintiff had alleged that the act was done to him and some 2500 other blacks on account of their race. Thus, the complaint came within federal jurisdiction. Given the finding that the registrar had acted illegally, the appellate court felt the issue of racial discrimination should be heard.

The wholesale purge of black voters from the rolls in several Louisiana parishes gave rise to another case that came before Judge Dawkins in late 1956.[8] That case also involved the registrar of Ouachita Parish. The plaintiff in that case was a black lawyer who had been retained to represent a black client whose registration had been challenged. The lawyer and client went to the registrar's office to investigate the matter. At this point the facts in the trial record were conflicting. The lawyer asserted that he was refused permission to inspect his client's registration card in the registrar's office and was directed to another room and another clerk where all the cards of challenged blacks were kept. The black attorney, Mr. Sharp, sued the registrar, seeking money damages for injury done to him in his profession as a lawyer. He also asked the federal court to enjoin the practice of keeping black voters' registration cards in a separate office.

Judge Dawkins viewed the case entirely as one involving the alleged infringement of the plaintiff's right to practice law, and such an allegation was properly heard in a state court. There was no problem here of racial discrimination. Registration cards of some blacks were kept in a separate room, and the plaintiff simply refused to inspect his client's card in that room. Dawkins dismissed the action with these comments:

7. 3 *RRLR* 229, p. 233.
8. *Sharp* v. *Lucky*, 148 Fed. Supp. 8.

There has been much controversy, in recent time, on many aspects of segregation, but we believe this is the first time any Court has been asked to enjoin the segregation of inanimate objects. No Court has extended the Constitution that far, and we certainly will not do so.

In the final analysis, what plaintiff asserts here is that, as a lawyer, he "lost his case," simply because of what he refused to do, not because of what defendant did or failed to do.[9]

Once again the Court of Appeals for the fifth circuit in a two-to-one decision (Judge Cameron dissenting as in *Reddix* v. *Lucky*) disagreed with Dawkins. This was not a case of interference with the plaintiff's rights as a lawyer, but a case arising out of restrictions placed on Sharp because he was black. On this basis, the complaint set out a cause of action maintainable in a federal court. The suit plainly alleged that Sharp and his client were refused service in the registrar's office solely because they were black. Judge Dawkins's comments about segregating inanimate objects notwithstanding, the appellate court cited its opinions outlawing segregation at a publicly owned cafeteria in Harris County, Texas, and at a publicly owned swimming pool in St. Petersburg, Florida.[10] The Supreme Court had also ruled against a segregated municipal golf course.[11] Thus, "it is too plain for argument that Ouachita Parish, Louisiana, may not, through its registrar of voters, operate a segregated registrar's office." [12] The case was sent back to Dawkins to be tried on those terms.

After the lower court judge took testimony and at the beginning of his opinion, Dawkins observed that the Court of Appeals permitted the plaintiff to change his position on appeal. Initially, Sharp sought relief in his capacity as a lawyer injured in the exercise of his profession. On appeal, Dawkins asserted, Sharp maintained his suit as a black person discriminated against solely on

9. 148 Fed. Supp. 8 (1957).
10. *Derrington* v. *Plummer*, 240 Fed. 2d. 922 and *City of St. Petersburg* v. *Alsup*, 238 Fed. 2d. 830, respectively.
11. *Holmes* v. *City of Atlanta*, 350 U.S. 879.
12. 252 Fed. 2d. 913.

account of his race. The judge had this to say of the appellate court's performance:

Notwithstanding its own prior rulings, and the great weight of authority everywhere holding that such an about-face will not be permitted, two members of a three-judge panel of the Fifth Circuit Court of Appeals reversed our ruling and not only allowed plaintiff to maintain his suit in his new capacity, but held that he could prosecute it as a class action in behalf of all other Negroes similarly situated. We are bound by that Court's mandate, which is the law of this case.[13]

In his opinion, Dawkins focused on the alleged racial discrimination, and he found that, while there had been a racial distinction made by the registrar, this distinction was not made for any "malicious" purpose. In fact, the comfort of the blacks was the motivating factor. Dawkins found that in late August 1956, after the registrar had sent out 1500 challenges (1000 to white voters; 500 to black voters), "voters of both races began pouring into defendant's office to answer them." The registrar's office and the corridor were filled with members of both races. Dawkins continued:

Of their own volition, and not because of anything done by defendant or her deputy, most Negroes stood back and allowed white persons to go ahead of them, with the result that the Negroes were not being fairly and adequately served.

Because of this, defendant made arrangements with Police Jury officials to use its room to handle the overflow; and since Negroes had not been receiving service on a "first-come-first-served" basis, it was decided to place the registration cards of those Negroes who had been challenged, from Wards 3 and 10, in the Police Jury Room. The substantially larger number of cards of all other Negro registrants from these two wards, and from the eight other wards of the Parish, were left in defendant's office.[14]

This separation was more comfortable for the blacks as well as

13. 165 Fed. Supp. 405, p. 407.
14. *Ibid.*

expeditious, and some black leaders expressed their appreciation of the arrangement:

So well did the system work, so advantageous was it to the Negroes, that several Negro leaders thanked defendant for having made it possible that a larger number of Negroes could answer challenges in a more comfortable manner; while many other Negroes showed their appreciation by bringing flowers and gifts of various kinds to defendant.[15]

As soon as the rush was over, the registrar returned the black registration cards to her office. Dawkins was confronted with a conflict in testimony as to what transpired when the black lawyer, accompanied by his client and another black citizen, Mrs. Hill, entered the registrar's office. The blacks testified that Mrs. Lucky told them she did not serve black people in her office and that they would have to go to the Police Jury Room for service by her assistant. Mrs. Lucky, on the other hand, testified that she simply told them that the client's card was in the other room. The court made its judgment:

From our observations of the demeanor of these witnesses on the stand, and having noted the "pat" version of the incident as given by plaintiff Tillman [the client], and Mrs. Hill, we believe Mrs. Lucky's version, for she impressed us, above all else, as a completely honest person.[16]

The controlling facts for Dawkins were that no purposeful racial discrimination was intended—such racial distinction as existed lasted for only three weeks—and there was no reasonable expectation that it would be repeated.

The black lawyer was not satisfied. He appealed, but this time the Court of Appeals fully backed Judge Dawkins.[17] The important matters were that the registrar fairly and justly administer

15. *Ibid.*
16. *Ibid.*
17. 266 Fed. 2d. 342 (1959).

her office in the future "in good faith, with good manners and with good will," and the trial record indicated that this would be done.

Few persons who followed civil rights developments in the South after the passage of the Civil Rights Act of 1957 believed that the newly created United States Commission on Civil Rights would receive full cooperation from Southern officials. The commission met its first challenge in Alabama when it attempted to obtain the voting records in Macon County and when certain local registrars refused to appear to testify. These conflicts resulted in protracted lawsuits in 1959 which were ultimately resolved in favor of the commission.[18] One such case arose out of plans to hold hearings in Shreveport, Louisiana, on July 13, 1959. Subpoenas were served on several registrars for Louisiana parishes, but on July 12 Judge Dawkins, on the motion of the registrars, issued a temporary restraining order against holding the hearings.[19] It was the issuance of this order that served as the occasion for Judge Dawkins's statement, "It is all part of the game." [20]

In his opinion, Dawkins expressly noted that he was attempting to give the commission as much opportunity as possible to defend its actions. This, he felt, was necessary "because of the national importance of the matters involved." An application for a temporary restraining order was normally decided *ex parte,* but Dawkins immediately notified the counsel for the commission "and its Vice-Chairman, Honorable Robert G. Storey (a personal friend of the Court's of long standing) of our information, and invited them to be present for a hearing on the applications." At the beginning of the hearing, he gave the commission counsel an hour and a half to study the registrars' complaints and briefs. Two hours of oral argument followed, and opposing briefs were filed. Two days later, Dawkins, noting the necessary need for expedition, issued the restraining order. He prefaced his findings by saying:

18. See Chapter Five.
19. *Larche* v. *Hannah,* 177 Fed. Supp. 846.
20. *1959 Report,* U.S. Commission on Civil Rights, p. 101.

Necessarily, because of the time element, we have been compelled, under great pressure, to consider the question rather hastily; and we reserve the right to alter our views, if necessary, after more mature deliberations.

The registrars' major objection was to the procedures of the commission. (The complaints also attacked the constitutionality of the Civil Rights Act of 1957.) The commission had set forth certain rules to govern its hearings: it would not permit cross-examination by those subpoenaed and would not divulge the source of its information pertaining to voting denials. Dawkins at once characterized the commission as an executive agency and thus subject to the provisions of the Administrative Procedure Act. The commission violated that act by not informing the registrars "of the matters of fact and law" involving the alleged denials of voting rights and by not permitting cross-examination. Not only did the Administrative Procedure Act require this, but these rights had traditionally been required by American courts "in hearings or trials of all kinds."

The registrars, Dawkins felt, should have been given the opportunity to protect their integrity and veracity as well as to help establish the complete truth. How could the latter be ensured if the registrars were not fully informed of the circumstances of the charges? How would they know what witnesses to ask to appear in their behalf?

Plaintiffs [the registrars] thus will be condemned out of the mouths of these [Negro] witnesses, and plaintiffs' testimony alone, without having the right to cross-examine and thereby to test the truth of such assertions, may not be adequate to meet or overcome the charges, thus permitting plaintiffs to be stigmatized and held up before the eyes of the nation to opprobrium and scorn.[21]

The question involving the constitutionality of the Act was serious enough, Dawkins felt, to warrant a temporary restraining order until a three-judge court could rule on the issues.

21. 4 *RRLR* 935, 941.

The three-judge court consisted of Chief Judge Dawkins, Circuit Judge Wisdom and District Judge Hunter. In a two-to-one decision, Wisdom dissenting, the court upheld Dawkins's views on October 7, 1959.[22] Inasmuch as the Civil Rights Act was constitutional, the case turned on two issues: did Congress, in creating the commission, specifically authorize it to adopt rules for investigations which would deprive parties investigated of their rights of confrontation and cross-examination and their right to be apprised of the charges against them? and if Congress did so authorize the commission, was such authorization constitutionally permissible? Judge Hunter wrote that Congress was silent on the particular rules adopted. In addition, the registrars were charged, in essence, with criminal conduct for which they could lose their jobs. The commission's duty was to investigate and to report to the President, "whose duty it is to enforce federal criminal laws." The Supreme Court's decision in *Greene* v. *McElroy*[23] required the protection of persons found in the position of the registrars. The purpose of the commission's hearing was to ascertain the facts. "Certainly, the surest way of finding out all the facts is to hear from everybody, and the surest test of a witness' veracity is his confrontation and cross-examination." [24]

Commission counsel urged the three judges to take judicial notice of the possible retaliation that could result to persons making complaints to the commission.

This Court does not know of a single instance where any such pressure has actually been brought. Some honest, sincere, and well-meaning people really believe this, but we are not going to assume (in the total absence of evidence) that the people of this State will be guilty of such a practice.[25]

22. 177 Fed. Supp. 816.
23. 360 U.S. 474.
24. 177 Fed. Supp., p. 827.
25. *Ibid.*, p. 828.

The Civil Rights Commission appealed the ruling to the Supreme Court, which heard arguments on January 18 and 19, 1960. A decision was issued on June 20 reversing the lower court, with Justices Douglas and Black dissenting.[26] Chief Justice Warren delivered the opinion of the court. *Greene* v. *McElroy* held that when the procedures of an inferior governmental agency raised serious constitutional questions, the issue had to be decided whether or not "the President or Congress within their respective constitutional powers, specifically has decided that the imposed procedures are necessary and warranted and has authorized their use." [27] Warren stated that congressional intent to permit the rules established by the commission was inferred from the deliberate refusal to adopt proposals limiting the commission in that respect:

We have no doubt that Congress' consideration and rejection of the procedures here at issue constituted an authorization of the Commission to conduct its hearings according to the Rules of Procedure it has adopted, and to deny to witnesses the rights of apprisal, confrontation and cross-examination.[28]

Given this finding, the Supreme Court then proceeded to hold that the rules did not violate due process of law. The commission dealt in fact-finding, not adjudication. Such agencies were not bound by procedures associated with agencies with the power to affect an individual's legal rights. Interestingly enough, the Supreme Court was as little impressed with the registrars' contention that they could lose their jobs and be criminally prosecuted as the lower court was with the commission's concern for possible pressure being brought against black complainants. Warren wrote:

That any of these consequences [loss of jobs and prosecution] will result is purely conjectural. There is nothing in the record to indicate that such will be the case or that past Commission hearings have had

26. 363 U.S. 420.
27. *Ibid.,* p. 507.
28. 363 U.S., p. 439.

any harmful effects upon witnesses appearing before the Commission.[29]

Justice Frankfurter's concurring opinion relied on his characterization of the Commission as "an investigatorial arm of Congress." "To require the introduction of adversary contests relevant to determination of individual guilt into what is in effect a legislative investigation is bound to thwart it by turning it into a serious digression from its purpose." [30]

The Supreme Court's two staunchest libertarians, Douglas and Black, voted to uphold Judge Dawkins. But whereas Dawkins saw his order as part of a game, Douglas's dissenting opinion expressed concern for the civil rights of black citizens. This concern, however, could not be used to sacrifice other civil rights, namely, the right to know the exact charges against the accused, the right to be confronted with witnesses, and the right of cross-examination. To Douglas and Black the commission was an executive agency, and one investigating possible violations of criminal law. The libertarians were not willing to permit what they considered to be a violation of basic safeguards of due process of law, even against Southern registrars accused of racial discrimination, however true those accusations might have been.

The Department of Justice "started Judge Dawkins's training off" with a suit alleging voting denials in Bienville Parish, Louisiana. "We knew we didn't have a [Judge] Skelly Wright or Frank Johnson," one attorney stated. "But we also felt that Dawkins was what you might say torn—a segregationist with respect for the law." And with these factors to work on, the government set out to prove that some 570 black voters were unconstitutionally purged from the rolls, that those blacks should be immediately restored to the rolls, that the registrar was engaging in a pattern and practice of discrimination, and that a voter referee should be ap-

29. *Ibid.*, p. 443.
30. *Ibid.*, p. 490.

pointed.[31] The case was filed in June 1960. The defendants included the registrar of voters for Bienville Parish, the Association of Citizens Councils of Louisiana, the Citizens Council of Arcadia, Louisiana, the Citizens Council of Gibsland, Louisiana, and seventeen individuals who were officers, directors, or members of the councils.

Dawkins was impressed by the thorough preparation of the government's case; he found virtually no dispute as to the facts. This finding was buttressed by the refusal of the defendants to cooperate on trial (all except the registrar claimed the protection of the Fifth Amendment) and the reliance by the government on the registrar's own records. The defendants had decided in a meeting on September 24, 1956, to purge most of the 595 registered black voters from the rolls.[32] The registrar assisted the others in this purge. Only thirty-five white residents were challenged under the state statute providing for this procedure.[33] Dawkins noted that in elections prior to October 1956 blacks "had engaged in the reprehensible practice of 'bloc voting,' " and this undoubtedly was a major motivation behind the purge. But Dawkins stated that he could not let this "alter one whit our duty under the Fifteenth Amendment to see to it, wherever we are called upon to do so, that there is no discrimination in voting registration because of race or color."

While Dawkins believed the testimony of Mrs. Lucky in the Reddix case, he was unable to accept the statements of Mrs. Pauline A. Culpepper, Bienville Parish's registrar:

While the Registrar, in her testimony, vehemently protested that she had never discriminated against Negroes because of their race, the

31. *U.S.* v. *Association of Citizens Councils of Louisiana, Inc.,* 196 Fed. Supp. 908.
32. There were approximately 6120 white persons and 4475 black of voting age. In September 1956, there were approximately 5284 whites and 595 black persons registered to vote.
33. The same statute was involved in *Reddix* v. *Sharp* reported above.

truth is that she has done so continuously, not only in the 1956 purge but even until the time this case was tried in November 1960.[34]

Since 1956 she had registered 925 white persons and no black applicants. More than one-third of the registered whites filled out application cards containing the same or similar errors which served as basis for purging blacks. Even during the purge, about 80 per cent of the white voters had the same kind of errors the blacks had, but only 1 per cent were challenged—and half of this 1 per cent had moved away from the parish. Dawkins was impressed that at the trial "the Government presented a veritable parade of Bienville Parish Negroes, holding bachelor's and master's degrees," who had been denied the right to register since 1956. White persons whose "level of education was far below" that of many rejected black applicants and whose application cards reflected this were nonetheless registered. The judge added:

It is to be earnestly hoped that in the future those Negroes who are qualified to vote will achieve a degree of political maturity so as to vote according to the best interests of their State and Nation rather than for their own selfish or venal purposes.[35]

Dawkins concluded that a pattern or practice of discrimination existed, but the appointment of a voting referee was not then necessary. The names of the illegally purged black voters were ordered restored to the rolls, and the registrar was enjoined from future discrimination. No injunction was issued against the other defendants as long as they did not "renew their unlawful activity." Dawkins asked the government to prepare a decree implementing the decision of August 17, 1961. The proposed decree was accepted by the court with one significant change. The government simply wanted the court to order the approximately 570 blacks restored to the rolls and to be so notified within fifteen days, "or

34. 196 Fed. Supp., p. 911.
35. *Ibid.*

at least three days before the next election, whichever is sooner." This was the way Judge Johnson had handled the matter a few months earlier in Alabama. Dawkins' decree in this respect, however, was much more detailed and put more responsibility on the blacks.[36] Finally, the decree required the registrar to report the completion of the task to the court, and permitted the government to inspect and copy, on order of the court, any or all voting records in the parish. The decree was entered November 3, 1961.

Dawkins's decree did not go as far as Johnson's by registering the blacks with "a stroke of the pen," nor was the registrar required to make detailed monthly reports, but the case did not involve the countless delays experienced in Mississippi. "Oh sure," one government lawyer stated in discussing the case with this writer,

We could have gotten a stronger decree, but you can see for yourself that this was not the worst kind of order we could have received. At least Judge Dawkins was on the right track, and that hearing told us that if we overwhelmed him with the facts, he'd come along. Slowly perhaps, but you'd have to admit that's better than not coming at all.

In the same month the decree was entered in the Bienville Parish case, the government tried a second suit before Judge Dawkins arising out of East Carroll Parish.[37] The case was filed seven months earlier, in April 1961. The government alleged that the registrar, Cecil Manning, required black citizens to fulfill virtually impossible conditions to establish their identity. Under Louisiana law, applicants for voter certificates were required to establish their identities to the satisfaction of the registrar. If the registrar had good reason to question the identity of the person, the regis-

36. The black citizens had to return the original registration cards. A certain number of days were provided, and specific responsibilities were placed on the blacks if the registration certificate was returned undelivered by the postal authorities.
37. *U.S.* v. *Manning,* civil action no. 8257.

trar could require him to produce two credible persons registered to vote in his ward and precinct to identify him under oath.

There were approximately 4183 blacks and 2990 whites of voting age in the parish. A new registration period began in the parish on January 1, 1961.[38] From that time to November 1961 about 500 white persons and no black persons had been registered. In fact, no black had been registered in the parish since 1922. On hearing the testimony in the case, Dawkins made the following findings of fact:

Manning has used the identification requirement to discriminate against Negroes. He restricts the possible means of identification to four: (a) He permits persons known to him to apply for registration without further identification. His standard of "knowing" is applied liberally in favor of white persons and arbitrarily with respect to Negroes. Not only does he "know" very few Negroes in the Parish, but he does not "know" those Negroes with whom he is in regular contact and those who have appeared repeatedly at his office.

(b) He permits white persons to apply for registration who are introduced to him by another white person known to him. He requires that Negroes be introduced to him by white persons since he "knows" very few Negroes. He will not permit one Negro to identify another.

(c) Manning permits persons to apply for registration without further identification if they have been previously registered in the Parish. This necessarily excludes Negroes, because none have been registered in the Parish since 1922.

(d) Manning permits persons to apply for registration who are identified by the affidavits of two registered voters from their precinct. This is tantamount to requiring Negroes to be identified by white voters, since no Negroes are registered. No white person has ever identified a Negro and, in fact, efforts by Negroes to get white people to identify them have been unsuccessful. Thus, by virtue of Manning's requirements, and the refusal of white voters to identify Negroes, the Parish has succeeded in excluding all Negroes from being permitted to register and vote for the past 40 years.[39]

38. At the end of the previous registration period on December 31, 1960, there were 2845 white persons and no black persons registered.

39. 7 *RRLR* at p. 478.

The Department of Justice had four major theories in its dealings
with the activity of registrars or state registration requirements in
the South which it sought to urge on Southern federal judges. First,
where a system of vouching or identification was found to exist
in those counties with few or no registered black voters, this should
be construed as constitutionally impermissible because of the extreme hardship it worked on blacks. In effect, it required blacks
to solicit whites in their efforts to register. This was the situation
in Bullock County, Alabama. Second, where the registrar required very stringent standards for whites and blacks alike in those
areas where very few if any blacks were registered, this amounted
to freezing the status quo. Third, the standards by which the
registrars should be guided in registering future black applicants
under conditions prevailing in the second situation should be those
standards used to register the least qualified white persons during
the period of racial discrimination. Fourth, where it was shown
that none or a very small percentage of the voting-age blacks were
registered over a certain period of time and where several black
people had attempted to register while a substantial majority of
the white persons of voting age were already registered, this evidence alone should support a claim for relief under the Fourteenth and Fifteenth Amendments and under the Civil Rights Act
of 1957 and 1960.

Judge Dawkins accepted at least the first and fourth theories
in his Manning opinion. He made a finding of a pattern and
practice of discrimination based on race. The particular ways by
which the registrar manipulated the identification requirement
amounted to discrimination per se. Consequently, he enjoined any
acts of racial discrimination, and specifically the identification requirements the registrar had been using. The registrar had "to
make reasonable inquiry as to the identity of Negroes seeking to
apply for registration." Blacks should be permitted to establish
their identity by use of driving, hunting, or fishing licenses, library cards or automobile registrations, as well as by military

papers, records of property ownership, rent receipts, and the like.

Then Dawkins assumed the role of overseer. He ordered the registrar to file monthly progress reports showing a list of new registrants, a list of persons "scratched from the rolls," a list of transfers, a list of names, race, and addresses of all applicants rejected on the ground of lack of identification, the kinds of identification each offered, and the reasons for its unacceptability. Finally, the monthly report was to contain a list of the names, race, and addresses of all persons whose applications for registration were rejected and the reasons therefor. Likewise, the government was given the right to inspect the voting records at any and all reasonable times. The judge did not appoint a voter referee.

Some lawyers for the Justice Department expressed the belief that Judge Dawkins was annoyed with the blatant fact that no black person had been registered in the parish in forty years. His sympathies were with the registrars because he abhorred the thought of a "black bloc vote." But he sincerely believed that all qualified persons, black or white, should be able to vote. One government attorney made the following observation:

I believe, also, in terms of the effect of a suit, that Dawkins [in the East Carroll Parish case] called the District Attorney [the counsel for the registrar] in his chambers and said something like, "Now listen, I want to save you as much embarrassment as possible, so you all get on over there and register those Negroes. I am not going to have those people running in and out of here. I'll order a referee if I have to, but I would rather you folks handled this yourself."
Of course, I don't know what he said to him, but I do know he called the DA into his chambers. And this is perfectly legal. He can call in the defendants and their lawyers only. I suspect this happened.

Some government lawyers felt that Dawkins "really didn't realize what a pattern and practice finding meant," while others believed that Dawkins would be a "strong judge," meaning forceful enforcement of voting rights. The former group was doubtful that he would make such a finding in the near future, since that was the "trigger for appointing a referee." The latter group voiced the opinion that he would respond favorably if the government continued to document the inequalities as well as it had in Bienville and East Carroll parishes. In addition, the government was able to impress Dawkins with the need for more detailed, monthly reports, which he did not order in the Bienville case. A vital consideration in Dawkins's development would be not only the kind of decrees he ordered, but the manner by which he would oversee the monthly activity of the registrars.

Most government lawyers believed that pessimism was not the frame of mind most conducive to success in arguing right-to-vote cases before Southern federal judges, and they were very encouraged when they saw the development by Dawkins in his progress from the East Carroll Parish decree to the Bienville order. The law said the case must be filed in the district court; there was no alternative. So in discussing Judge Dawkins, one government attorney summed up in the following manner: "I'd agree that he's torn—just like so many other white Southerners, not just judges. But, as I say, we work with them. Help bring them along. I guess you could say, help put the pieces together—on the right side."

Effort to influence the courts is not new,[40] but it was new, as far as is known, with Southern federal district courts on racial issues. Some of the more prevalent practices were probably not available to the government—*amicus curiae* briefs and law articles in major law journals. Therefore, the Justice Department relied on what was probably the strongest determinants in any event— the basic respect of the judge for the law and the persuasive presentation of a well-documented body of evidence.

40. See Clement Vose, "Litigation as a Form of Pressure Group Activity," *Annals of the American Academy of Political and Social Science,* Vol. 319 (September 1958); Chester A. Newland, "Legal Periodicals and the United States Supreme Court," *Midwest Journal of Political Science,* Vol. 3 (February 1959); Note: "Private Attorneys-General: Group Action in the Fight for Civil Liberties," *Yale Law Journal,* Vol. 58 (1949).

8 Intimidation: The Courts and "Political Termites"

The foundation of our form of government is the consent of the governed. Whenever any person interferes with the right of any other person to vote or to vote as he may choose, he acts like a political termite to destroy a part of that foundation. A single termite or many termites may pass unnoticed, but each damages the foundation and if that process is allowed to continue the whole structure may crumble and fall even before the occupants become aware of their peril. Eradication of political termites, or at least checking their activities, is necessary to prevent irreparable damage to our Government.[1]

One thesis of this study is that the problem of intimidation of black voters or would-be voters is probably the biggest problem in this entire field of voting rights. It is a big problem not only because of the prolific existence of the practice in some areas, but because the problems of legal proof are so great. Intimidation is essentially of two types, physical and economic, with the ever-present existence of a third factor pervading both—the fear on the part of black people that intimidation of either or both types will result if they try to register or vote.

This chapter examines material covering both types, but it puts the problem into four categories based on some assumptions of

1. *U.S.* v. *Wood*, 295 Fed. 2d. 772 (1961).

the difficulty of proof. It is the assumption of this study that proving intimidation becomes more difficult as we move from the first through the fourth category: (1) physical reprisals, (2) economic reprisals by large numbers of people against large numbers of blacks similarly situated, (3) relatively long-term and consistent economic reprisals conducted by several persons against one black person, and (4) a single act of economic reprisal performed by one individual against a black person.

President Kennedy took note of all four of these forms of action in his special message to the Congress on February 28, 1963, when he stated:

Too often those who attempt to assert their constitutional rights are intimidated. Prospective registrants are fired. Registration workers are arrested. In some instances, churches in which registration meetings are held have been burned. In one case where Negro tenant farmers chose to exercise their right to vote, it was necessary for the Justice Department to seek injunctions to halt their eviction and for the Department of Agriculture to help feed them from surplus stocks. Under these circumstances, continued delay in the granting of the franchise —particularly in counties where there is mass racial disfranchisement—permits the intent of the Congress to be openly floated.

Federal executive action in such cases—no matter how speedy and how drastic—can never fully correct such abuses of power. It is necessary instead to free the forces of our democratic system within these areas by promptly insuring the franchise to all citizens, making it possible for their elected officials to be truly responsive to all their constituents.[2]

Physical Reprisal and Intimidation by Prosecution

A situation arose in the summer of 1961 in Walthall County, Mississippi, which provided an illustration of the first type of intimidation coupled with a legal effort by the local authorities against a black voter registration worker. The black, John Hardy, had come to town along with a few other members of the Student

2. Special Message to Congress from the President, 1963, p. 3.

Non-Violent Coordinating Committee (SNCC) to conduct a voter registration drive among local black citizens. At that time there were 2490 blacks of voting age in the county, none of whom was registered. There were 4530 white persons of voting age in Walthall County, a substantial majority of whom were registered. Hardy had completed two years of college in Tennessee. He and his co-workers canvassed the black community, established voter registration classes, and proceeded to teach local blacks how to qualify as registered voters.[3] As many as twenty-five to fifty persons attended the classes each evening. Hardy began to accompany small groups of "graduates" to the registrar's office on August 30, 1961—five one day, three another; "driblets," one SNCC worker said, "but don't play it down when you write about us. You've got to establish the habit."

On September 7 Hardy accompanied a sixty-three-year-old black woman and a sixty-two-year-old black man, both owners of eighty-acre and seventy-acre farms, respectively. The registrar, John Q. Wood, told them he was not registering anyone. "You all have got me in court and I refuse to register anyone else until this court is cleared up." The registrar then took his revolver from his desk drawer and ordered Hardy from his office. The following account was reported in the opinion of the Court of Appeals:

According to the affidavits of the [U.S.] Government, Hardy had given Wood only his name when Wood got up and said, "I want to see you, John." He then brushed past Hardy into the main room and from the drawer of a desk took out a revolver. Holding the gun down by his right side he pointed to the door going outside and said, "Do you see that door, John?" Hardy replied, "Yes." Wood then told him, "You get out of it." Hardy said OK, and turned to go. Wood followed him,

---

3. "You have to understand," stated James Forman, executive director of the Student Non-Violent Coordinating Committee, "that when we go into one of those black-belt areas, we have to spend most—this is true—most of our time just trying to overcome the fear. The fear of just simply going down to that white man's courthouse. This is something new to many of those people. . . . Why, in Greenwood, one old lady told us she didn't know where the courthouse was."

and just as Hardy got to the door, Wood struck him on the back of the head, saying, "Get out of here you damn son-of-a-bitch, and don't come back in here."

Hardy and the two other blacks rushed from the office, sought medical aid for the SNCC worker, talked to the editor of the local newspaper, and met the sheriff on the street. The sixty-three-year-old black woman gave the following account in her affidavit:

They met right where I was standing [Hardy and the sheriff] and the sheriff asked, "What happened to you, boy." John told the sheriff what had happened. The sheriff told him he didn't have no business in that courthouse. Wilson [the 62-year-old black man] walked up at this time. The sheriff then said to John, "If that boy [pointing to Wilson] wants to register he know how to go down to that courthouse and he don't need you to escort him. You didn't have a bit of business in the world down there. You is from Tennessee, you was in Tennessee and you ought to have stayed there." The sheriff told him to "come on." John asked him, "Are you arresting me?" The sheriff said, "Yes." John asked, "On what charges," and the sheriff said for disturbing the peace and bringing an uprising among the people. John said, "Will you allow me to tell my side of the story?" The sheriff said, "don't give me none of your head, boy, or I will beat you within an inch of you life." After the sheriff took John, I went home.[4]

Hardy was formally charged, questioned extensively about his voter registration activities, and released on bond the following morning. Trial was set for September 22.

The government filed a suit before Judge Cox in the Federal District Court on September 20. The government sought a temporary restraining order against the local officials in the disturbance-of-the-peace case against Hardy. The second claim of the United States charged a conspiracy to deprive black citizens of the county of the right to vote. Judge Cox refused to issue an order. The government immediately appealed, and after a hurried airplane flight to Montgomery, Alabama, by a U.S. Attorney to petition circuit Judge Rives for a stay of the state prosecution, Mississippi agreed

4. Affidavit in files of Justice Department.

not to prosecute Hardy pending the government's appeal of Cox's decision.

The government's argument was that the state and local authorities should not be permitted to prosecute Hardy, that such a case was, in fact, motivated by an attempt to intimidate local blacks in the exercise of their right to vote. It was not any right of Hardy's that the government sought to protect; indeed, in oral argument, the government asserted that the assumption could be made that Hardy would receive a fair trial. But the entire circumstances—conviction or acquittal of Hardy—were calculated to discourage further attempts by blacks to attempt to register. If the state prosecuted Hardy, other black people in Walthall County would be afraid to apply for registration for fear they would be subjected to unjustified official acts, including arrest and prosecution. Assuming acquittal, the government contended that few blacks could afford the time and expense—not to mention the lack of competent black counsel in the state—of a trial. Until the time of the incident on September 7, eleven blacks had applied for voter certificates; no black citizens had applied after then. The government's brief stated:

On the basis of the record in this court [the appellate court] and in view of the conditions and circumstances prevailing in Mississippi, it is most unlikely that if the appellees are allowed to proceed with Mr. Hardy's trial, further Negro registration will take place. The blunt truth is that it can really not be expected that Negroes who have lived all their lives under the white supremacy conditions which exist in that area of Mississippi will continue their efforts to register and otherwise to exercise their rights and privileges of citizenship if, in addition to being threatened and beaten, they will also be prosecuted in state court with all that such a prosecution entails.[5]

Before disposing of the case, the Court of Appeals had to decide a jurisdictional point—was such an appeal allowable? The court concluded that statutory and case authorities answered this in the

5. Government's brief before appellate court in *U.S.* v. *Wood*.

affirmative. Normally, the denial of a temporary restraining order was not such an order refusing an injunction. But the government had argued that this case was an exception. If the government could not appeal, then the Hardy trial would be held and the damage done. The appellate court agreed that the Civil Rights Act of 1957 gave the United States a cause of action for "preventive relief" where a person had intimidated or had attempted to intimidate another in the exercise of the latter's right to vote.

The fact that it was a state criminal proceeding that was to be restrained was not controlling in light of the statutory authority and the overriding "national interest" involved. The court proceeded to balance the equities. It specifically declared that it was not deciding the merits of the government's case for a preliminary or permanent injunction against alleged racially discriminatory acts of intimidation, but merely that the factual circumstances (presented by government affidavits and not contradicted by the local authorities) when weighed against the mere "temporary postponement of trial of a misdemeanor case before a justice of the peace" warranted a temporary restraining order. The appellate court (Judges Rives and Brown concurring; Cameron dissenting) indicated at this point that the issue of intimidation raised by the United States was important enough not to be allowed to become moot by holding Hardy's trial. A breach of peace charge on the local level could wait until a full hearing could be had in the federal courts as to whether or not "political termites" were at work in Walthall County in 1961.

The county officials dropped the breach of peace charge against Hardy in April 1963 and returned the black man's bond money.

Mass Economic Retaliation: The Tennessee Sharecroppers

One characteristic associated with intimidation as a method of deterring black voting is the relatively wide publicity such acts receive. Flagrant discriminations by registrars of the kind witnessed in the Alabama counties were periodically publicized, but they were not dramatic, headline news stories. A bombing of a church which served as a meeting place for voter registration drives in Georgia or a shooting of a voter registration worker in Mississippi received national news coverage and invariably provoked comment by the President at his next press conference.[6] Occasionally such acts of intimidation took an economic form and lasted longer as front-page items of national attention. Such was the situation in the autumn and winter of 1960–61 in two black-belt counties in Tennessee. This situation was magnified, of course, because it involved hundreds of black people who had registered or attempted to register to vote.

Fayette County, Tennessee, had in March 1961 a black population of about 7500. Prior to 1959 no more than ten of the blacks were registered to vote. When registration began for Tennessee's 1959 state and local primaries there was a marked increase in the number of blacks who sought to enroll. Still, the number of black persons registered was under a hundred. On election day in 1959 when eligible blacks attempted to vote, they were turned away from the polls. Each man or woman was handed a printed slip informing him that this was an "all-white primary" and that black voting was illegal. Twelve black citizens filed suit against the Democratic committee in the county, charging that they had been

6. President Kennedy made the following statement at his press conference on September 13, 1962: "I don't know any more outrageous action which I've seen occur in this country for a good many months or years than the burning of a church—two churches—because of the effort made by Negroes to be registered to vote. . . . To shoot, as we saw in the case in Mississippi, two young people who were involved in an effort to register people, to burn churches as a reprisal with all of the provisions of the United States Constitution—at least the basic provisions of the Constitution guaranteeing freedom of worship—I consider both cowardly as well as outrageous. . . . I commend those who are making the effort to register every citizen. They deserve the protection of the United States Government, the protection of local communities, and we'll do everything we possibly can to make sure that that protection is assured. And if it requires extra legislation, and extra forces, we shall do that." *New York Times,* September 14, 1962.

barred illegally from exercising their franchise. They won their case.[7]

This incident was followed by the formation of the Fayette County Civic and Welfare League by the twelve blacks. The first stated purpose of the league in its articles of incorporation filed at Nashville read, "To promote civil and political and economic welfare for the community progress of Fayette County." The first job the league undertook was to get more black people registered to vote. The leaders canvassed the sharecroppers, tenant farmers, and day workers, and their efforts resulted in hundreds making their way to the courthouse in Somerville, the county seat.

Shortly after the mass registration drive began, leaders of the league began to suspect the existence of a secret blacklist of their membership. One day the list was discovered—a list of those who had been registered—with a special "x" by the names of those who were the leaders in the movement. When the blacks went to stores where they had traded for years, the white owners or managers scanned the list under the counter. If the black person's name appeared on the list, the manager refused to sell to him. Gas stations refused to sell gasoline to blacks who were suspect. Doctors and clinics in the county no longer would treat their black patients. It became necessary for the black people to travel forty miles or more when in need of medical care. Crop production loans were withheld from many blacks who had previously obtained them through the Department of Agriculture.

Some—not many—of the white people in Fayette County were inclined to be charitable if not sympathetic toward the black movement for equality in voting rights. But any manifestation of this feeling frequently brought reprisal to them as swiftly as it did to the black people. "There's lots of white men in Fayette County who aren't free either," an elderly black clergyman said. "He

7. U.S. v. Fayette County Democratic Executive Committee, no. 3835 (1959).

doesn't dare not conform when the [white] Citizens Council tells him to."

The Presidential election of 1960 neared. Pressure on the black population, especially those who were now registered voters, grew heavier and more oppressive. Now they had to drive one hundred miles back and forth to get gasoline and oil for their automobiles and tractors. Most blacks found it impossible to purchase a gallon of gasoline in the county. Deliveries of bottled gas, fuel for their home heating and cooking, were halted.

November 8, 1960, came, and the black voters went to the polls. No attempts were made to turn them away. Fayette County had a long record of voting safely in the Democratic column. When the ballots were counted, the county gave its vote to the Republicans. The blacks, more than 1200 of them, had swung the balance of power.

Retribution was not slow in coming. On some of the large plantations, on farms in the back districts of the county, summary notices to "get off my land" were given to blacks even before all the states had completed the tabulation of their votes. In almost every instance, the commands were verbal, because in Fayette County there were no written leases or contracts between the landlord and the blacks who farmed as tenants or who sharecropped. Some eviction notices were peremptory—"get the hell off by Saturday." Others were more charitable and gave some families until January 1, 1961, to find a new home and a new way to support themselves and their families. An important legal factor was that many landlords made no secret of their malice, bitterness, and motives. In all, 345 families were given eviction notices, and blacks began to double up with relatives in already overcrowded shacks. The league actively sought families to take in those who had been made homeless.

At this point, a dramatic element was introduced by the erection of "Tent City." Some families were unable to find accommodations.

The solution was a cluster of fourteen green canvas tents set up in a clearing off the highway on the property of a black farmer, Shepard Towles. The "city" was born December 14, 1960, with eleven families—twenty adults and fifty-six children. Late in January the tents got wooden floors. Before that, the floors had been the bare ground or sheets of cardboard. Kerosene oil lamps furnished the illumination after sunset before the families went in bed to keep warm. Later, an electric line was installed. Wood-burning stoves served for heating and cooking. Outside, great black kettles stood over wood fires for laundry purposes and the family wash was draped over convenient bushes to dry. Tent City (referred to in some civil rights circles as Freedom Village or Liberty Lane) became a symbol for many civil rights groups throughout the North. Food and clothing drives were mounted in many urban areas to supply the needy families of the Tennessee area.

The following statement was taken by the Department of Justice from a Mrs. Georgia May Turner, fifty-eight, a black resident on one farm in the southeast corner of the county for fifty years. She was a charter member of Tent City:

I've plowed with mules, I've chopped cotton, I've pulled fodder. I guess I can do anything on a farm except to drive a tractor. I raised my family on that farm. My oldest daughter picked thirty pounds of cotton when she was four years old.

When the old Mr. M_____ died, I fell to his son. After he died, I fell to his lady. I loved them and I thought they loved me. Then my daughter and my friends told me I should register so I could be a real citizen. Some of my white friends told me, "Georgia, you register, you'll be in trouble."

But I registered because I want to be a citizen and I want my freedom, not just for me but for my children and those little ones you see here. After that I voted and the boss lady told my son, "You and Georgia have to get off my land." When he told me, I borrowed bus fare to go see her and ask her herself because I couldn't believe she would do that to us.

She told me, "Georgia, you voted and done wrong and now you have to get off my land but you can stay until the first of the year 'til you find a place." I thanked her and that was all I could say 'cause I didn't want her to see me cry.

I went home and I cried all night 'cause this was the only house I'd ever had for thirty-eight years and I didn't know where to go. But I knew the Lord will always open the way for us and He led me here [Tent City], praise His name.

But I still loves my boss lady no matter what she done and I'll never say one bad word about her because she was good to me and it wasn't her fault I voted.[8]

Tent City was not without its violence. On December 28 occupants from a speeding car fired shots blindly into the community. One bullet ripped the tent of twenty-five-year-old Early B. Williams and his family and tore into his arm. Two nights later, three white youths fired into the community, but no one was hit. Some of the Tent City residents fired on the intruders and gave chase. The young men were later caught by the sheriff but were released after he lectured and reprimanded them. An appeal that some of the Tent City men be deputized to protect themselves against the violence was rejected by the Fayette County sheriff's office.

A second tent community was put up isolated from any main road and for some time its exact location was unknown to most people, white or black, in the county.

The Department of Justice began its investigation of the situation in the late spring of 1960. In the adjoining county of Haywood, there were no tent cities, but similar acts of eviction and economic reprisal were taking place. Out of these investigations came three suits covering the two counties. The government filed a suit on September 13 against twenty-nine defendants in Haywood County. On November 18 it amended its complaint to include thirty-six more defendants.[9] The defendants included the mayor of Brownsville, the sheriff, the school superintendent, and various bankers, merchants, and landowners of Haywood County.[10]

8. Affidavit in files of Justice Department.
9. *U.S.* v. *Beaty,* civil action no. 4065.
10. 6*RRLR* 201.

In December 1960, a vitrually identical action was brought in the same court against ten other defendants.[11] Then on December 14, 1960, the United States brought an action against eighty-two defendants, including the mayor of Somerville, the general sessions court judge, and the representative to the state legislature, a bank and various insurance agents, wholesale grocers, gasoline dealers, cotton ginners, and landowners of Fayette County.[12] The actions were filed under Section 1971(b) of Title 42, USC to enjoin the several defendants from causing threats and intimidations of an economic nature to be made against black residents because of their status as registered voters.

On December 2 the government applied for a temporary restraining order against defendant landowners who allegedly had mailed notices of eviction as of January 1, 1961, to black tenants in Haywood County. The eviction notices were alleged to be a further means of intimidation because of the acts of voter registration. The district court on December 16 denied this application but set December 19 for a hearing on the United States application for a preliminary injunction.[13] Then on December 23 the district court entered an order temporarily enjoining thirteen of the defendants "pending the hearing of this cause, from engaging in any threats, intimidation, or coercion . . . of any nature for the purpose of interfering with the right of any other person to become registered to vote in Haywood County, Tennessee, and to vote for candidates for Federal office," but denying other relief asked in the application:

The court refused to extend the injunction to include evictions or refusals to renew leases of Negro tenants for purposes of intimidating them in the exercise of franchise rights, stating that the Civil Rights

11. *U.S.* v. *Barcroft*, civil action no. 4121.
12. *U.S.* v. *Atkeison*, 6 RRLR 200.
13. *Ibid.*, p. 202.

Act did not "vest the courts with authority to adjudge contracts and property rights." [14]

The United States immediately petitioned the Court of Appeals for the sixth circuit for an injunction pending appeal. The government was concerned that unless such an injunction were issued, the January 1, 1961, date would pass, the evictions would occur, and the case would become moot. The district court was concerned that it was being asked to do something for which it basically had no authority. The lower court stated:

In effect, it seems to the Court the plaintiff is asking that the Court make new rental contracts for certain of the parties in this litigation. It ought to be evident to all that relief of this type cannot be awarded, especially on application for temporary injunction. The Congress, it is plain to see, did, in passing the Civil Rights Act, intend to protect the voting right but it did not, as the Court reads the statute, vest the Courts with authority to adjudge contracts and property rights, and this is the main problem inherent in this very broad application by the Government.[15]

On December 30 the Court of Appeals entered an order restraining the landowner defendants from intimidating, threatening, or coercing any black tenants for the purpose of interfering with their right to vote, and from evicting, removing, or refusing to renew leases as to such tenants for the purpose of intimidation or coercion, or to punish them for exercising their rights to register or vote. The appellate court felt that the evidence in the case warranted a temporary restraining order against the landowners until the cases could be heard on the merits.

On the same day, in keeping with the appellate court's opinion, the district court ordered the landowners of both Haywood and Fayette counties restrained and enjoined from intimidating, threat-

14. *Ibid.*
15. *Ibid.*, p. 205.

ening, or coercing any black tenants for the purpose of interfering with their right to vote, and from evicting, removing, or refusing to renew leases of tenants for the purpose of intimidation or coercion, or to punish them for exercising their rights to register or vote.

The United States then proceeded to appeal the lower court's ruling of December 23. The Court of Appeals rendered an opinion in that cause three months later on April 6. It did not believe that the district court judge should have been required to grant an injunction back in December that would have caused him "to adjudicate or declare contracts or to specifically enforce them." And the language of the Court of Appeals on December 30 should not be so construed. Instead the appellate court wanted to issue an order that would not offend the substantive rights of the defendants and at the same time would substantially protect the rights of the black citizens. This was the intent and operation of the restraining order. The appellate court said:

It should, however, be understood to empower and require the District Judge to inquire, by a hearing, at which interested parties are given an opportunity to be heard, into any situation where a defendant landowner evicts or threatens to evict a Negro tenant or refuses to deal in good faith with said tenant for a continuation of occupancy and tenancy, and if said eviction, threatened eviction or refusal to deal in good faith is found to be for the purpose of interfering in any way with the right of such Negro tenant to become registered or to vote in Haywood County, Tennessee, and to vote for candidates for federal office, or as punishment for having previously registered or voted, such conduct would constitute a violation of the prohibitions of the order.[16]

This kind of order was sufficient to safeguard the rights of any blacks evicted as a result of having registered or voted, the court felt. A landowner so acting would be subject to punishment for contempt, and the Court of Appeals stated that it did not "think

16. 288 Fed. 2d. 657–58.

the District Judge will withhold adequate punishment for any contempt of his injunction."

One year and one month later, on May 2, 1962, the Court of Appeals entered a consent decree of final judgment enjoining the defendants from using threats or coercion for the purpose of interfering with registration or voting. The injunction was not limited to specific acts, but it expressly prohibited terminating employment, refusing to sell goods or services, refusing to lend money, and evicting or changing the customary terms of tenancy for the purpose of interfering with voting rights.[17] This decree related to Haywood County, but on July 26, 1962, a final judgment in identical terms was entered concerning Fayette County.

The final order, however, did not actually decide the merits of the case. It merely enjoined the named defendants from violating Section 1971(b) of 42 USC. The second paragraph stated in part:

Now, therefore, without final trial or adjudication of this cause upon the merits, and without this Final Judgment constituting evidence or an admission by any of the Defendants with respect to issues of fact, and upon consent of the parties as aforesaid, it is hereby ordered, adjudged, and decreed. . . .[18]

This meant that if a black person were subsequently evicted, it would be incumbent upon the government to show that such act was in violation of the injunction. The situation that initially led to the action by the department was not adjudicated.

The Commission on Civil Rights, in its Report in 1961 before the final decree, pointed out the great importance of the Tennessee cases:

In at least one respect these suits are the most important cases that have arisen under the 1957 Act. Considering the large number of counties in the South where Negroes are almost completely dependent upon white persons for employment, economic sanctions

17. 7 *RRLR* 484.
18. *Ibid.* p. 485.

could prove to be a serious obstacle to enforcement of the fifteenth Amendment. Assuming a favorable result in the Haywood and Fayette cases, the Government will have established an important precedent against the use of economic retaliation to deter Negroes from efforts to register and vote. How long and effectively the remedy in such cases can provide protection for a large group of Negroes so dependent economically on the whites is another question.[19]

One might conclude that if such a decree resulted in blacks not being evicted or being denied goods and services, then the legal action was successful. This might be a valid argument for the particular case at the particular time, but it has less value for future instances. It would have much more of a deterrent value if a specific precedent could be cited where the court had said that such acts in that setting constituted a violation of the Civil Rights Acts. It is not unlikely that economic retaliation against masses of blacks attempting to register or vote will be a frequent practice in many Southern areas, as the Civil Rights Commission pointed out. The stronger the precedent in terms of court decrees with specific findings of fact, the easier it would be to deal with such acts when they occurred.

The Economic Squeeze: A Louisiana Farmer

These cases of intimidation are more difficult to prove than discriminatory action by state legislatures or local registrars because of the acts of intimidation (or rather, alleged intimidation) involve not only competing rights but questionable motives. On the one hand, the right of blacks to register and vote should be protected against unlawful acts of coercion and threat, but at the same time, it may be difficult to connect an eviction from the land or a refusal to extend medical services or commercial services with voting rights, especially when this society places such a high value on the right of private property and freedom of choice. Over-zealousness

19. *1961 Report,* U.S. Commission on Civil Rights, p. 96.

in protecting one right might illegitimately infringe on the other. This, of course, involves motivation. The courts certainly have examined legislative motives. They did so with the grandfather clause, in the Tuskegee gerrymander case, and other instances. But most of these actions were flagrantly supported in their unlawful intentions by recorded statements of legislators as to their purpose or by standards that left virtually no room for doubt. When this evidence was presented in *Gomillion* v. *Lightfoot,* the competing right of a state legislature to redraw its local boundaries was not a difficult matter to adjudicate, even for such an advocate of judicial self-restraint as Justice Felix Frankfurter, who wrote the opinion for a unanimous Supreme Court. But an eviction supported by private right (as the right not to renew a rental contract) offers grave difficulties when weighed against an allegation that such an act was predicated on an unlawful intention to violate another's right to vote.

These difficulties are mitigated somewhat when the acts occur as they did in the context of Haywood and Fayette counties. Many individuals were involved on both sides, thus offering greater opportunity to search out possible incriminating statements and other pieces of evidence showing intent. But these difficulties are magnified when the acts are perpetrated not against a mass of individuals similarly situated, as the Tennessee sharecroppers, but against one black person. This was the situation in which Mr. Joseph Atlas, a fifty-five-year-old black farmer in East Carroll Parish, Louisiana, found himself and his family in the autumn of 1960. In September 1960 he was subpoenaed by and testified before the Civil Rights Commission at hearings in New Orleans. He testified to the years of denial of voting rights to blacks in his parish—a parish that had 5330 blacks of voting age and not one registered. (There were 3220 white citizens of voting age and 2845 registered.) From October 1960 to February 1961 Mr. Atlas was caught in an economic vise that threatened to result in financial ruin for him and his family.

Atlas and his wife lived on their sixty-five-acre farm in East Carroll Parish with two of their twelve children and two grandchildren. He had lived in the parish all his life except for three years in an Alabama school. Of the twelve children, three were schoolteachers, two in the army, one a nurse in Chicago, one a bus driver in Chicago, and three were in college in 1960. Five of his children had received college degrees and one was then in high school. Atlas himself had three years of high school training at Tuskegee Institute in Alabama, where he learned the plastery and brick masonry trades. His father, who died in 1958, owned over a hundred acres of land. Atlas had been a farmer ever since he returned from school in Alabama. He was a member of the Progressive Baptist Church in Lake Providence, had been a deacon for thirty years, superintendent of the church Sunday school for twenty years, and treasurer of his church for three years. He was a past president of the PTA in Lake Providence.

He purchased his sixty-five-acre farm in 1942 for $4580, and his farming business consisted of raising cotton, soybeans, small grain, and cattle. In the fall of 1959 he borrowed several thousand dollars from the Farm Home Administration to repair and remodel the house, including the installation of indoor toilet facilities. The farm was adjacent to the land previously owned by his father. In 1960 Atlas owned one-eighth of it (inherited upon his father's death), the remainder being owned by his brothers and sisters. In 1959 he grossed about $10,400 from the farm. About $7300 was from the sale of cotton and $1900 from the sale of soy beans.

In 1948 certain blacks in East Carroll Parish organized a voters' league. Atlas served as secretary of that organization and was a member of a committee that met with the sheriff to discuss registration and voting of blacks in the county.

On September 23, 1960, he received a subpoena to appear before the Civil Rights Commission in New Orleans on September 27. His testimony read, in part:

Vice Chairman Storey: Have you ever made any attempt to register?

Mr. Atlas: I have.

Storey: When was the first time, and tell us the circumstances.

Atlas: Well, as near as I can recall, the first time we made an effort to register was when the primary case was broken in Texas and we went before the officials—what gave Negroes the right to participate in white primaries—we went to the officials of the town and questioned them about that, and they refused us.

Storey: Do you remember about what year that was?

Atlas: Well, as near as I can recall, it was in 1948.

Storey: Well, did they give you any reason for not letting you register?

Atlas: Well, I would consider them random.

Storey: You mean not satisfactory?

Atlas: That's right.

Storey: Did you ever make any further attempt to register?

Atlas: I did.

Storey: When?

Atlas: As I recall, I believe in 1950, we went to the registration office, and I applied for a registration card, and the lady gave it to me, and I filled it out as best I knew how, and she looked at it and said it was incorrect. So as I recall. . . .

Storey: In what respect, did she say?

Atlas: She did not tell me what.

Storey: All right.

Atlas: So I had to leave; so I came back on another occasion; what distance that was apart, I don't recall.

Storey: Well, about how long; a year or two?

Atlas: No; it wasn't a year; it was right around a month or maybe two months.

Storey: What happened then?

Atlas: I filled the card correctly, and she told me to get three electors to identify me.

Storey: Did you make an effort?

Atlas: So I made an effort. I contacted some I thought was my friends, one man I had been doing business with.

Storey: White or colored?

Atlas: No colored is registered there, so had no ground.

Storey: Did they require that you get a registered voter to identify you?

Atlas: That's right. So they told me, one told me, politics, and he didn't want to have anything to do with it. And the other one say, "Well, the position I hold, I couldn't have anything to do with it."

Storey: Did the registrar know you personally?

Atlas: Well, now, I really don't feel safe in saying that she knows me personally.

Storey: But you went back to see her two or three times, didn't you?

Atlas: I did. Two times.

Storey: Did you have any trouble identifying yourself to the bank or stores or anybody else in your parish?

Atlas: Not that I can recall.

Storey: Then when is the next time you went back?

Atlas: Well, I didn't go back any more.

Storey: Didn't go back any more? Have you ever filed a suit or made any further efforts with any other group?

Atlas: Well, I was with the group that did file a suit in 19——I don't remember the exact or what year it was.

Storey: Was that the one Reverend Scott testified about?

Atlas: That's right.

Storey: You were a party to that suit?

Atlas: I was a part of that suit.

Storey: Have you been back this year?

Atlas: Well, I was with the group, but I didn't go before the registrar of voters because I had met so many of them, and they told me the results and I didn't see where it was necessary.

Storey: You say you were with the group. When was that? A group when?

Atlas: That was this last July; July 25.

Storey: July this year?

Atlas: That's right.

Storey: About how many went?

Atlas: About 21, as I recall.

Storey: You found out that some of them couldn't register?

Atlas: That's right.

Storey: Did any of them register?

Atlas: No, not a one.

Storey: And when it came to your turn, you just gave up, did you?

Atlas: I didn't feel like it was necessary.

.   .   .

Storey: Why do you want to vote, Mr. Atlas?

Atlas: I am a taxpayer. I want a voice in the government in which I live. I feel that is my constitutional right, and I just feel

like it is my responsibility as a citizen to take whatever—if I
can share it as a taxpayer and other reasons, I think I
should vote.[20]

Mr. Atlas's testimony before the commission on September 27
received wide publicity in the Monroe, Louisiana, and New Orleans press.

The following evening, September 28, the sheriff of East Carroll
Parish came to Atlas's home to tell him that the cotton ginners
in the parish did not wish Atlas to bring his cotton to their gins
any more. Atlas asked why; the sheriff replied, "civil rights." Atlas
later talked to the owners of the Olivedell gin where he had his
cotton ginned for several years. He was told that the ginners had
all agreed, and the owner asked him if he had been subpoenaed
to testify in New Orleans. The next day another gin owner came
to Atlas to tell him not to bring his cotton to the gin, that it would
embarrass him. Atlas's affidavit continued:

I asked him why, and he said "pressure." He said there had been
meetings held and pressure had built up so. I asked him who it was
that was having the meetings, but he didn't answer. I asked him
wasn't it his gin and what has other people got to do with it. I told him
I was worrying about it, and he said that it wasn't worth getting into
such a worrying condition. He didn't have no suggestions about it
though.

Atlas sought out another cotton ginner in the parish who had
asked him to bring some of his cotton to that gin earlier in the
year. This ginner told him that the ginners' association had agreed
not to gin his cotton because he had done something "not in the
best interest of the Parish and that from now on, I'd have to hustle
for myself." Again, this ginner asked him if he had been subpoenaed to go to New Orleans, and he finally advised Atlas that
he "was stuck with a hot potato."

Atlas owed the Tallulah Production Credit Association about

20. *Hearings,* U.S. Commission, New Orleans, 1960–61.

$6000. The debt was secured by a chattel mortgage on his crops. One of the cotton ginners told him that the Olivedell gin would gin his cotton if the Tallulah Production Credit Association told them to do so, and they would gin the cotton under the name of the Production Credit Association.

On October 15 Atlas went to a gin in West Carroll Parish, asked if they ginned cotton from outside the parish and was told that they did. Then the manager asked who owned the cotton. When he answered, "Atlas," the manager replied, "Oh, no, we won't gin that." Another gin owner in East Carroll Parish told Atlas that someone had called the gin to tell them that they should not gin Atlas's cotton. Then the black farmer went to the Tallulah Production Credit Association and told them his story. They read his contract and indicated that under it the only way they could "come in" was if he abandoned the crop. Mr. Atlas's affidavit read in part:

Around the 27th of October, 1960, I went to the Farmer's Seed and Feed Store in Lake Providence with a purchase order from the ASC Office to buy some grass seed. The Government will pay a portion of the cost of the seed. However, Mr. Reed who is a clerk in the store told me that he had orders not to handle it and I would have to see Mr. Norris who is the manager.

On the next day I returned to the Farmer's Seed and Feed Store to see Mr. Norris. I told him what Mr. Reed said. Mr. Norris said yes, I gave him the order. He said, "I have enough customers without you. I do not need your business. I would appreciate it if you don't come back." I asked him why, and he said, "I just don't need your business."

I asked him if that went for the grain elevator and he said yes. The grain elevator is the Terral–Norris Seed Company at Lake Providence. Mr. Norris owns part of the elevator.

After Mr. Norris told me he didn't want my business, he turned over my old account of $580.10 to a lawyer for collection. I have paid this amount in full and the matter is settled except that the lawyer says I still owe some twelve dollars in costs.

The John Deere Company also turned my account over to a lawyer and I received a letter from their lawyer. I have settled this account. The company was sending me collection letters last summer.

At the beginning of November 1960 Mr. Atlas took his story to the United States Attorney in Shreveport, who advised him of the Outpost gin eighteen miles from his farm. Atlas spoke to the manager who said he would be happy to gin the cotton. When he asked why the cotton was being brought so far, Atlas told him there was a misunderstanding with the ginners in Lake Providence. The Outpost gin manager said he would be glad to gin all of Atlas's twenty-five to thirty bales of cotton. Atlas borrowed a truck from a neighbor—eighteen miles was too far for a tractor and trailer—and had four bales ginned on November 3 and two bales ginned on November 5. On election day, he took two more bales and at that time the manager said to him, "Joe, I can't do it." Atlas related:

He [the manager] said they got him on Saturday and Sunday and he couldn't gin it. I asked him why, and he said it was the pressure from the people. The manager told me that some people had gone to Mound, Louisiana and talked to the owner of the gin, Mr. Yerger. He said that Mr. Yerger had contacted him and instructed him not to gin Atlas' cotton. I offered him more money to gin the two bales I already had there, and he said he couldn't do it. So I brought the cotton back home.

The story was the same with all the other cotton ginners in the area.

Mr. Atlas started heating his house with butane gas in 1953. He generally purchased gas on credit from the Planters Butane Heat and Power Company in Lake Providence. After the cotton ginners started refusing to gin his cotton, Atlas received a letter from the power company advising him that if he did not pay the $150 he owed the company, legal proceedings would be instituted against him. Just prior to Christmas, his tank was running low, and he went to Planters to order gas. The clerks in the office took his order, but the gas was not delivered. He made several trips to the office and each time his order was taken, but no gas was delivered. Finally, a clerk told him he had to see the owner of the company, Mr. Baxter Deal. This required several days, and when he was able to see him, Deal told him, "No, Joe, I can't carry no gas out there." The black man went to another butane company in town and was asked to whom the gas was to be delivered. He replied, "Atlas," and was told by the manager that the company was out of gas.

His gas ran out just before Christmas, and he started heating the house with a $4.75 wood stove. Mrs. Atlas began cooking on a $72.00 wood kitchen stove that her husband had to purchase. Atlas also had to take care of his soybean crop. He related in January 1961:

Early in the Fall, I arranged with Irving Jackson, a colored man who owns a combine to combine my soybeans for one-fifth of the sale price.

In the middle of November, the beans were ready to be harvested. It was a pretty good crop, as good as last year. I went to Irving Jackson but he said, "Joe, I can't do it." He said, "I am afraid the white people might take reprisals against me for helping you combine your beans."

He suggested that I contact Mr. Warren of Warren and Coody Grain Company, Lake Providence, about combining the beans. Warren and Coody Grain Company is an elevator to whom I have sold beans in the past. It also operates combines. But Mr. Warren said he couldn't handle it.

I contacted another Negro who owns a combine and he agreed to do it as soon as he finished harvesting his own bean crop. But his combine burned and he has not been able to do it.

I contacted Rev. Otis Virgil, a Negro. Virgil also owns a combine. He told me that Mr. Warren said he would not buy my beans. Virgil told me he asked Mr. Warren about the possibility of buying the beans in the field and then combining them and selling them to Mr. Warren. According to Rev. Virgil, Mr. Warren said he wouldn't handle it that way either. My beans are still in the field. I am afraid over 50% of the crop is lost. I think I may be able to borrow a combine and when I can get into the field I will harvest what is left of the crop.

Atlas was able to get two bales of cotton ginned in the name of a friend. In January 1961 he had picked about thirteen bales of cotton which he was unable to gin and it was stored in two old tenant houses on his farm. About six bales remained unpicked because he had no place to store the cotton. He tried to work out an arrangement with the Production Credit Association that would permit ginning of the cotton and applying the proceeds to his indebtedness. There was nothing final on this. His soybeans began shelling in the field.

The United States stepped into this situation, and in January 1961 filed an action under Section 1971(b) against several defendants, including the cotton gin companies, grain elevator operators, gas companies, and feed and seed stores—twenty-two defendants in all.[21] The government sought a temporary and permanent injunction to enjoin the defendants from engaging in acts of economic intimidation against Joseph Atlas. The reprisals, the complaint alleged, were directly connected with Atlas's efforts to become a registered voter—more specifically with his appearance before the Commission on Civil Rights and the investigations of that body into voting denials in East Carroll Parish. The United States argued that unless the injunction was issued and the ordinary business channels were opened to Atlas, he would be forced out of business, and registration and voting by blacks in East Carroll Parish would never become a reality. The economic squeeze, if successful, would instill such fear in the black citizens that they would not run the risk of attempting to register and vote.

On January 30 the defendants filed a motion to dismiss. Firstly, they urged, the burden was on the government to show by pleading, affidavits, or otherwise, that the complaining witness was about to exercise the right to vote which included the registration process. This was a necessity under Section 1971(b), and by the complainant's own admission he was not in such a position. Atlas had already sworn, contended the defendants, that he had joined earlier in a lawsuit to register and was not successful. The record showed undeniably that he did not possess the qualifications to

21. *U.S.* v. *Deal,* civil action no. 8132.

vote. The unsuccessful lawsuit was "the most dynamic and convincing self-assertion that the complainant could make which would divulge his inability to register because of insufficient qualifications or otherwise." [22] So at the outset the government's charge that the acts were perpetrated for purposes of coercing Atlas in regard to his voting rights was not tenable.

Secondly, the defendants argued that they were under no legal or contractual obligation to gin Atlas's cotton, buy his beans, or sell him gas. The defendants had an absolute right to refuse to perform these acts. "These rights to refuse are property of the defendants as the term property is used in the Fifth Amendment." [23] To require them to perform these acts would amount to a direct taking of private property without due process of law and without just compensation. The defendants again stated that this contention had especial validity for purposes of Section 1971(b), inasmuch as the failure of the named defendants to act had not the remotest connection with the conduct of a federal election.

While these formal pleadings were being prepared and filed, the Department of Justice, typical of its procedure in many of the right-to-vote cases, was busily attempting to work out an agreement with defendants in the case. The government's primary purpose was to bring about a situation whereby Joseph Atlas could pursue his business of farming in the normal way in East Carroll Parish. If this could be accomplished outside the courtroom through private negotiation and settlement, then that was satisfactory. Indeed, the Justice Department officials frequently indicated that that kind of settlement was preferable to the expensive and sometimes emotional method of a lawsuit.

On February 3, 1961, Judge Ben. C. Dawkins, Jr., before whom *U.S.* v. *Deal* had been filed, held a conference in his chambers at Monroe. Present were the attorneys for the Department of Justice,

22. The circumstances and outcome of that case were reported earlier in this study.
23. Defendants' Motion to Dismiss filed in U.S. district court in *U.S.* v. *Deal* on January 30, 1961.

attorneys for the defendants, and the defendants. Judge Dawkins opened by saying that he understood an agreement had been worked out to the satisfaction of all the litigants in the case.[24] The defendants had agreed that arrangements would be made for the prompt ginning of all of Atlas's 1960 cotton crop, purchase of his 1960 soybean crop and furnishing him the needed supply of butane gas. Atlas was to be solely responsible for harvesting and transporting to market his cotton and soybean crops, and he was to pay cash money at the time of delivery of all supplies of liquefied petroleum gas.

The second part of the stipulation was a statement that the defendants agreed not to intimidate, threaten, coerce, or perform any other acts for the purpose of interfering with Atlas's right to vote in a federal election. The third and final section contained the following statement:

The agreements herein contained are for the purpose of compromise only, and in no wise constitute or are to be interpreted as an admission by any party-defendant of the truth of all or any part of the allegation of the captioned complaint, or of any statement or declaration contained in the Affidavit of Francis Joseph Atlas.

Judge Dawkins read the agreement aloud, received the affirmative replies of all the defendants that they understood the agreement and entered into it in good faith. Dawkins stated that he would not dismiss the suit but would merely postpone it "with the understanding that if good faith compliance with this stipulation is made by you [the defendants] and each of you, that somewhere down the line, if this matter becomes moot, in the sense that there is no longer any need for the Court to retain jurisdiction, that the case will be dismissed."

At this point, one of the cotton gin owners raised a question. This was as close as any official documents came to an intimation on the part of the defendants that there was a community problem

24. The full stipulation is set out in the Report of the Civil Rights Commission of its hearings held in New Orleans in 1960 and 1961.

of possible economic retaliation against anyone who serviced Mr. Atlas. The ginner asked:

Where defendants are in the same business, in order to protect them in the operation of their business with their other customers, there has been discussed the possibility of share and share alike, which with reference to the hauling problem, could be a little complicated. Is it satisfactory with the court that we work that out ourselves in good faith?

The judge assured them that a good faith, non-prejudicial agreement was the object. Dawkins then stated that reaching such agreements in an amicable manner was always the "general philosophy" of his court," so that this Court would not be in the position of having to force anybody to do anything." He then reiterated that the United States had demonstrated as far as he was concerned that its purpose was not punitive but merely to provide relief for Atlas.

Attorney John Doar re-emphasized that point at the conference. He likewise stated that the government merely wanted to assure "that come next fall when Mr. Atlas takes his crops to market, he can get to market in the ordinary course of business. I understand you people indicated you will see that that happened, and that is fine with us." Doar was talking about Atlas's 1961 crop, and since the agreement specifically mentioned only the 1960 crop, he wanted the record to show that the government's concern was not confined to one-season relief.

That this agreement was not a decision of the case on the merits was pointed out by Judge Dawkins, and the stipulation "in no way prejudices these defendants from raising legal defenses further down the line, if that becomes necessary, and I hope it will not." He made this statement at the request of the attorney of one of the defendants. Dawkins then said on this point:

For your information, the Court has formed no set opinion one way or the other as to whether this section of the Act [1971b] is applicable or not, or is unconstitutional. We will keep our mind open in that respect. We wanted all of you to know that, because that, I am sure, is one of the reasons for the stipulation having been entered into. I think both sides have been well represented by counsel, and I am very happy we have worked it out on this basis. I hope this is the last we hear of this, except to dismiss the suit.

The conference ended with an attorney for the defendants restating, as he put it for "caution and clarity," that the agreement in no way obligated any specific defendant to perform any specific act, "but his obligation under the good faith arrangement is to see to it, by all defendants working together, that the man is provided the service he needs, provided it is in the normal course of business and he can pay the normal, usual price for it."

Once again the case was not decided on its merits and it did not provide a full test of the new provision—Section 1971(b). What constituted an actual economic reprisal in interference with voting rights remained to be adjudicated, although in the specific instances examined in this study (and the only ones filed in court, incidentally) the victimized blacks received relief.

We have seen in these cases as well as with those handled by Judge Johnson that the apparatus of the new civil rights laws had been used to accomplish the desired ends, although the specific prescriptions of those laws were not invoked. Blacks were registered under Judge Johnson without voter referees, and the blacks in Tennessee and the one black farmer in Louisiana received relief without an actual determination under Section 1971(b). Some of the proponents of a judicial approach argued that the courts were capable of such operation. Those who opposed the judicial approach were probably convinced that significant solutions could not result from a reliance on the courts' equitable powers or on the informal arrangements worked out under the supervision of the courts. It may be that this method has more to recommend it than may appear at first glance. It may be tactically wise to enact relatively wide legal powers and remedies, and thereby provide room for maneuver and manipulation by those who have to enforce the laws.

To Hire and Fire: The Mississippi Schoolteacher

Mrs. Ernestine Denham Talbert was a thirty-three-year-old native Mississippian, a resident of George County, a teacher by profession, mother of one son, and a holder of a B.S. degree from Alcorn A & M College in Mississippi. She had six hours of graduate work in business education at the University of Minnesota and eighteen hours in library science at Jackson State College in Jackson, Mississippi. Mrs. Talbert had taught in the Mississippi public school system for ten years prior to 1962 when the events in this case took place. She normally taught commerce courses and served as school librarian. She was employed as a new teacher at the Greene County Vocational High School in this dual capacity under a one-year contract in September 1961. All the teachers, returning and new, were hired on one-year contracts. There were twenty-two teachers in all.

Mrs. Talbert, her husband (a brickmason), and son lived in adjoining George County. She commuted to her job daily.

On January 6, 1962, at 11:30 a.m., Mr. and Mrs. Talbert went to the registrar's office in George County to make applications for voter certificates. There were several other black applicants in the office filling out registration forms at the time. They were told to return after lunch and did so at 2 p.m. The registrar, a Mr. Green, gave them the application forms and the oath, and he asked Mrs. Talbert to read and interpret Section 50 of the Mississippi constitution. She gave her interpretation of the statute. Mr. Green then asked if they knew their county officials. Mr. Talbert began to name them. The registrar then asked if they knew the fifteen members of the election commission, the group that determined the eligibility of applicants for registration. They did not know those members. Mr. Green then asked several questions connected with the election commission, the answers to which the Talberts did not have. Green then advised them that there was "a lot to voting that people don't realize." At that point, he told them that the election commission, after its meeting in March 1962 would inform them if they were qualified to vote.

The Talberts waited until April 2 and returned to the George County registrar's office to inquire about the status of their application. There was another black couple present for the same purpose. The registrar informed them that he had given their applications to the election commission, but the commission wanted to talk to them personally. Mr. Green indicated that he could register persons whom he personally knew, but otherwise the applicants had to meet with the commission. Mrs. Talbert asked him if this was the normal procedure. The registrar replied, "If you want me to disprove of your application, I guarantee you I can do that. But I thought you were interested in becoming a registered voter." He then advised them that the commission would be in session again in August. The Talberts stated that they wanted to vote in the state primaries in June. The other black woman applicant then noticed a notation in a ledger on the counter that the commission would meet again on June 4.

On April 13, 1962, the United States filed a suit against the registrar of George County and the state of Mississippi under Section 1971(a) of 42 USC alleging denial of voting rights to blacks on account of their race.[25] The complaint charged racial discrimination in the registration process. Mrs. Talbert and five other blacks gave affidavits in that case attesting to their inability to become registered. On April 17 wide publicity was given to the suit in Mississippi newspapers and in the press of Mobile, Alabama. The names, addresses, and educational levels of the six blacks were published with the news stories. One week later, the

25. *U.S.* v. *Green et al.*, civil action no. 2540. There were 580 blacks of voting age in George County of whom ten were registered voters. Substantially all of the 5276 whites of voting age were registered.

press again published the identity of the blacks in connection with a temporary restraining order issued by the United States district court.

The established practice in the hiring and rehiring of teachers in Greene County where Mrs. Talbert was employed was for the principal of the school to make his recommendations to the superintendent of education of the county. If the superintendent approved the recommendations, he would, in turn, give the recommendations to the county board of education which had final approval. The superintendent, however, could refuse any recommendation given him by the principal and require the latter to make a new recommendation. The superintendent was under no obligation to account for his rejection either to the principal or to the person rejected.

On March 21, 1962, Mrs. Talbert's principal, a Mr. Macarthur Hayes, recommended all of the twenty-two teachers, including Mrs. Talbert, for re-employment for the 1962–63 school year. He submitted these recommendations in writing to the superintendent, Evans J. Martin. On April 25 at a special meeting of the board of education of Greene County, the superintendent overruled Hayes's recommendation of Mrs. Talbert and suggested to the board that she not be rehired for the 1962–63 school year. The remaining twenty-one teachers were approved. On the same day, Mr. Hayes informed Mrs. Talbert of the board's action. He stated, "Mrs. Talbert, the superintendent just called and told me he didn't accept my recommendation on you." Mrs. Talbert asked why. Hayes replied, "The superintendent didn't say why. He just said it was in the best interest of the school."

The following day Mrs. Talbert was in the principal's office on school business. Hayes stated, "Mrs. Talbert, I don't know how you feel about what happened yesterday, but I feel very bad about it. I recommended you. I recommended all of the teachers and all of them were accepted except you." Hayes said he could not give any reason for her release because he had never said anything unfavorable about her to the superintendent. He told her, "I think you have done a good job in your departments, and I'm satisfied with your work." He promised he would recommend her highly to any other prospective employer. Mrs. Talbert thanked him and left.

On Saturday, April 28, after she had learned that her teacher's contract would not be renewed, Mrs. Talbert returned to the registrar's office in George County and was successfully registered.

On June 16 the United States filed a suit against the board of education of Greene County, the board members, and the superintendent of education of Greene County under Section 1971(b) of 42 USC. The complaint alleged that the refusal to reappoint Mrs. Talbert as a teacher for the 1962–63 school year was directly connected with her activities relating to the voter registration effort in George County. Such a refusal, the government urged, was an attempt to intimidate, threaten, and coerce her and other blacks in their attempts to become registered and vote. The refusal to rehire her was not based on any consideration of her ability or performance as a teacher. Likewise, the United States contended, the refusal served as an obstruction to the work of the Department of Justice in the performance of its duty of prosecuting voting denials, inasmuch as the failure to rehire, if successful, would effectively deter other blacks from coming forth to attest to racial discrimination. The fear of losing their jobs or suffering some other form of economic retaliation would be too great. The government asked for a preliminary and permanent injunction against the defendants and requested the court to require the board of education of Greene County to offer Mrs. Talbert a contract of re-employment for the ensuing 1962–63 school year. The case was filed in Judge Cox's court at Hattiesburg, Mississippi.

Affidavits were taken from Mrs. Talbert, Evans J. Martin, the superintendent, and Macarthur Hayes, the principal. Martin stated in his affidavit that he personally investigated each new teacher hired for 1961–62. He said that his refusal to recommend Mrs.

Talbert for a new contract had nothing whatsoever to do with her efforts in connection with voter registration in George County. His observations of her led him to conclude that she "did not have good professional and social relations with some of the other teachers." His affidavit contained the following conclusions on which he based his decision:

She would not accept her responsibilities in extra-curricular activities such as home room teacher, and she complained if occasion arose when she had to stay at school other than her regular teaching hours to take part in school activities which are a necessary part of the duties and responsibilities of a teacher and a necessary part of an educational program and in the education of a child. The action of Ernestine Denham Talbert in not accepting her responsibilities as other teachers did caused dissension among some of the other teachers. Also, Ernestine Denham Talbert had very poor personal and social relations with the principal, Macarthur Hayes, toward the end of the school year.

Thus, Martin decided, if she were recommended by the principal, he would not concur. He insisted that while her involvement in the George County voter registration suit was known after Hayes recommended her and he heard about it "just prior to my recommendation to the board," this had no influence on his decision.

Undoubtedly, the role of the black principal would be important in a case of this nature. Black public school teachers, school principals, and county agents are not held in high esteem by many black social activists in the South. They are frequently referred to as "captive leaders." [26] They owe their jobs directly to a white-

26. See Daniel C. Thompson, *The Negro Leadership Class.* (Englewood Cliffs: Prentice-Hall, Inc., 1963.) In this case study of New Orleans, Thompson writes: "Depending as they do upon white officials, public school teachers have been greatly restricted in their leadership role. . . . Several laws passed by the Louisiana state legislature, as well as rules and regulations adopted by state and local school boards in recent years, have made it almost impossible for Negro teachers to identify with racial uplift organizations, or even to participate actively in the civil rights movement. This is definitely an important reason why some teachers have remained inactive and silent during heated controversies over civil rights"; p. 46.

controlled educational system, and yet in many instances, they are called upon by that system to serve as spokesmen for the black community. They generally say what their employers, who are segregationists, want and expect to hear. Obviously this image and, in most instances, accurate description angers and embarrasses some of the more militant teachers. There are, of course, several exceptions to this generalization. We have noted teachers and a principal serving as government witnesses in a voting discrimination case in Forrest County, Mississippi. One can only speculate as to why economic retaliation is not exerted against some of these activists. In some instances, it may be that the school board does not object and is able to protect the teachers from pressure from the white community. This requires a particular political situation in the county consisting of several factions, which is not too infrequent in some Southern counties. Another reason may be that the action-oriented teachers are relatively small in number and thus pose no major threat to the political status quo. In fact, such a situation could be advantageous, especially when local officials can reply that "we even have Negro teachers who vote and believe it or not, some of them belong to the NAACP."

Mrs. Talbert's principal gave an affidavit which read, in part:

Ernestine Denham Talbert came to me well recommended. However, during her employment for the 1961–62 school year, I had ample opportunity to observe her work, and found that she did not produce in her work to the extent that the other teachers of equal ability and training produced. Her classroom work was satisfactory. However, as a librarian, she was very lax on the job and did not perform her duties as she would have. After spending four hours per day in the library at the end of the school year, she still had not catalogued the library and only a few of the books were displayed in order. On one occasion during the 1961–62 school year, I instructed Mr. Randall, one of my male teachers, to assign home rooms to the teachers. When he assigned a room to Ernestine Denham Talbert, she became angry and did not speak to him for the balance of the school year, according to reports made to me by him. Toward the latter part of the 1961–62 school year—for about the last eight weeks, Ernestine Denham Talbert avoided me and I noticed a definite change in her attitude toward me.

When the time came to recommend new teachers, I recommended all the teachers. If there were any other teachers available to take the place of Ernestine Denham Talbert, I was not aware of it.

Mr. Hayes signed this affidavit on June 21, 1962, and he stated that at no time had the matter of voting activities of teachers been discussed between himself and the superintendent. He further indicated that this was not the first time a recommendation of his had been rejected by the superintendent. As we shall see, the statements in this affidavit are not entirely consistent with the principal's testimony given in open court just one month later.

The trial on the merits was held on July 25. At the outset, the defendants objected to the introduction of any documents relating to the George County case, but the court overruled the objections and permitted the government to introduce as exhibits the complaint in the George County case, Mrs. Talbert's affidavit in that case, and various other motions and orders.

Mrs. Talbert was the first witness. The attorney for the government, John Doar, questioned her extensively about her educational and teaching background. The defense attorney objected to questions relating to the condition of the library at the beginning of her employment in September 1961, but the court allowed the line of inquiry to help establish what Mrs. Talbert had done in her capacity as school librarian. The school had never had a librarian, so Mrs. Talbert had to set up an entirely new library. This consisted of ordering supplies, getting the vocational agriculture teacher to build new shelves, cataloguing all the books, and discarding old textbooks. Doar was attempting to establish that in fact she was not, as the principal stated in his affidavit, lax in her duties as librarian. There was detailed testimony in the trial record about purchase orders for library supplies, her typing ability, her duties as a home-room teacher for sixty-three pupils, her job as occasional clerical assistant for the principal, as well as her duties as keeper of the lunchroom records and various funds relating to athletic events throughout the school year.

Doar had to ask Mrs. Talbert repeatedly to speak louder so that everyone in the courtroom could hear. At one point, Judge Cox interrupted her testimony and said, "I can't understand about half you're saying. If you're trying to keep it a secret from me you're succeeding admirably. I can't understand your enunciation at all." Mrs. Talbert testified that neither Hayes nor Martin had visited her classroom during the entire year, and neither had spoken to her regarding their dissatisfaction with her work in the library.

Finally, Doar questioned her about her voter registration efforts in George County and about her conversation with the principal in the latter's office the day following the board's refusal to renew her contract. Her testimony read:

> Hayes said, "I feel awful about it," he said, "I didn't sleep last night for thinking about it." He said, "Why didn't you tell me about this?" And I told him because I knew he would object and he said, "Well, I can't swear that that was why you were fired, but I don't know of any other reason. . . . I believe you have done a good job in your department." And he said he wished he had all teachers like me.

The principal did not specify his reference when he spoke of telling him "about this."

The government's next witness was the principal. In addition to describing his duties and the general operation of the school, his testimony continued:

Doar: Now, Mr. Hayes, have you had an opportunity to examine and review the work that Mrs. Talbert did in the library last year?

Hayes: Well, I had an opportunity to examine if after school.

Doar: What did you find?

Hayes: Well, in the outset, I was of the opinion that Mrs. Talbert's work had not come up to par, but in all fairness I talked to a lady who had been in the business a number of years, Mrs. T. C. Rounsaville. And I told her what had been done and what I had expected, and her answer was that she thought Mrs. Talbert had done about as much as could be expected of a teacher over that period of time. I said to her, "Well, I'd have to back your judgment—let your judgment be here and not mine." And she said, "Well, I think she has done enough here now to justify that." In fact, I made a statement to that effect, but I would have to decline after finding that I was wrong, because I don't want to falsely accuse anybody.

Doar: Did you ever discuss with Mr. Martin prior to April 25th anything about Mrs. Talbert's performance in the library?

Hayes: Let me see, I believe I did.

Doar: Well, did you make any complaint about her work?

Hayes: Seems that I was still complaining at that time.

Doar: What were the circumstances of that?

Hayes: That I can't recall.

Doar: When was the discussion?

Hayes: I couldn't be specific of the date.

At the close of all testimony, a colloquy developed between Judge Cox and Doar which highlighted the fundamental difference in their respective approaches to the case. The government, according to Cox, was in essence asking the court to require the board of education of Greene County to enter into a contract with Mrs. Talbert. Courts over the centuries had consistently refused to make contracts for parties. They simply interpreted contract rights of agreements parties made with each other. There may have been "indirect implications, involvements, or coincidental things" as a result of the refusal to contract, but these were not sufficient to require the court to rule for the government. It was clear to Judge Cox that this was a matter of private contract rights "where the situation simply, incidentally, affects the civil rights area." By asking that the court compel the defendants to make a contract with the teacher, the United States was seeking mandatory relief. Cox understood the civil rights acts to provide only preventive relief. Mrs. Talbert had a one-year contract; she fully performed, and was fully paid. She had no vested right to a new contract. "Now what right does somebody else have to come in here—the United States or anbody else—and assert some vested right when there is no existence of any such vested right even on her part if she were suing? That's the question that's in my mind," Cox stated.

John Doar argued that the interest of the United States was not solely that Mrs. Talbert be given a job for the next year, but that all citizens had the right freely to vote. Not giving her a new contract was an act of intimidation and retaliation for her registration activities.

The court reminded government counsel that Mrs. Talbert's position had been filled by a new appointment for the coming year. This would make preventive relief difficult. And then the court talked about the connection between Mrs. Talbert's involvement in the voter registration suit in George County and the subsequent refusal to renew her contract. Judge Cox said:

Now you say that there's some question in evidence here about whether these defendants were to some extent influenced. And I say at least to some extent. But they probably were influenced by the fact that she was participating in some litigation which had some effects which were not regarded as too wholesome, particularly when this school board looked unfavorably on all kinds of litigation, even debt litigation and had gone so far as not to renew contracts I believe of two teachers in a prior year who were involved or would be involved in some litigation. And they didn't consider that in the interest of the school.

Thus, although the defendants swore under oath they were not influenced by the George County suit, Judge Cox concluded otherwise, but offered grounds or justification for the defendants.

Doar argued that preventive relief meant to put a stop to further acts of intimidation, and it seemed unfair for the court to contend that it could do nothing since she was discharged and someone else hired in her place.

For all practical purposes, the colloquy and the case ended when Judge Cox interrupted Doar and admonished:

Mr. Doar, you don't seem to get the impact of what I'm saying. You keep using the word "discharge." If she were discharged, you'd have

a very much stronger case here. She wasn't discharged. She filled her
contract. She simply wasn't rehired and you're just trying to get the
Court to rehire her.

The court entered its final order dismissing the complaint on
August 29 on the grounds that the plaintiff had failed to show a
connection between the board's refusal to rehire Mrs. Talbert and
her voter registration activities. The formal opinion was largely a
reiteration and elaboration of the points made by the judge in the
discussion with Doar in open court. The opinion nowhere mentioned the Beaty case, but there was discussion of it in court. Cox
expressed an interest in what the Court of Appeals for the sixth
circuit had to say on the matter of the district court not making
contracts for private parties. Doar took the opportunity to sum-
marize the Beaty case for the court, "inasmuch as I just finished
working on that case up in Tennessee." When the Court of Appeals stated that the district court did not err in not ordering the
landlords to enter into contracts with the tenants, this, according
to Doar, was perfectly understandable, "because effective relief
could be made or accomplished without such an order because
the tenants were still on the land and because, for the second
reason, it was a preliminary injunction." Doar went to considerable
lengths in explaining the Beaty case in his summation. Counsel for
the defendants emphasized that the Beaty case was not an authority for ordering parties to make contracts, because that order was
not a hearing on the merits, as the appellate court clearly pointed
out.

The government filed notice of appeal in December 1962, and
the case was argued before the appellate court on April 3, 1963.
The Court of Appeals supported Judge Cox in 1964.[27]

Some Justice Department lawyers were not particularly san-
guine about the possibility of winning these cases. One attorney
observed that a case like the Talbert one was much more difficult

27. 332 Fed. 2d. 40 (1964).

to prove because only one person on each side was involved. It was easier to prove an unconstitutional motive when a large number was involved—statements were made, meetings held. One lawyer for the Justice Department expressed the difficulty, frustration, and impatience of others when these situations arose:

In Dallas County [Alabama] thirty-six teachers were fired after we went in and investigated. **Jet, Afro-American** and the **Courier** [black magazine and newspapers] and places like that are overzealous in drawing inferences. But these things are very difficult to prove. Only four of those teachers were connected with voter registration directly. Now, it's difficult to single out these four and say the firing was for voting and the thirty-two were not. My opinion is that the firing of most of the thirty-two was to keep from paying them full retirement benefits since most of them were rather old and near retirement. This was not legitimate in any mind, but it was not connected with voting either.[28]

The department had been criticized by some Southern black voter registration workers, especially the Student Non-Violent Coordinating Committee, for what the latter considered to be laxness in prosecution and catering to local white sentiment. Justice officials invariably answered that legal proof acceptable in court was a much greater requirement than "those on the front line" could sometimes appreciate.

28. Interview at Justice Department.

9 White Judges and Black Ballots: Some Observations

The material presented in this study has shown that many of the apprehensions toward utilizing the federal courts were not justified. Judge Frank M. Johnson's handling of the voting cases in Macon, Bullock, and Montgomery counties was anything but slow, reactive, passive, or negative. True, he was reluctant to appoint voter referees where he had made a finding of a "pattern and practice" of racial discrimination, but this reluctance stemmed not from the nature of the judicial process, but rather from Judge Johnson's persistent efforts to accomplish the goals of the law without imposing what he considered more federal authority over local officials than necessary. This restraint was a judicious consideration of local attitudes without doing injury to the basic purposes of the law. He did not tolerate long delays, and the number of blacks registered by him or as a result of his firm orders was not inconsequential.

I categorized Johnson as an aggressive judge largely because he took the initiative in a manner that some critics of the judicial approach did not visualize. He issued orders of a positive nature, and he established procedures to determine if those orders were being implemented. He provided alternative ways of action to both the old and newly concocted practices of the registrars. In other words, he did more than reconcile, caution, and suggest by implication, as one commentator predicted. The fact is that those who predicted that "judicial decisions here [in the field of voting rights] . . . are not likely to make any major departure from the norms of the community" were too pessimistic as the significant results in Alabama have shown. Granted, Johnson's court possessed no "self-starter," but there is validity in stating that once a case or several cases had been tried and decided in his court, a pattern was established that had considerable repercussions for the other counties in his judicial district. Couple this pattern with a strong inclination on the part of the Department of Justice to push the starter button, and one found a combination that added up to the effective elimination of many, if not most, of the obstacles to black voting.

One could conclude from the cases examined in this study that, as one observer noted, "the willingness of the federal judge to carry out the law" was more important to the success of the judicial approach than the "inherent complex nature of the judicial process." At least this criterion was centrally important in dealing with the discriminatory tactics of local registrars. There was little complexity involved in the Alabama cases. Judge Johnson simply did not permit innumerable motions on the part of the state—motions that compounded the cumbersome process and contributed to endless delays.

One critic of the judicial approach feared that such an approach would not be sufficient to "go into the backwoods" to get blacks to come to the registrars' offices. One could question whether this specific function was the responsibility of government. Perhaps the mere removal of obstacles was all that could be expected of federal legislation and implementation. A strong case could be made that it was incumbent upon the blacks themselves—specifically the black leadership groups—to perform the task of encouraging and directing black citizens to register.

The Trial Situation as Impetus

Another aspect of this phenomenon must not be overlooked. While the judiciary could go out to solicit prospective black registrants, the judicial approach did have an effect not mentioned by the critics in 1957 and 1960. Many black Southern leaders will attest to what they call the "booster effect" of the filing of a federal suit. Dr. Aaron Henry of Clarksdale, Mississippi, president of the state NAACP and a long-time worker for voter registration in the Mississippi delta counties, was fond of describing what he called a theory of federal presence, "It's important to establish the fact that if constitutional rights continue to be violated, then the federal government will step in. This encourages the Negroes and it puts the whites on notice." Many black people in the South believed that two factors were central to their struggle for civil rights—widespread publicity of the injustices and federal intervention. In the right-to-vote field, that intervention was felt most strongly in a lawsuit filed by the Justice Department. When department investigators came to town and local registrars were forced to answer questions in open court, black citizens saw that they were not alone in competing against an almost impregnable wall of Southern white resistance. This was especially utilized by voter registration workers, who then had an answer when blacks asked "What's the use?"

Attorney David L. Norman of the Justice Department used the trial situation for another, but related, purpose. He gave the following description:

I have a technique I use and I used it in the Madison Parish, Louisiana case. I got the registrar on the stand and the galleries were packed with Negro leaders in the county. So I asked her questions for the benefit of the Negroes. Questions like: Now what are your office hours? What days are you in your office? Now just what do you require of persons who come in to make application to register? etc. And the Negroes are sitting right there and they leave the courtroom armed with all that information. Plus, you see, I purposely ask the registrar if she intends to register all persons who come in and who are qualified.

Now, we just recently tried that case before Judge Dawkins and he is nowhere near a decision, but the next week seventy Negroes were registered. I expect they'll get a thousand Negroes registered in that Parish and it won't make much difference what sort of ruling we get from Dawkins.[1]

This, again, is an illustration of the executive branch working in conjunction with the judiciary to provide a kind of self-starting mechanism. All the results of the judicial approach did not have to come from specific action of the judges alone. As was noted at the beginning of this study, the orientation and actions of the executive branch, specifically the Department of Justice, were very important in contributing to the success or failure of this approach.

Can one say that community pressures against black voting deterred judicial action? There is no evidence to substantiate this conclusion. In fact, one can conclude that these community pressures either did not exist or were ineffective in Judge Johnson's district. There is evidence that he received public support from leading local newspapers, notwithstanding their basic rejection of federal intervention. Perhaps this was due to a belief on the part of some Southern opinion leaders that the right to vote stood apart from some other aspects of the race relations revolution enveloping the South. This recognition may have stemmed from the fact that the constitutional prohibition against racial discrimination in voting was more explicit than, say, the desegregation of public schools, or it may have stemmed from the fact that Congress, and not the Supreme Court, was the source of the guides set up for the lower federal courts to follow. Both of these factors may have been operative.

In an earlier chapter I cited the editorial reaction of the *Birmingham News* to Judge Johnson's order in Montgomery County wherein he personally registered over 1000 blacks. Other leading

1. Interview at Justice Department, January 1963.

Alabama newspapers editorialized in favor of equitable voting practices. On February 2, 1960, Alabama's *Lee County Bulletin* commented on the proposal to provide federal registrars:

It is simply a bill drawn by the attorney general and approved by the
President which rescues thousands of colored voter applicants from
a hopeless situation. Nothing is to be gained by crying foul. It is true
that this matter ought to be handled by the states. But the states have
failed to act fairly and honorably. Alabama, along with several others,
has asked for what it is getting. At the time of the Civil Rights Commission hearings in Alabama last year, this paper pleaded that Alabama officials ought to act in good faith in this matter of registering
voter applicants regardless of race or color.

On May 17, 1960, one of the two major daily newspapers in Alabama, the *Montgomery Advertiser,* editorialized:

Negro voting and Negroes butting their way into white schools where
they are not wanted are organically different matters. It's not a federal dispensation, but the **law of Alabama enacted by Alabamians** that
qualified Negroes are entitled to vote. Qualified Negroes are entitled
legally and morally to vote.
Qualified Negroes are going to vote in Alabama and the south in
growing numbers. Some unhappy consequences undoubtedly will attend this condition; they will surely vote in blocs for an indeterminate
period, though finally the bloc will fragment like any other group vote.

The Fate of Registration Obstacles

The material in this study leads to the conclusion that the federal
courts virtually nullified all possible legal means to deter black
voting. The term "legal" is used here to denote the duly-constituted
agencies of the state whose function it is to register all qualified
persons without regard to race, color, or previous condition of
servitude. Various devices concocted by state legislatures and local
registrars either met their death or their demise was not far off.
In those areas where applicants were required to interpret constitutional sections, the courts either insisted that this requirement

be administered indiscriminately or, if the evidence showed that the statute was being unfairly administered, declared it void.

The greatest problem with these legal barriers lay in those areas where judicial resistors engaged in delaying tactics and weak court orders. But this was a matter of time, and presumably either higher court decisions or corrective congressional legislation or both would help bring recalcitrant Southern federal judges into line. Southern federal courts—aggressors, resistors, and gradualists—continued to show great sympathy for the feelings of local registrars. Everything possible was done to permit the registrars to continue operating the registration process themselves, but one could also expect aggressive jurists like Johnson to continue to prod slow-moving registrars. One did not find large-scale appointment of voter referees, but if the judge chose to assume the task of a vigorous overseer, this was not necessary.

Judge Johnson's actions showed that many, if not all, of the objections to the judicial approach were not valid. Blacks in large numbers were registered through the Southern federal court.

It is no valid argument that many of these blacks were not qualified to vote under state literacy laws, because the simple fact was that on the whole they were just as qualified as most of the whites who were registered. And if the Justice Department could persuade the courts (as it did in Bullock and Montgomery counties) that the previous standards applicable to whites were the standards that should be applied to blacks, then not very many black people would be unable to qualify. This was an interesting result of past Southern attitudes and practices that had as its practical manifestation the belief that the least prepared white person outranked the vast majority of blacks. It is no argument to state that because they were perhaps illiterate, neither should vote. The fact is that this society has decided that notwithstanding other requirements and qualifications, racial identity should not be a factor in granting or withholding the privilege to vote, and this was the sole issue before the courts in these cases.

The aggressor judge in these voting rights cases saw his role more as an enforcer, an overseer. It did not take much to convince him that registrars were discriminating on the basis of race, and he was concerned largely with prodding the registrar to mend his own ways. The resistor, on the other hand, approached these cases more as a judge would hear a criminal case. The defendant was clearly innocent until absolutely proven guilty beyond a reasonable doubt. The process then was slow and deliberate; the judge sifted through the facts.

The judicial aggressor emphasized the comparatively equal abilities of those blacks rejected and those whites accepted. If the evidence showed the former equal to the latter, then the blacks must be registered. The judicial resistor talked about how he knew for a fact that most blacks were inferior to most whites and this broad generalization along with other stereotyped ideas influenced his judgment in disposing of particular black applicants before him.

The judicial aggressor did not talk about the political consequences of wholesale black voting, while this factor was obviously uppermost in the mind of the judicial resistor. The latter feared that blacks would bloc-vote and that this would be an uninformed, unsophisticated vote, so the resistor applied as many tactics as possible to forestall this event or to mitigate it by issuing weak decrees.

The judicial gradualist presented different characteristics. He had the fears of black bloc voting possessed by the resistor, but he ordered the blacks registered and hoped for the best. In short, he seemed to share the social and political opinions of the resistor, but he tended to reach the results of the aggressor. He did not like the particular law, but he abided by it because he respected the law. He did not engage in the various delaying tactics of the resistor. In all likelihood, if the cases coming before the gradualist constantly concerned blatant examples of racial discrimination, there was a good possibility that this type of judge would become an aggressor. He would do so not so much to protect blacks but to maintain and protect the integrity of the law he was called upon to apply. Certainly one important factor in the development of this type of judge was the extent to which the Justice Department could work with him and "bring him along."

The Department of Justice continued to attempt to "train" the judges in a point of view more compatible with the intent of the Civil Rights Acts of 1957 and 1960. This matter of influence was not entirely a one-way street, however. As indicated earlier in the chapter dealing with Judge Johnson's actions in Alabama, the Department of Justice was definitely influenced by Johnson's predilections in disposing of the cases. The department came to recognize that he was not prone to appoint voter referees but rather preferred to give specific standards to guide the registrars. Subsequently, in the third case filed before Johnson, the department did not bother to request the appointment of voter referees, but asked instead that the court set up standards similar to those applied in Bullock County. This is what Burke Marshall meant when he wrote:

While it is still too early to write confidently of all these effects of a voting case, clearly the first case in a judicial district is educational for all concerned. The courts, we, and defense counsel know better the materials that will be subject matter of any subsequent controversies. We know each other, too.[2]

There is no positive evidence that the influence of the judges extended beyond this point. But frequently lawyers in the Justice Department commented on the necessity of understanding that such judges as Cox and Clayton were not entirely in accord with the purpose of the civil rights laws. This meant that the government lawyers simply had to expect the delaying orders, the motions to make more definite, and the "weak" orders. One did not receive the impression from talking to these lawyers that they were influenced by these views. Indeed, as was shown in the Mississippi cases, the appellate briefs of the United States clearly indicated steadfast disagreement with the positions of the district court judges. Aside from the prob-

2. News release of Southern Regional Council in March 1963.

lem of how to deal with the registrars once a finding of a pattern and practice of discrimination was established, as in Alabama, one could conclude that the Justice Department had not been influenced by the judges. A clear illustration of this was found in the reaction of one government lawyer, noted earlier, to Judge Cox's ruling in the Jefferson Davis County, Mississippi, case. He stated: "I believe Judge Cox wanted to simply create another delaying device."

On what issues could the judge attempt to exert his influence? Would the existence or nonexistence of discrimination be such an issue? Judge Johnson found the evidence to be "abundantly clear" that discrimination existed. The government lawyers in the Mississippi cases were convinced that the documented data in the counties in that state were no less compelling. Should the Justice Department be influenced by the bloc-vote fears of Cox, Clayton, and Dawkins? Should they, as a result of these fears, drop the prosecution of some cases where such a bloc vote might materialize? The proper answer, it seemed, and the one adopted by the United States government is that these considerations had no place in proceedings before the courts under the civil rights laws. Given the clear, fundamental purpose of the laws—the elimination of race as a factor in determining voter qualifications—it was difficult to perceive any legitimate grounds, aside from that referred to in connection with Johnson, for attempted influence of the Justice Department. It was not the function of the government as plaintiff or the judges as triers of fact to debate the wisdom of the laws. As was pointed out, that judgment had been made, and whatever debate proceeded on this subject was more properly conducted in places other than in a trial court where the issue before the court was one simply of racial discrimination.

There was one area where one might suggest that the government's views could have been influenced by the judges. That concerned the problem of intimidation. By bringing the action in the case of the Mississippi school teacher, was the Justice Department going too far and thus infringing on the contract rights of the school board? In its action to halt the eviction of the Tennessee sharecroppers, was the government invading the property rights of the landlords? And the same question was applicable to the case involving the Louisiana farmer who testified before the Civil Rights Commission. In the briefs and arguments of the specific cases reported, there is no indication that the government was so influenced. And in interviews with the government lawyers, one did not receive the impression of any such influence. Indeed, the only conclusion drawn by most of the lawyers was that "these are very tough cases." The fact was that where the Department of Justice had not been convinced by the available evidence that a strong case of intimidation based on race could not be made, it refused to prosecute. This was shown by the statement of one government lawyer cited earlier concerning the firing of thirty-six black teachers in Dallas County, Alabama. The evidence simply was not strong enough to show a connection with voting. Admittedly, this left the Department of Justice in the middle, accused by black leaders of laxness in prosecution and by Southern spokesmen of federal intervention. This was never a preferred position, but it was an unavoidable one faced by a government agency sensitive to the rigorous requirements of the legal profession.

10 The Voting Rights Act of 1965 and Beyond

Protest and Politics

In the Preface to this book, the observation was made that the Voting Rights Act of 1965 was not enacted in a political vacuum. Thus far, we have examined the tedious work of the Southern federal courts in dealing with the civil rights laws. Now it is important to link that story to the period immediately following and to describe the political action that led to the Civil Rights Law of 1964 and the Voting Rights Act of 1965. The final section of this chapter will briefly describe the progress that has been made in registering black citizens throughout the South and particularly in the specific counties covered in this study. In addition, attention will be paid to some major problems that still persist in 1973, sixteen years after the Civil Rights Act of 1957.

On February 28, 1963, President Kennedy submitted a relatively mild message to Congress that called for continuation of the Commission on Civil Rights and the tightening of loopholes in previous laws in regard to voting rights. But shortly afterwards, the country began to experience one of the most dramatic and sustained periods of civil rights protest in its history. Blacks and whites began to demonstrate in Birmingham, Alabama. The protests dealt mainly with legal segregation and discriminatory employment practices in that city, but protest demonstrations spread throughout the country, sometimes in sympathy with the Alabama protests and sometimes directed against segregation and discrimination in the particular indigenous area, North as well as South. In less than six months, demonstrations had occurred in approximately 800 cities and towns, and these reached a climax on August 28, 1963, with a march on Washington in which roughly 200,000 people participated.

Many people have suggested, and probably correctly, that what had come to be called "the civil rights movement" reached its peak in mobilization, visibility, and effectiveness during that "simmering summer of '63."

On June 13, 1963, Kennedy amended his proposals of the previous February and asked the Congress to pass a much more comprehensive law covering voting and segregation in places of public accommodations. In July a provision concerning fair employment practices was added. There is little doubt that this change in the President's legislative plans was an immediate result of the growing direct-action protest movements by civil rights groups across the country.

One of the major fights developed over the section concerning public accommodations. What would be the constitutional basis for congressional prohibition of racial discrimination in hotels, motels, restaurants, and similar places? Some argued that the time was ripe to base the provision on the Fourteenth Amendment; others (civil rights groups and the Department of Justice) advocated the "commerce clause": in other words, these places could be considered as doing business that affected interstate commerce, and therefore subject to congressional regulation.

Another crisis centered on fair employment. What businesses should be covered? Should there be such a provision in the bill at all? The Kennedy administration objected to including it, fearing it would weaken the chances for passage of the rest of the bill. The civil rights groups insisted on its inclusion as constituting a mean-ingful response to some of the major disadvantages confronting blacks. The House Judiciary Subcommittee added a proposal "that Congress empower the Attorney General to intervene in or to ini-tiate civil proceedings to prevent denials to persons of any rights, privileges or immunities secured to them by the Constitution of the United States."

After the assassination of President Kennedy, Congressman Howard Smith's Rules Committee appeared to be delaying the bill, and a discharge petition was attempted. President Lyndon B. John-son called for action. Smith announced in December 1963 that he would hold hearings on the bill "reasonably soon in January." After extended hearings in that committee, the bill went to the House floor, where debate was held for an unprecedented nine days. More than a hundred amendments were proposed, most of them aimed at crippling or weakening the bill. All but a very few were defeated.

The political forces and strategies of the civil rights proponents were more organized than ever before. Unlike the situation in 1960, the liberals had their leaders, mapped their plans, and literally manned their posts. The major groups were the Leadership Con-ference on Civil Rights, consisting of major black organizations; the big industrial unions of the AFL–CIO, led by the United Auto Workers; Protestant, Catholic, and Jewish church groups; liberal congressmen in the House Democratic Study Group (DSG); the White House; the Department of Justice; and a small band of Re-publican congressmen known as the Republican Legislative Re-search Association.

When key votes were taken on the floor, the lobbyists had spot-ters in the galleries to check the presence and performance of con-gressmen. The DSG instituted its "buddy system," whereby each of twenty members was assigned five or six congressmen and checked on their attendance and how they voted. The DSG had congressmen stationed at the head of the teller line on the House floor to see who voted. One account of the tactics was as follows:

Whenever a crisis arose over an amendment, a signal would be made from one of the two DSG leaders on the House floor. [Representative Frank] Thompson [New Jersey] or Representative Bolling, Democrat of Missouri, and the Justice Department, civil rights groups and labor leaders in the galleries would come down for a strategy conference off the floor. . . .

At the start of each day of the debates, basic strategy and planning meetings were held, first of the entire Leadership Conference on Civil Rights and then, in Mr. Thompson's office, of the key civil rights and union operatives together with Justice and White House representatives.[1]

The bill passed the House in February 1964 by a vote of 290 to 130.

Democratic Majority Leader Mike Mansfield of the Senate announced that he would propose that the bill be placed on the Senate calendar "without referral to committee," that is, Senator Eastland's Judiciary Committee, the traditional graveyard of many civil rights bills. This passed by a respectable vote of 54 to 37. It was then clear that the liberals held commanding power. The tide had turned. The Southerners began a filibuster in March 1964, but this time there was a difference. Instead of letting the opposition talk unceasingly, the bill's proponents decided to answer the arguments point for point. Debate, frequently repetitive, droned on for seventy-five days, and it became clear that only a vote of cloture would end the filibuster, a vote which had never been successful in congressional struggles concerning civil rights. On June 10, 1964 the Senate, for the first time in history, invoked cloture to limit debate on a civil rights bill. The vote was 71 to 29. The Senate subsequently passed an amended bill. It went back to the House for quick approval (how different from 1957!), and on July 2, 1964, President Johnson signed the bill.

The new law had a provision to speed up trials alleging denial of the vote; it prohibited racial discrimination in places of public accommodation; the Attorney General was empowered to sue to

1. *The Washington Star,* February 16, 1964.

desegregate schools (a provision that failed to pass in 1957). Federal funds to local areas could be cut off if racial discrimination was practiced. There was a provision prohibiting discrimination by employers or unions with more than a hundred workers, this to be scaled down to twenty-five workers by 1968. And the law established a mediating agency, the Community Relations Service, for communities involved in racial problems.

Thus, within a span of seven years, the Congress and the country had moved to a point where legislative responsibility for civil rights was recognized and accepted.

In the latter months of 1964 the general thinking among many civil rights leaders and liberal congressmen was that no new significant civil rights legislation would be proposed in the next Congress. "We will spend our time," one civil rights lobbyist said in November 1964, "seeing if the present legislation can be made to work." But just as Birmingham and subsequent events had changed legislative plans in 1963, Selma, Alabama, was the dramatic protest catalyst in 1965 that led to a new law on voting rights.

Dallas County (Selma) was in the jurisdiction presided over by Federal District Court Judge Daniel H. Thomas. Unlike his colleague, Frank M. Johnson, in the adjoining district, Thomas was not willing to impose strict enforcement procedures on a new board. He readily admitted that the board of registrars that operated in Dallas County up to 1961, did so in a racially discriminatory manner. But in January 1961 a new board was appointed and it proceeded to apply very rigid standards to both races. As noted earlier, Johnson did not permit this device. Thomas, however, saw nothing wrong with this new method for Dallas County, and, in fact, suggested that the practice should be emulated throughout the United States. The net effect, of course, was to frustrate and slow up, if not entirely impede, the registration process.

Dr. Martin Luther King, Jr., and his organization, the Southern Christian Leadership Conference (SCLC), began a series of mass protests in Selma to highlight the frustrations and aimed at getting

Congress to enact a more effective law protecting voting rights. The mass demonstrations attracted world-wide attention, and they were marked by violence on the part of local white citizens and officials against the protesters.

A twenty-six-year-old Selma black man, Jimmie Lee Jackson, died on February 26, 1965, from wounds allegedly inflicted eight days before by Alabama state troopers. A thirty-eight-year-old white Unitarian minister from Boston, the Reverend James J. Reeb, died March 11 of skull fractures received from a beating by local whites in Selma on March 9. Approximately forty demonstrators were seriously injured by state troopers in an abortive protest march on March 7 when the troopers used tear gas, whips, and horses to break up a demonstration. All these violent events received nation-wide (in some instances, world-wide) publicity. A white housewife from Detroit, Mrs. Viola Liuzzo, was killed on a highway in neighboring Lowndes County. She had been transporting marchers from Montgomery back to Selma.

Tension was extremely high and sympathy was building throughout the country for legislation that once and for all would end denial of the right to vote. The Selma protests made it clear that no large number of black people would be registered quickly as long as the Southern federal courts were relied on to implement the process. Legislative activity focused on remedying this situation.

The liberals in Congress mobilized again. They had experience and a strong issue, but more important, they had the political strength, thanks to a landslide Johnson victory over Senator Barry Goldwater in the Presidential election of November 1964. Some of the previous methods were used, including the buddy system. One staff member of the DSG stated:

There were a few older members [of Congress] who resented the buddy system. They thought that the White House was working with us on the teller system, but this was not true. Some thought that the White House was using the names of those who did not vote to exact reprisals in the way of withholding patronage, projects, etc. This was not true, but they didn't know, and we really didn't say anything to discourage the rumor.[2]

There were, however, substantial differences in the politics of the 1965 bill from that of the 1964 law. According to Clarence Mitchell, many more pressure groups were actively involved in 1964 because that bill included more separate titles and people wanted to be sure that their particular interests were protected—voting, fair employment, public accommodations, education. The 1965 bill, by contrast, dealt only with voting and was more regional in its application. Another difference stemmed from the fact that the 1965 effort was mostly devoted to closing loopholes in voting legislation, whereas the 1964 law included new items altogether: a fair employment provision that the Kennedy administration at first did not intend to include; federal cut-off of funds to contractors who practiced discrimination, which the administration was willing to yield on if necessary in order to save the section on public accommodations. Pushing for a ban on state poll taxes was new in 1965, but basically, attention centered on taking the implementation of the right to vote out of the Southern federal courts. The new law accomplished that goal. In his testimony before the House Committee on the Judiciary, Attorney General Nicholas Katzenbach painted a record of low achievement by the Southern federal courts. He stated:

In Alabama, the number of Negroes registered to vote has increased by 5.2 between 1958 and 1964—to a total of 19.4 per cent of those eligible by age and residence. . . .

In Mississippi, the number of Negroes registered to vote has increased at an even slower rate. In 1954, about 4.4 per cent of the eligible Negroes were registered; today, we estimate the figure at about 6.4 per cent. . . .

And, in Louisiana, Negro registration has not increased at all, or if at

2. Interview with Mr. William G. Phillips, Staff Director of the Democratic Study Group, Washington, D.C., October 12, 1965.

all, imperceptibly. In 1956, 31.7 per cent of the eligible Negroes were registered. As of January 1, 1965, the per cent was 31.8.[3]

On August 6, 1965, President Johnson signed into law the Voting Rights Act of 1965. The major provisions of the law were as follows:

1. The Attorney General could send voting examiners into a state or political subdivision to register all persons they found qualified to vote.

2. Examiners could be sent into any area where the Attorney General determined that a literacy test or similar device was used as a qualification for voting on November 1, 1964 and the Director of the Census determined that less than fifty per cent of the persons of voting age residing in the area were registered to vote on that date or actually voted in the 1964 presidential election.

3. Literacy tests or similar voter qualification devices would be suspended when the Attorney General and Director of the Census determined that a state or political subdivision came within the coverage of the law as spelled out in the previous paragraph.

4. New voting laws enacted by state or local governments whose voter qualification laws had been nullified under the bill would be approved by the Attorney General or federal courts before they could take effect.

Clarence Mitchell pointed out the significance of the intervening Presidential and congressional elections of 1964. He said:

Meanwhile, there had been an election. Many people who had been in congress in '64 who were question marks—therefore we had to work hard to answer those question marks—were not present in '65. The state of Iowa is a good illustration of that. All of the Iowa House delegation with the exception of congressman Gross went out of office in '64. And of those who were replaced, we got their votes alright in '64, but in many instances there were question marks about what they would do. In '65 there were no question marks, because these people

3. U.S. Congress, House Committee on the Judiciary, Hearings, Voting Rights, 89th Congress, 1st Session, 1965, p. 4.

had run on commitments to support the principle of civil rights. Also they were administration stalwarts.[4]

Virtually no stone was left unturned in persuading congressmen to vote for either the 1964 or 1965 bills. At one point in the 1965 struggle, the black congressman from Detroit, Charles Diggs, who was chairman of the Civil Rights Committee of the DSG, held a luncheon for the Michigan Democratic delegation to which he invited Clarence Mitchell. All of the congressmen generally supported civil rights, but a few had doubts about certain provisions in the proposed bill. After a free exchange of views, they went along out of respect for the data and opinion of their colleague Diggs.

Many observers concluded in 1965 that although the Congress had not said all it could or would be called upon to say on civil rights and race relations, one very important factor had been established—it no longer was extraordinary to see the Congress act. It could and would act if the votes were there and if the President provided firm leadership.

Progress and Persistent Problems

The record of voter registration of black citizens in the South is not one of complete failure. As Tables II and III indicate, in the eleven Southern states, only two states, North Carolina and Tennessee, show a decline in the percentage of blacks registered from just prior to the passage of the Voting Rights Act of 1965 to 1971. Some states have shown rather dramatic increases: Alabama, from 19.3 per cent to 54.68 per cent; Arkansas, from 40.4 to 80.89; Georgia, from 27.4 to 64.24; Mississippi, from 6.7 to 59.37.

The country has begun to expect periodic reports of black political "firsts" in the South, such as a black mayor in a predominantly black town, a black sheriff, congressional representatives from Atlanta and Houston. These are clearly results of steady, persistent

4. Interview, Washington, D.C.

Table I

Voter Registration in the South*

STATE	WHITE VAP	BLACK VAP	WHITES REGISTERED	BLACKS REGISTERED	PER CENT WHITE VAP REGISTERED	PER CENT BLACK VAP REGISTERED
Alabama	1,353,058	481,320	860,073	66,009	63.6	13.7
Arkansas	850,643	192,626	517,897	72,604	60.9	37.7
Florida	2,617,438	470,261	1,819,342	183,197	69.5	39.0
Georgia[1]	—	—	1,130,385	161,958	77.0	30.9
Louisiana	1,289,216	514,589	993,118	159,033	—	6.2
Mississippi	636,046	386,095	—	23,801	—	38.2
North Carolina	2,005,955	550,929	1,861,430	210,450	92.8	—
South Carolina[1]	—	—	479,711	57,978	—	64.1
Tennessee	1,779,018	313,873	930,198[2]	150,869[2]	83.5[2]	33.7[3]
Texas	4,884,765	649,512	1,973,217[2]	174,387[3]	50.9[3]	23.0
Virginia	1,876,167	436,720	866,794	100,499	46.2	

* Except where otherwise indicated, the source is: *1961 Commission on Civil Rights Report, Voting.* VAP stands for voting-age population.
1 Source: Margaret Price, *The Negro and the Ballot in the South* (Atlanta, Southern Regional Council, 1959). Figures are for 1958.
2 Totals for 63 counties out of 95.
3 Totals for 213 counties out of 254.

Table II

Voter Registration in the South, 1965*

STATE	WHITE VAP[1]	BLACK VAP[1]	WHITES REGISTERED	BLACKS REGISTERED[2]	PER CENT WHITE VAP REGISTERED	PER CENT BLACK VAP REGISTERED
Alabama	1,353,122	481,220	935,695	92,737	69.2	19.3
Arkansas	848,393	192,629	555,944	77,714	65.5	40.4
Florida	2,617,438	470,261	1,958,499	240,616	74.8	51.2
Georgia	1,796,963	612,875	1,124,415	167,663	62.6	27.4
Louisiana	1,289,216	514,589	1,037,184	164,601	80.5	31.6
Mississippi	751,266	422,273	525,000	28,500	69.9	6.7
North Carolina	2,005,955	550,929	1,942,000	258,000	96.8	46.8
South Carolina	895,147	371,104	677,914	138,544	75.7	37.3
Tennessee	1,779,018	313,873	1,297,000	218,000	72.9	69.5
Texas[3]	4,844,765	649,512	—	—	—	—
Virginia[4]	1,876,167	436,718	1,070,168	144,259	61.1	38.3
Totals	20,057,450	5,015,983	11,123,819	1,530,634	72.9	36.8

* Before the Voting Rights Act of 1965.

1 The source of all population data in this table is the 1960 census; VAP stands for voting-age population.

2 The source of all data on registration before the passage of the Voting Rights Act of 1965 is the Information Center, Commission on Civil Rights, Registration and Voting Statistics, March 19, 1965.

3 Figures showing pre-act state-wide white and black registration are not available. No county figures by race are available for Texas.

4 State-wide figures are from Voter Education Project News, September 1967.

Table III

Voter Registration in the South, 1971*

STATE	WHITE VAP	BLACK VAP	WHITES REGISTERED	BLACKS REGISTERED	PER CENT WHITE VAP REGISTERED	PER CENT BLACK VAP REGISTERED
Alabama	1,744,166	530,461	1,369,542	290,057	78.52	54.68
Arkansas	1,126,952	212,952	674,000	165,000	61.39	80.89
Florida	4,169,196	606,429	2,695,121	320,640	64.65	52.87
Georgia	2,324,304	700,519	1,598,268	450,000	68.76	64.24
Louisiana	1,693,186	626,116	1,315,981	354,607	77.72	56.64
Mississippi	962,782	452,126	670,710	268,440	69.66	59.37
North Carolina	2,720,007	672,488	1,648,254	298,427	60.60	44.38
South Carolina	1,235,472	450,201	614,383	206,394	49.73	45.84
Tennessee	2,291,478	373,789	1,542,135	245,000	67.30	65.55
Texas	6,518,694	844,137	3,700,000	575,000	56.76	68.16
Virginia	2,599,634	528,446	1,550,000	275,000	59.62	52.04
Totals	27,385,871	5,997,664	17,378,394	3,448,565	64.97	58.61

* Due to the addition of eighteen- to twenty-year-olds and the usage of the 1970 Census Data as the basis for estimating the Voting Age Population (VAP), the percentage of black registered voters for all states excluding Arkansas and Georgia is lower than estimated in the 1970 report. Voter registration statistics shown are the most reliable estimates available as of the following dates: Alabama—January 1972; Arkansas—May 1972; Florida—October 1971; Georgia—May 1971; Louisiana—December 1971; Mississippi—December 1971; North Carolina—December 1971; South Carolina—December 1971; Tennessee—February 1972; Texas—January 1972; and Virginia—January 1972.

Source: Voter Education Project, Inc.

efforts over the last decade and a half, and one can expect more
such developments. In various places, especially in the more popu-
lous Southern urban areas, one can expect black voter registration
and successful black candidates to increase.

By contrast with earlier years, these developments are indeed
impressive. But it is easy to misread the voting picture in the South.
The fact is that there are still very many instances of blacks still
being hampered in their efforts to register and to vote free of racial
discrimination. An organization known as the Washington Research
Project issued a documented study of such instances in 1972 entitled, *The Shameful Blight*.[5] The study presented numerous cases,
especially in Mississippi, where registrars used delaying tactics to
hold down the number of black registrants. No longer could registrars use literacy tests to disqualify applicants, but they could
hold their registration hours at inconvenient times and in inconvenient places. The following are some rather typical practices still
prevailing in the 1970s:

Irregular or nonexistent hours for registration interfered with a registration drive in Noxabee County. In March 1971 it was reported to
the VEP that in the second week we [the Noxabee County Voter Education Project] will not be able to register anyone because our court
is in session and he [the circuit clerk] will not allow the lady he has
in his office to register anyone.[6]

The inaccessibility of the registrar's office was considered a deterrent
to registration in Clay County. According to the county voters league:
It had been rather difficult to register [more than one-third of the
black voting age population] because the physical location of the
registrar's office is located in the corner of the county, therefore
many people have to go as many as thirty miles in order to register.
As a result, those who do not own cars do not bother to register; also
it is rather expensive for those who own cars to make very many trips
to town to get people registered.[7]

5. *The Shameful Blight: The Survival of Racial Discrimination in Voting in
the South* (The Washington Research Project: Washington, D.C., 1972).
6. *Ibid.*, p. 15.
7. *Ibid.*

Registration hours from 8:00 a.m. to 4:00 p.m., Monday through Friday, according to the Yalabusha County for Better Education Organization, present problems for working people. The organization tried to get the hours extended to at least one evening a week, or Saturday mornings, but was unsuccessful.[8]

In some Mississippi counties, all registered voters are required to re-register. This has meant that those black citizens who have become registered since 1965 must now go through the process again, and many observers have asserted that the entire process has worked against any sizable black registration gains. The re-registration requirement in all cases followed state redistricting.

It is useful to examine briefly the work of the Nixon administration in implementing the Voting Rights Act. This will be done by looking at the record in three situations: (1) the appointment of federal examiners; (2) response to state re-registration requirements; and (3) what is known as Section 5 procedures, that is, that part of the Voting Rights Act requiring approval before a revised state or local election requirement could be instituted.

In all three instances, the Department of Justice under the Nixon administration has proceeded with less than vigorous, aggressive action.

(1) The Voting Rights Act of 1965 permits the Attorney General of the United States to send federal examiners into an area covered by the law to register citizens if he believes that such action is necessary to ensure non-discriminatory voter registration. Under the Nixon administration, from 1969 to 1972, examiners had been assigned to counties in only two states: Louisiana and Mississippi. (Under Lyndon B. Johnson, examiners were assigned to five states: Mississippi, Alabama, Louisiana, Georgia, and South Carolina.)

The policy of the Department of Justice under the Nixon administration has been to rely on persuasion and a standard of fairness. The Department prefers to use examiners sparingly. Acting Assistant Attorney General David L. Norman of the Civil Rights Di-

8. *Ibid.*

vision of the Department of Justice explained the practice in his testimony in 1971 before the Civil Rights Oversight Subcommittee of the House Judiciary Committee:

It is done on a county basis. What we do is to make surveys routinely prior to and during registration periods, prior to elections, to determine whether there are any unreasonable barriers to black registration and voting. . . . If we find that there are barriers, there are grounds to do so . . . we would send Federal examiners. If we find, for example—and these examples are hard to come by these days because it happens so rarely—that they are registering people in basically white precincts but they are not going into the black precincts, we would appoint an examiner and put him in the black precincts, in all probability. The standard is whether they are being fair on a racial basis.

This approach relies on a judgment based on notions of fairness. The United States Civil Rights Commission prefers, instead, to implement a hard and fast, more automatic rule. It suggests that where there is less than one-half of the eligible black citizens registered, this should serve as an automatic trigger for the appointment of examiners. The Department of Justice rejects this suggestion. There is no question that the present law authorizing examiners could be quite effective, but the law also permits the executive branch to act on its discretion. If the Department of Justice chooses not to use examiners prolifically, which is the case with the Nixon administration, there is virtually nothing that can be done under present statutes to require otherwise. In fact, the Washington Research Project concluded:

. . . the Department is unconcerned with short or inconvenient hours of registration and with inaccessible registration places, both of which are more burdensome for blacks than for whites and make it especially difficult for blacks to overcome the effects of past discrimination. . . . The way the examiner program is now administered, it is no longer a relevant part of the Voting Rights Act, since the Department rarely uses examiners and since examiners do not list a substantial number of persons when they are used. These difficulties could be overcome. The examiner program could be used to eliminate all barriers to voter registration for minority group members in the specially covered jurisdictions. Greater flexibility in the hours and locations of examiners and greater publicity concerning their presence could yield better results.[9]

(2) In Mississippi in 1971, district boundaries in several counties were redrawn and voting precincts were changed. In many counties there was the requirement that all voters re-register. Some civil rights groups argued that in the context of present-day Mississippi, with its history of racial discrimination and voter denials, such a re-registration requirement worked an undue hardship on black citizens who had struggled for years to register. The Department of Justice under the Nixon administration has taken a different view. It has assumed that re-registration will be conducted in a non-discriminatory manner, and the Department will not act unless specific complaints are received. The burden, then, is on the citizen to prove discrimination. This attitude comes rather close to the resistant stance adopted by Judges Cox and Clayton when they were hearing cases of voting denials. Indeed, it is ironic, but nonetheless accurate, to say that black citizens were better protected in their efforts to register by an aggressive judge like Frank M. Johnson than by a hesitant Department of Justice in the Nixon administration. The conclusion is that the change from a judicial approach to an executive approach might have resulted in a slow-up of registration efforts in some instances—perhaps not in the jurisdictions presided over by resistant judges, but certainly in areas where aggressive and even gradualist judges were sitting. The Nixon administration puts great emphasis on the good will of the Southern officials, but the essence of years of experience is that such trust, without firm enforcement *practices,* is not entirely warranted.

(3) In passing the Voting Rights Act of 1965, Congress certainly was aware of the history of Southern practices as described

9. *The Shameful Blight,* p. 58.

in Chapter Two. The practice of devising new schemes to replace old ones was well known. We saw this most clearly with the Southern efforts to protect the existence of the white primary, which efforts were finally defeated by the federal courts. The ingenuity of some Southern legislators to devise legal road blocks to increased black voter registration seemed almost limitless. Therefore, the new law provided that if a jurisdiction covered by the law sought to change its voting requirements, it would have to get prior approval either from the Department of Justice or from the federal district court in Washington, D.C. This was stipulated in Section 5. But from the beginning of the Nixon administration, this safeguard has been, first, under attack from the executive branch, and then casually enforced. In 1970, the Nixon administration sought to change Section 5 to require the Attorney General to bring a suit in the federal district court if he felt that a change in local laws was discriminatory; *prior* approval of the change would not be necessary. The effect of such an amendment would have been to revert to a judicial approach and to put many potential black voters at the mercy of some resistant judges once again. The Congress refused to follow the Nixon administration's proposal. In fact, however, Section 5 has been quite loosely enforced. At times, Southern states have not waited for prior approval, and when this has been the case the Department of Justice frequently has not objected. Likewise, even where the Department has objected but the state proceeded nonetheless, as in Warren County, Mississippi, in 1971, and elections were held under new districting laws, the Department took no action to stop the election.

The record of executive enforcement of the Voting Rights Act, especially since the beginning of the Nixon administration in 1969, has been, at best, an uneven one. One important factor is that the law does not operate automatically. That is, the Attorney General has the *discretion* to appoint federal examiners or to approve changes in electoral laws. This means, quite obviously, that the discretion will reflect not only the legal opinions but the political preferences of the executive branch. If a particular presidential administration sees political advantages accruing from a soft approach to Southern white officials (an approach, that is, that relies more on persuasion and cajoling than on forceful enforcement of the law), then it is safe to assume that a soft approach will be chosen, with procrastination the result. Thus, even with the present legislation, which is the most far-reaching ever enacted by Congress on the subject, the discretionary features provide an opportunity— if an executive branch wishes to so avail itself—to forestall the too rapid and too widespread increase of black voter participation. The Nixon administration prefers to file lawsuits against authorities rather than to move by executive fiat. *In one important sense, then, although the law is on the books, the present Department of Justice has virtually reverted to a pre-1965 judicial approach.* This has resulted in many of the disadvantages (delay, frustration, sparse results) of that approach and very little, if any, of the advantages.

John Lewis, Executive Director of the Voter Education Project with headquarters in Atlanta, Georgia, has observed that the system of dual registration should be abolished. That is, in some Southern areas, citizens are required to register separately for city and county elections. This imposes a hardship on persons who must go to separate places at separate times to register. In addition, Lewis contends that still in many places, especially in rural areas, white registrars continue to act as if they are doing a favor for black citizens if they register them. There is still an atmosphere of contention surrounding the registration process. In many places, in the minds and manners of some persons—white and black—the fact is still *not* established that voter registration is a constitutional right, that it is *not* to be treated as if the potential registrant were applying for credit at a local grocery store. In spite of the years of legal and political struggle and the present Voting Rights Act, in all too many places there is still an atmosphere of tediousness and laborious testiness surrounding the voter registration process of black citizens. The tension and hesitancy (on the part of black applicants and white registrars) still prevail. Lewis believes that a more summary system should be instituted throughout the country, one that relies only on identification of residence and age. If a citizen presents reasonable evidence that he or she is eighteen or over and lives in the voting district, this alone should be sufficient to qualify that person to vote in all elections.

The most difficult problem before the Voting Rights Act of 1965 was passed and the one that still persists is the problem of intimidation—economic and physical. The clearest, simplest way to state this is that many black citizens in Southern communities will lose their jobs and their livelihood if they register and vote. And many more believe that this will happen to them; thus they do not even make the effort to register. One account of elections in Mississippi on November 2, 1971, was as follows:

The apathy normally associated with low income and education undoubtedly played a part in [the low black turnout], but the evidence leaves little doubt that the factor of **fear**—whether justified or not— was also deeply involved. Despite the absence of explicit race-baiting in the gubernatorial campaign, tensions were clearly high during the campaign. In the months preceding the election, four racial slayings occurred in the Delta alone, most notably the murder of young Jo Etha Collier. Though not directly related to the elections, these slayings contributed to a climate of apprehension. The threat of economic pressures had the same effect. Black applicants for loans in some areas were instructed to "go see Charles Evers." The fact that the election took place in the middle of the cotton-picking season only intensified the problem; for many blacks believed they would jeopardize their meager jobs if they voted. Black turnout was therefore low, particularly in those counties where blacks are most dependent on local whites for their income. . . .

This is, in fact, the real dilemma of black politics in Mississippi and the rural South. Outright fraud and ballot-box stuffing were probably not necessary to defeat black candidates. Economic dependence and fear of economic pressures were sufficient.[10]

10. L. Salamon, "Mississippi Post-Morten: The 1971 Elections," *New South* (Winter 1972), pp. 43, 46–47.

To continue to treat this problem as one of legal evidence and substantial proof is insufficient. The procedures and results of the judiciary are too rigorous and too tenuous for the solution of such a prominent but subtle problem. The answer lies in the realization that many social, political, and economic conditions must change first. Universal suffrage is no solution, because the fear of voting will remain. Strengthening the laws by imposing heavier penalties is no solution, because the methods of intimidation are too subtle and the problems of proof will remain. One cannot expect the courts to overlook completely the possibility that other rights (e.g., property, contract) might be invaded, and yet it is clear that the process of governmental attempts to maximize equality (in this case, non-discriminatory voting rights) usually are exacted at the cost of increased regulation of individual freedom—in this case the freedom of employers to hire and fire, or of creditors to make loans. Surely, however, the federal courts should not be required continuously to strike this balance between equality and freedom.

Without question, there must be built into the economic structures various protective mechanisms for the now vulnerable blacks —namely, the protection afforded by union organization with its guarantees of job security. In addition, there must be much more effort expended toward creating self-sustaining credit unions and similar forms of local, indigenous cooperative ventures. As long as sizable numbers of blacks in the South remain economically dependent on the most personal of terms to a white economic apparatus that wishes to protect against socio-political change, those blacks will never be able to bring about that desired change. There are serious limits, procedural and political, to what courts can do, and there are certainly political limits to what the executive branch is willing to do. The greatest hope, it would seem, for alleviation of these difficulties lies in a sustained effort to create structures of economic independence which will provide a base for political leverage.

The irony is that normally a powerless people must rely initially on those resources most available to them for bringing about changes in their condition. With Southern blacks in some areas, this primary resource constitutes the ballot. The same is no less true in other sections of the country. But the problem of utilizing a franchise model for change in some Southern areas is aggravated by the woeful economic condition of many black citizens. The economic obstacles to the ballot box are clear, and they must be removed before it is legitimate to talk about a free vote in the South.

Unquestionably, federal government intervention is one of the best ways to ensure the removal of such obstacles. As the evidence throughout this book indicates, black citizens historically have had to rely on such external assistance, whether in the form of federal court decisions or the executive branch. It is now clear that such help in the form of providing at least a modicum of economic independence is needed. The proposed Family Assistance Plan which was defeated in the Congress in 1972 would have been a significant step in this direction, if only because it would have provided guaranteed direct payments from the federal treasury to citizens in local communities. At least the families would not have been *totally* dependent on the good will of some local hostile whites.

Equally clear is that the formation of various kinds of economic cooperatives should be encouraged. In 1969, the Southern Regional Council issued a special report entitled *Cooperatives and Poor People in the South*. Its author, Al Ulmer, came to the conclusion that:

There are approximately 40 cooperatives owned by poor people in the South. Fifteen of these are large enough and long-established enough to be called significant efforts. Between 10,000 and 15,000 people are being affected by the cooperatives. Almost all are black people over 45 years of age. All but a few co-ops are in the rural South. None are in large urban centers. Only two co-ops have over 1,000 members, most having between 50 and 300.[11]

11. Al Ulmer, *Cooperatives and Poor People in the South* (Atlanta, Georgia: Southern Regional Council, 1969), p. 30.

One of the larger co-ops is the Southern Consumers Cooperative in Louisiana. As a producer co-op, it has dealt in mail-order fruit cakes, fresh doughnuts and pies. It has established a finance company, "created to fill members' needs for low-interest credit and consumer counseling." Ulmer stated: "Southern Consumers is large enough to be a political force in Southwest Louisiana. Candidates ask for its endorsement." [12]

The Southwest Farmers Cooperative Association (SWAFCA) is another example of a relatively large, but struggling venture. "SWAFCA was an outgrowth of the voter registration drives undertaken in the Black Belt during 1964 and 1965 and the famous Selma-to-Montgomery 'March for Freedom.' " [13] It received a grant from the Office of Economic Opportunity over the opposition of the Alabama governor and the Alabama congressmen. Community services such as adult education, self-help housing, and day care centers were part of the plans of the co-op. It has had to rely on "soft money" from a fast disappearing federal anti-poverty program and on very limited funds from foundations.

In Chapter Eight, the economic intimidation of Tennessee share-croppers was described. Many blacks who had registered to vote were unable subsequently to buy petroleum products. But, growing out of this voter registration experience, the Mid-South Oil Consumers Cooperative was formed in 1965, covering a three-county area in Tennessee. Prior to that time, the blacks had to travel long distances to Memphis and northern Mississippi for supplies. Professors Ray Marshall and Lamond Godwin wrote:

This experience caused a small group of black farmers, led by E. R. Shockley, a retired black county extension agent, to establish their own petroleum business. They began as a small buying club and raised $4,700 by selling preferred stock and $100 membership fees. In the fall of 1965 MSOCC obtained a charter and secured a $49,000

12. *Ibid.,* p. 12.
13. Ray Marshall and Lamond Godwin, *Cooperatives and Rural Poverty in the South* (Baltimore: The Johns Hopkins Press, 1971), p. 45.

loan from FHA for a building, bulk storage facilities, tanks, pumps, and two trucks to bring gasoline from the Missouri Farmers Cooperative in Memphis to its members at a savings of about 5 cents per gallon.[14]

14. *Ibid.,* p. 69.

All these ventures are relatively small and they face tremendous problems of capitalization and effective managerial skills. These cooperatives by no means can answer all the problems of economic vulnerability facing Southern black citizens, but they certainly are efforts to be encouraged. As noted, some of the enterprises were direct spin-offs from the intense political activities in the local areas. Many black voter-registration workers in the South knew all along the important relationship between politics and economics in the daily lives of black people. But scarce resources—financial and human—made it difficult to operate on too many fronts simultaneously. A major lesson of the civil rights struggle, certainly in the South but no less in the North, is that that struggle must begin to give greater attention to solutions that link political and economic concerns.

Appendices

Appendix A

ALABAMA—1972

1. Macon County
   Black Registered Voters— 7035
   White Registered Voters— 2769

2. Bullock County
   Black Registered Voters— 4561
   White Registered Voters— 2700

3. Montgomery County
   Black Registered Voters—20,000
   White Registered Voters—60,866

4. Dallas County
   Black Registered Voters—11,600
   White Registered Voters—14,269

Appendix B *

MISSISSIPPI—1972

1. Bolivar County
   Black Registered Voters—10,000
   White Registered Voters— 9000

* Information received from Mississippi Institute of Politics.

2. Jefferson Davis County
   Black Registered Voters—   2000
   White Registered Voters—   4300

3. Walthall County
   Black Registered Voters—   1880
   White Registered Voters—   5120

4. Forrest County (as of March 31, 1972)
   Black Registered Voters—   6000
   White Registered Voters—18,350

Appendix C

LOUISIANA—1972

1. Ouachita Parish
   Black Registered Voters—   4502
   White Registered Voters—37,827

2. Brenville Parish
   Black Registered Voters—   2922
   White Registered Voters—   5452

3. East Carroll Parish
   Black Registered Voters—   803
   White Registered Voters—   3341

4. Madison Parish
   Black Registered Voters—   3388
   White Registered Voters—   4036

Appendix D *

TENNESSEE—1972

1. Fayette County
   Black Registered Voters—   5000
   White Registered Voters—   3307

2. Haywood County
   Black Registered Voters—   2641
   White Registered Voters—   4900

* Figures as of early 1972, Dr. Haddad, Chairman, Registration Committee, Fayette County.

Index